SOCIOLOGY: AN INTRODUCTION

SOCIOLOGY | An Introduction

JACK H. CURTIS, Ph.D.

JOHN A. COLEMAN

RALPH LANE, Jr., Ph.D.

THE BRUCE PUBLISHING COMPANY / MILWAUKEE

Library of Congress Catalog Card Number: 67–22558

Preface

OUR society is preoccupied with its problems — racism, crime, suburbanization. For this reason we often overlook the fact that a structure of knowledge exists which addresses itself to the why of society. Statistics on crime, prostitution, and drug use, read with case histories of deviants, make engrossing courses for students. But, by themselves, without a systematic *relating of this material to the structure of American society,* they are superficial and cause little real growth in the student.

This book is intended to be the first exposure of the student to systematic sociology, an analysis of the why of society. The basics are stressed. Concepts, definitions of terms, and the principles of scientific social inquiry are given prime attention. But we do not use a question and answer style. Rather we infer the basics through considering problems, both those of sociological analysis and those of American society

The Introduction, about sociology as a science and its uses, is brief. While such an orientation is necessary, of course, the authors feel that the remaining chapters, contacts with the fascination of social analysis, will be most meaningful. Our analysis of American society is both systematic and systemic in keeping with the latest thinking in American sociology. Part One deals with cultural and personality systems. Part Two deals with social systems. Part Three deals with the kinds of social problems mentioned at the outset of this preface.

Out of our many combined years of teaching sociology at the secondary and college levels of education we are convinced that this problems' approach is best: logical, developmental, and most stimulating for the student. John A. Coleman contributed Chapters 2, 3, 7, 11, and 12. Ralph Lane, Jr., contributed Chapters 8 and 9. I am responsible for the overall organization of the book and contributed Chapters 1, 4, 5, 6, and 10. Together we hope that our work will help to develop the intellectual competence of students in understanding society.

JACK H. CURTIS
The University of San Francisco

Contents

SOCIOLOGY: AN INTRODUCTION

Chapter 1

Sociology, Man, and Society

WHAT is sociology and what are the reasons for studying it? This two-fold question begins your study of the science of society. Sociology forms a basis for understanding the social world in which we live. This "understanding" should supplement your moral and ethical beliefs about the way you, as a social individual, can help to shape a better social world.

Sociologists characteristically describe their science as *objective*. They like to contrast sociology with philosophy. Neither better nor worse, perhaps, than philosophy, sociology is a different kind of inquiry. Sociology is not as *speculative* as philosophy. By this it is meant that sociology is based upon the *empirical* methods of science. Nothing should be accepted as sociology until research and experimentation have verified it. Universal conceptions of the good, the true, and the beautiful lie in the province of philosophy and esthetics. The tested facts of experience limit the generalizations of sociology to a description and analysis of society as it is.

But sociology summarizes its research findings into logically related propositions which attempt to explain society. The end result sociologists call *theory,* the best existing explanation of a thing. Sociological theory is *nonethical,* and a moment's reflection will reveal the reason why. Sociology is not an extremely advanced science. Hence, its explanations (theories) are valid *as far as they go.* You would not wish to take an ethical position on the basis of sociological theory alone. What if further investigation revealed facts that would cause you to change your mind? Ethical and moral judgments have such grave consequences that it would be better to look upon sociological theory as an aid, rather than as a determinant of moral judgments. For example, crime in modern society has some "integrative" effects upon the non-criminals. That is to say, sociologists have found that law-abiding citizens are drawn closer together because of the threat of crime and violence. Of course, you are not going to be foolish enough to advocate more crime in cities whose inhabitants need more social consciousness! The truly useful thing accomplished by this sociological fact is rather to raise a question, "How can a community develop more social consciousness while eliminating crime?"

Sociology should be of increasing value because its theory is *cumulative:* new theories do not merely replace old ones. Sociology is "getting somewhere." New theories correct, extend, and refine older ones.

Nor is sociology the only social science. It is the science of society, and it is concerned with *all* of society. Why then do we have political science, economics, and the other social sciences? The answer is that sociology is the "geometry" of the social sciences. It is concerned with human relationships, wherever they occur. Politics and economics are valid studies in themselves but sociology studies man in all of his social relationships. Psychology studies man also, but it concentrates upon the *individual* man. Sociology studies *man in relation to other men*. It studies man the social animal.

Let us turn now to the object of study of sociological science so that all of this discussion may become clearer to you.

MAN AND SOCIETY

Man's intelligence has created his societies. This social world of man covers the inhabitable areas of the physical world like a cloak. In creating this *social* world man also created a different kind of environment than that of the lower animals, the environment of groups and societies. Thus, in his quest for effective adaptation to the physical environment as part of nature's "survival of the fittest," man has created social structures which require continued creative adaptation. Sociology is one of man's tools for helping himself to solve the problems of physical and social adaptation.

From the dawn of history man, through his commonsense reasoning, has been aware of his need for community life. Many proverbs of primitive and ancient societies testify to the universal awareness of humans that ours is a social existence. The sociologist Sumner in his book *Folkways* offers hundreds of illustrations of the primi-

Bettmann Archives

This Babylonic bas-relief illustrates one aspect of man's social "shared" existence. Here King Assurbanipal celebrates a victory with his wife.

tive's awareness of his social nature. While primitives were not philosophers, they had myths and fables about social welfare and every man's stake in it. They were well aware that men do not live in isolation but rather in groups. The proverb, "the link has no ring excepting in the chain," illustrates this notion that what is important in an individual is his connection to the tribe. This is true not only of the small bands and tribes of antiquity but also of the great multitudes which make up modern societies. The social, or "shared," dimension of man's life is so indispensable to his existence that we can speak of man as the *social animal*.

But we must make an important distinction between the shared existence of man and that of lower animals, many of whom live in colonies. Man's social nature is unique because man's consciousness is unique. Intelligence and reason distinguish the social forms of man from the settlements of animals. Ants, for example, have developed a highly complex societal structure. There are classes of ants and a relatively complex division of labor exists in colonies of ants. But each colony developed by ants of the same species is a carbon copy of every other such colony. Not so with man!

Of all the myriad number of societies that have existed on the face of the earth, no two are the same. Each one has elaborated into a unique social structure with its own "way of life," or culture. But, like all statements in social science, this one needs to be qualified. Despite their uniqueness, all societies which have survived efficiently have developed certain uniformities. These uniformities are imposed by *human nature*.

In the first flush of discovery of the wide variety of social forms and culture, social scientists were once prone to discard the concept of a universal human nature. The diversity among societies and the seemingly infinite variety of human cultures dazzled social scientists to the point where they could not see underlying uniformities in all human societies.

But more prolonged and careful study revealed to social scientists that *human needs* establish a basis for all societies. The confusion came in the complexity of the different ways in which societies solved their problems of human need. Societies must have children or they will not survive — procreation and education into the society's *way* are therefore human needs. Societies must make adaptations to the environment for the physical needs of their members. Order, both internally, and to regulate relations with other societies is another human need. The need to relate the two worlds of the natural and supernatural, the secular and the sacred, probably accounts for more social forms than any other need. Hence, there is a continuity among all societies from the most primitive to the most advanced. This continuity is provided by the fact that all can be considered solutions to the problems of human needs. These human needs, then, are the foundations on which societies are built.

SOCIAL ANALYSIS

Sociology has a long history in one sense and a short history in another. If every kind of thinking about society is sociology, then sociology is as old as the human race. You have already seen that the most primitive of societies have proverbs about the social nature of man. These grew out of the storehouse of common sense which is the prize possession of every society. The accumulated experience, or wisdom, of each society testifies to the historical presence within these societies of men and women who have been able to think creatively about social life. Sometimes mystically, sometimes in a down-to-earth practical way, contributions to *social lore* are part of the human heritage from its beginnings.

Auguste Comte was convinced that all decisions about social reform should be based on scientific evidence.

Bettmann Archives

Social philosophy, on the other hand, is a much more recent development in human history. Plato's *Republic* was not the first work that could be called social philosophy. In the oriental and occidental worlds there were many others besides Plato who could be considered social philosophers. But for our purposes *The Republic* will serve as a good example. Plato (427–347 B.C.) was one of the first thinkers in our western civilization to relate human needs to social forms. Social philosophy differs from social lore in that social lore must be gleaned from proverbs or inferred from accounts of life in a given society. Social philosophy, on the other hand, represents the attempts of philosophers to analyze social life in the light of principles. Just as men are now, Plato was preoccupied with the principle of justice. He and other social philosophers are concerned with the "good" society, the society that would best meet the needs of men.

Modern sociology, in comparison to social lore and social philosophy, is a very recent newcomer to man's thinking about society. As with Plato and social philosophy, we could offer evidence that sociology did not begin with Auguste Comte. But like Plato, Comte offers a good illustration of, in this case, scientific sociology. He gave the discipline its name. He combined the Latin word *socius* meaning "companion" to the Greek ending *logia* meaning "the science of." Thus he gave us the new word "sociology" for the new scientific discipline which he believed would replace social lore and social philosophy as valid means of gaining insight into society.

Auguste Comte (1798–1857), like so many other nineteenth-century scholars, was so impressed with the accomplishments of the natural sciences that he went overboard in his enthusiasm for the idea of a science of society. From this time on he wanted mankind to base all decisions about social reform on scientific evidence. This sounds perfectly acceptable, but, briefly, it did not work.

The main problem stems from Comte's philosophy of *positivism*. Positivistic thinking holds that "that which is can be studied scienfically." This is not at all the same thing as sociology today. If you will recall, we said earlier that sociology is empirical, theoretical, cumulative, and nonethical. Hence, to some extent modern sociology has *some* of the flavor of positivism — it strives to be scientific. But in growing of age from its positivistic infancy it has achieved a certain degree of humility. Sociologists claim a far more limited territory than the "everything" which Comte staked out for the new field. There are many other problems with positivism. However, you are probably interested more in studying sociology and society than in studying positivism. So we can discuss briefly only those aspects of positivism that are of contemporary sociological significance.

Modern sociology agrees with Comte regarding sociology as a science. But in terms of religion, philosophy, and esthetics, sociologists are as diverse as you can imagine. There are Christian, Jewish, agnostic, atheistic, and, yes, even positivistic sociologists (those for whom science is everything). But, by agreement, good sociology follows the procedures of science. It has a healthy concern for the facts, even when these facts do not look good for the sociologists' commitments to other, nonsociological, conceptions of the good life. No one is betraying his principles. The sociologist is actually re-affirming by his scientific work his attachment to certain ideals. Among these are truth, justice among men, and the utopian idea that his work will help himself and other men to know more about society. All agree, at least in principle, with the Comtean ideal of a better society. To Comte, with all of his philosophical defects, sociologists owe their battle cry "to understand is to have the power to change." To understand society and to change it for the better — this is the commitment of sociologists.

We have discussed sociology and its concern with man and society at a very broad level. We needed to know something about the broader objectives of sociology. However, you probably are curious about the specific questions that are asked by sociologists. If you are practical you may already be asking if sociology has produced anything worthwhile. So in the remainder of the chapter we shall consider the kinds of questions that sociologists ask, and how they get answers to these questions.

WHAT QUESTIONS DO SOCIOLOGISTS ASK?

In the main, sociologists ask questions which occur to them as they study their specialties within sociology. Every sociologist, to be qualified, must master general sociological theory and sociological research methods. This is expected of him before he even undertakes to become a specialist. So before we can meaningfully discuss specific questions about specialized topics it is best that we consider *general theory, the research process,* and the relationship between them.

General Theory

The objective of any science is to build an organized body of knowledge about the things it studies. The general theory of sociology is the best existing explanation of the *structure* and *function of groups* and *the relations between groups.* The objective of sociology is to build a cumulative body of knowledge about these things. A group consists of any aggregate of people who share norms which enable them to pursue common goals. Sociologists ask questions about the internal workings of groups. These questions concern the way in which the group is organized. What are the main parts of the group (structure) and in what way does each part work (function), toward the performance of the group as a whole?

This general theory of sociology allows sociologists to range over the entire human population. Sociologists can ask meaningful questions about a glee club, a football team, a predominantly Negro neighborhood, or the economic system of the United States! But this wide latitude in subject matter does not mean that the sociologist is a man of all knowledge, of music, football, Negro life, or economics. He is primarily concerned with the *people* who are involved in these activities and the degree of *social organization* which they achieve.

Sociological Research

General theory is the concern of every sociologist regardless of his specialty. Most sociologists do research. Even those who do not participate in research are interested in it because sociological theory is cumulative. To keep up with the field we must be aware of the latest research. The research process consists of (1) seeking out general questions from the existing body of theory; (2) forming hypotheses about the structure and function of groups and the relationships between them; (3) observing social behavior; and (4) analyzing the results of the research to see if the hypotheses are borne out by the data. The end result is that the researcher extends and expands existing sociological theory or, unhappily, he has failed and must develop different and more fruitful hypotheses.

The relationship between theory and research can be illustrated by a simple diagram:

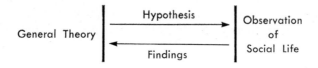

We can illustrate the way sociologists ask questions with actual examples. If you keep in mind that all sociologists are concerned with maintaining and building a general theory of society we can kill two birds with one stone. We can break down sociology into its main specialties and then you can see the theory-research process as it actually occurs.

ECONOMIC SOCIOLOGY

The analysis of social systems. The study of the structure and functions of groups and the relationships between groups, is, as you can already see, the same thing as general sociological theory. A chapter of this book (Chap. 5) is devoted to this kind of analysis.

The analysis of specific social systems is, of course, more specialized. Economic sociologists ask questions about the structure and function of groups performing economic activities and the way in which this economic activity forms the *economic system* of our society. For example, an economist is concerned with such abstract questions as supply and demand. The economic sociologist is concerned far more with patterns of group behavior. He wants to know the social relations of people who enter into economic activities. Do they work solely for economic gain? Sociological theory holds that people's behavior is importantly influenced by their positions in groups and their status in the eyes of others in the group. Applying the research-theory diagram we can see how the economic sociologist formulates and asks his questions and how he gets answers to them.

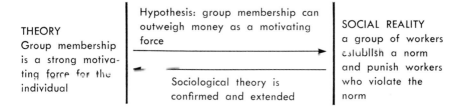

The economic sociologist was faced with a conflict between sociological theory and the incentive concept of economics. His hypothesis was, like all hypotheses, a purely *tentative* and *unproved* proposition. But once he had observed a work group whose norms prohibited doing too much work he was able to affirm his hypothesis. Group membership *can* outweigh economic incentive. The discussion of the Bank Wiring Group in Chapter 5 develops this example further.

POLITICAL SOCIOLOGY

So sociological theory can be a valuable supplement to economics. The same holds true for political science. Political science (among other things) explains how people elect officials in the American political system. Political sociologists (among other things) ask questions about why people vote the way they do. For example, Paul Lazarsfeld extended sociological theory farther through voting studies. Let us start with the same theorem from general sociological theory — group membership is a strong motivating force for the individual. It is generally held by nonsociologists that radio and television political campaigns and propaganda sway the voter. Lazarsfeld's study went like this:

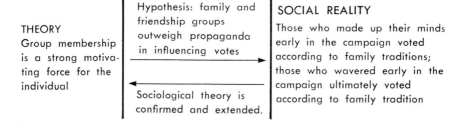

In other words, Lazarsfeld's and other voting studies demonstrated that groups (family and friendship cliques) explained voting behavior far better than the previously accepted idea in politics that the kind of campaign waged is the dominant factor in voting results.

FAMILY SOCIOLOGY

But sociological theory and research do not merely conflict with and supplement economics and political science. Often it is *social lore* that is corrected by sociological analysis. Family sociologists find that marriage and family life as conceived of by many Americans and the family system in sociological theory are poles apart! Romantic love, individual choice of a mate, and an idyllic married existence together are all conceptions which have a tight grip on Americans and their mass culture.

Fortunately, sociologists doing research on dating, engagement, marriage, and family life have been able to perceive a more solid system at work than movies and television plays would lead us to believe existed.

OTHER MAJOR SOCIAL SYSTEMS

The economic, the political, and the family systems are ways in which society is organized to meet the needs of its members and their needs as a total society. Other such group solutions are the religious system, the stratification system, and all of the other systems which account for the fact that the society works. Those systems which hold together a society are its organizational systems. You will see all of this much more clearly in the following chapters. You will also see that all of these systems can be considered as one great system, *the society as a whole*. While we use other societies for purposes of comparison, the study of American society is our primary objective. Therefore, in this book, you will be undertaking a sociological analysis of American society as a social system made up of the major organizational systems of the *religious,* the *political,* the *economic,* the *family,* and the *stratificational* system.

By now you have seen something of the sociological approach to social organization. The economic sociologist looked at the work group from a distinctive point of view in our example. The same distinctive point of view was illustrated by an example of political sociology where voting was viewed in the light of its group aspects. We also gave an example of research in family sociology which revealed again a distinctive point of view — marriage and family groups meet basic needs if they are successful. This distinctive point of view also applies to the sociology of religion. We do not study the *content* of religion for its own sake, but sociologists do study the ways in which *individual* and *social needs* are met in religious groupings. The same thing holds true for the study of social stratification. Sociologists are not snobbish because they study the way America is organized into social classes. Rather the emphasis in social stratification studies is again one of developing a distinctive point of view. How do social class distinctions meet the needs of individuals and the groups into which they are organized?

By now you can grasp the distinctive point of view which the sociologist takes toward society. He wants to know *how society is organized*. As a member of society he does not stop there. He then goes on to inquire about what can be done to create an even better society. When he does this, he looks to broader ethical, philosophical, and theological conceptions of the good society. Sociology has outgrown Comte's early conceptions of sociology as an all-encompassing ethical, philosophical science.

But the sociologist is securely within his competence in studying social problems as disturbances of social organization. He does not claim that he can blueprint the perfect society. He can study his society and point out imperfections in the ways that social systems are functioning. Malfunctions of social systems are called "social disorganization."

SOCIAL DISORGANIZATION

Probably before you took this course you had been exposed to social lore about the sociologist and what he does. In the popular view the sociologist is conceived of as a social physician who travels to the slums and to other colorful problem areas and dispenses prescriptions for social ills. There is a grain of truth in this. Many sociologists do specialize in social disorganization. Sometimes this specialization is called "social problems" and sometimes "social pathology." But whatever the sociologist's interest in social disorganization is called, one thing should be kept in mind. If he does not have a good grasp of social organization, it is difficult to see what he would have to offer as solutions for disorganization.

Many students begin their study of sociology by studying social problems. There can be no quarrel with this. No one can deny the intrinsic interest of this list of topics:

juvenile delinquency	drug addiction
suicide	prostitution
crime	divorce
poverty	broken homes
disease	sex deviation

And the list could be greatly expanded. But this list is sufficient to illustrate our point. From studying social *organization* you can understand any problem on this list better than if you had analyzed mountains of interviews and/or statistics which merely illustrated the magnitude of the problem. By studying the family system as it works you can better understand what happens when it breaks down. Not one of the social problems listed above can be understood without an understanding of the religious, the family, the economic, the political, and the stratification systems of American society.

We shall study social problems in this book and suggest projects for the outside study of disorganization. But we hope you are convinced that thorough study of social organization, the main emphasis of this book, is the prime requisite for intelligent understanding of social problems. This is why the book concludes rather than begins with the topic of social problems. This leads us to a related question — whether to consider sociology "pure" or "applied."

SOCIOLOGY — PURE OR APPLIED

This brings us to one last consideration. Where do *you* fit into sociology? What part can or should it play in your life? One can be aware of sociology as an important aid in his educational development. By taking sociology in high school and college one can become more socially aware. Many persons who finish their schooling without a course in sociology go out into the adult world unprepared to discuss and participate actively in areas of social tension. You have only to hear conflicting views on family life, crime, and race relations to realize that Americans can ill afford to be educationally unprepared for such important social responsibility.

It is characteristic of the American mentality that when we find something wrong we want to do something about it. We are activists.

Consequently, we have had two extreme positions on the question of the practical use of sociology. First, social reformers flooded to sociology in the first phase of its development in America. Then there was a reaction to the "crackpots." The scholars began to resent the undisciplined energy of the social reformers. They wanted to build a better sociology before attempting to build a better society. This made good sense because those who studied social problems without learning sociology first, did more harm than good. Good intentions are no substitute for knowledge. No one would think of letting an untrained person operate on a human body. Because of our American activism, however, no one seemed perturbed at the number of enthusiastic but untrained people who wanted to operate on the social body!

American sociologists, if for no other reason than that they are American, however, will not be permitted a purely passive role. They cannot stand on the sidelines and study social life as if they were not a part of it. So, really, there is little or no real validity in the oft-repeated distinction between pure and applied sociology. What is learned in pure research will soon be applied in social work, medicine, economics, politics, family life, and religion. The real question, then, relates to how this comes about. Do sociologists work in all of these areas or do they leave it to others to apply sociology? The answer is that they do some of both.

SOCIOLOGY AND SOCIAL WORK

Sociology is most often confused with social work. Students arriving in college often decide that a sociology major is a "do-gooder." In contrast to this cynical approach, the more idealistic high school youth tends to gravitate to sociology as a college major because it seems to offer an outlet for altruistic career motives.

Social work is not the same as sociology, although an undergraduate major in sociology is an excellent preparation for a future social worker. In all fairness, psychology and any of the social sciences, together with a minor in sociology are also acceptable academic preparations for training as a social worker. Often a course or two in undergraduate social work is provided in college so that the student of sociology can get some exposure to practical problems of social reality. But such courses are no substitute for the knowledge, or theory, of society provided by the science of sociology.

WHERE DO YOU FIT?

In summary, then, let us return to the question "Where do *you* fit in?" This book is written for two kinds of students, those for whom sociology is part of a general education and those whose future careers will be in or related to the field of sociology. At this point you may not have made up your mind as to which kind of student you are. If this is true, the book was written with you especially in mind. Its purpose is to provide the student with knowledge where his thinking may now be unclear. What is sociology and where do you fit into it? You will begin learning answers to these in the chapters on culture and personality which make up the first part of this book. You will penetrate more deeply into the way our society is put together (organized) in Part Two. In Part Three you will see how the understanding of social organization can lead us to an increased understanding of social disorganization (social "problems"). When you have finished the three parts we feel that you will have some answers to your questions about sociology and where you might fit with it.

Major Concepts in Chapter 1

1. *Objective:* Without bias, preconception, or prejudice, the ability to view evidence with detachment. Viewing facts in the light of reason and not emotion.

2. *Empirical:* Employing methods based on experience. Validated through observation. Not the only valid form of knowledge but the primary scientific mode of knowledge.

3. *Theoretical:* Summary of many scientific observations into abstract, logically interrelated propositions which attempt to explain causal relationships. In sociology, theory attempts to explain causal relationships in society.

4. *Cumulative:* Theories built upon one another. Newer theories refine older ones.

5. *Nonethical:* Deals with what is, rather than what ought to be. In sociology the aspiration for scientific status imposes this restriction. The sociologist is expected to be ethical as a person and especially in his observations of the canons of scientific inquiry.

6. *Social lore:* The social thought of a people which has grown out of its experience. Roughly equivalent to common sense in the individual.

7. *Social philosophy:* The interpretation of social phenomena in the light of ethical principles. Both social lore and sociology provide relevant material for such interpretations.

8. *Sociology:* The scientific study of social phenomena. Analysis of the structure (parts and their interrelationships) and function (the workings of parts) of society.

9. *Culture.* The complex whole which consists of everything we think, do, feel, and have as members of a particular society (see next two chapters).

10. *Religious systems:* Interrelated patterns of belief and behavior which relate a supernatural being or beings to man and his society.

11. *Economic systems:* Social patterns which are addressed to the problem of sustaining and promoting the material welfare of a society.

12. *Political systems:* Social patterns which are addressed to attainment of social goals both internal and in relation to other societies. Government.

13. *Stratification system:* The establishment of strata (layers) within a society. These social "classes" are formed on social definitions of inferiority and superiority of social status or standing.

14. *Social Work:* A helping profession which through services and counseling enables troubled individuals to achieve personal and social adjustment.

Review Questions

1. Is sociology truly a science? Are sociologists too ambitious in describing it as such? The attributes of scientific procedures are the following:
   a) They are objective.
   b) They are nonspeculative.
   c) They are empirical.
   d) They are theoretical.
   e) They are cumulative.
2. How does the term "theory" as used in the chapter differ from the layman's use of the term?
3. In what ways are sociological theories helpful in forming ethical judgments?
4. In what way is sociology the "geometry" of the social sciences?
5. Define political science, economics, history, and psychology, and try to distinguish them from sociology.
6. In what way can it be said that "man's intelligence has created his

societies"? Are any societies the most intelligent that could have been created?

7. Why call man *"the* social animal" when herds and colonies are so common among the infrahuman species?
8. Why are human needs considered the basis of society?
9. Distinguish among social lore, social philosophy, and sociology.
10. Is social lore generally accurate?
11. In what ways does Plato's analysis of society differ from the approach sociologists would take?
12. Why was Auguste Comte wrong in thinking that sociology would replace social lore and social philosophy?
13. How do modern sociologists differ from Comte's position (positivism) since they accept his dictum that sociology is a science?
14. What is meant by "general theory" in sociology?
15. What are the steps in the research process?
16. Contrast general theory and economic, political, or religious sociology.
17. Give examples of ways in which sociology could conflict with social lore; with social philosophy.
18. What is the stratification system of a society?
19. What are social organization and social disorganization?
20. What is the main social problem of your city?
21. Distinguish between pure and applied sociology. In the last analysis is it a valid distinction?
22. Distinguish between sociology and social work.

Discussion Questions

1. Discuss: "Sociology only tells people what they already know from common sense."
2. Should philosophers rule society as Plato suggested?
3. Should sociologists engineer society as Comte recommended?
4. Is social work a good career choice?
5. Can there ever be a perfect society on earth?

Bibliography

*Berger, Peter L., *An Invitation to Sociology: A Humanistic Perspective* (Garden City, N. Y.: Doubleday & Company, Inc., 1963).
*Cameron, William B., *Informal Sociology: A Casual Introduction to Sociological Thinking* (New York: Random House, 1962).
Faris, Robert E. L. (ed.), *Handbook of Modern Sociology* (Chicago: Rand McNally & Company, 1964).
*Gendell, Murray, and Hans L. Zetterberg (eds.), *A Sociological Almanac for the United States* (New York: Charles Scribner's Sons, 1964).

----

* Also published in paperback edition.

Homans, George C., *The Human Group* (New York: Harcourt, Brace and Company, 1950).

*Inkeles, Alex, *What is Sociology? An Introduction to the Discipline and Profession* (Englewood Cliffs, N. J.: Prentice-Hall, Inc., 1964).

*Jowett, B. (trans.), *Plato's The Republic* (New York: Random House, 1930).

*Lazarsfeld, Paul F., *et al., The People's Choice* 2nd ed. (New York: Columbia University Press, 1948).

*Lynd, Robert S., *Knowledge for What? The Place of Social Science In American Culture* (Princeton, N. J.: Princeton University Press, 1939).

*Mills, C. Wright, *The Sociological Imagination* (New York: Oxford University Press, 1959).

Parsons, Talcott, *et al.* (eds.), *Theories of Society: Foundations of Modern Sociological Theory* 2 vols. (New York: The Free Press of Glencoe, Inc., 1961).

*Petersen, William (ed.), *American Sociological Patterns* (Garden City, N. Y.: Doubleday & Company, Inc., 1956).

Sibley, Elbridge, *The Education of Sociologists in the United States* (New York: Russell Sage Foundation, 1963).

*Sumner, William Graham, *Folkways* (New York: Ginn and Company, 1940).

PART ONE

CULTURE AND PERSONALITY

Chapter 2

Cultural System

FACT OF CULTURAL DIVERSITY

IN EVERY one of our largest American cities there are neighborhoods which include small enclaves of foreigners: Russian, Italian, Chinese, Polish, Lithuanian, Puerto Rican. These ethnic groups, situated in ghettoes like San Francisco's Chinatown or New York's Spanish Harlem, are striking reminders of variety in human ideas and customs. Spend a day wandering through your own city's foreign section, the Little Mexico or Little Italy; take in some of the strange

Even in our own country, cultural diversity is a fact.

Joseph Muench

21

San Francisco's Chinatown has the largest Chinese community outside of the Orient.

San Francisco Chamber of Commerce

sounds, smells, and sights; interview some of the immigrants about their customs, and your immediate reaction will be to exclaim: "How different these people are from us!" Usually, like most Americans, you assume a position of superiority, as if your customs are the "right" ones and foreign ways are inferior.

This feeling of superiority when confronted with strange and different behavior patterns is a universal tendency in human groups. Herodotus noted it among the ancient Greeks. The biblical prophets continually inveighed against alien customs, reiterating solemn warnings about the danger of the "flesh pots of Egypt." One African tribe calls its neighbors by a name meaning "monkeys," while the word for "man" is exclusively used to refer to members of its own tribe. Americans are not immune to this universal tendency. How often have you heard tourists who have traveled to other countries, in Europe or Mexico, for example, or even to remote parts of our own country, like the Ozarks, make remarks about the quaint or odd people they met on their journeys?

It is impossible with our twentieth-century communications media to be unaware of the vast diversity in human behavior patterns. We all know, for example, that Hindus abhor the killing of animals, revere cows, believe in reincarnation, and organize their society into a multilayered caste system. In any given week, news magazines like *Time* discuss the complexities of tribal organization in Nigeria or political experimentation in Pidgin-English-speaking Papua in New Guinea. Even a country as close to us in cultural background as France is revealed to differ from us in many political, economic, and familial institutions.

This *fact* of cultural diversity — the wide variety of human ideas, behavior patterns, social institutions, and beliefs among the peoples of the world — becomes *the problem* of cultural diversity only when we ask several questions about it. (1) Is our way of life the human, natural, or best way while all other peoples' customs are unnatural or inferior? (2) If there is a common humanity shared in by all men, how do we explain the almost infinite variation in the way men think and act? This chapter on cultural system attempts to provide satisfactory answers to both of these questions.

THE PROBLEM OF CULTURAL DIVERSITY: ETHNOCENTRISM

While weighing solutions to the problem of cultural diversity, we must be on our guard against narrow-minded prejudice. For, the fact of cultural diversity simply ceases to be a problem at all if our own culture values are taken uncritically as standards for judging other societies. Eugene Burdick's best-selling novel, *The Ugly American,* pointed up the dangers inherent in viewing foreign people's actions and motivations through the eyes of American culture only. Similar warnings come from Peace Corps personnel throughout the world who repeatedly urge us to get inside other peoples' viewpoints. The warning is clear. Unless we see East African or Burmese problems the way the natives there see them, we will never light upon solutions to their problems which will be acceptable to *them.*

Sociologists call the inability to get inside other peoples' viewpoints by the name of ethnocentrism. Derived from two Greek words meaning group-centered, ethnocentrism is the tendency to measure and judge the way other people act in terms of the ideas and norms prevailing in the society with which I am most familiar. The ancient Egyptians with their pantheon of many gods condemned the monotheism of nearby Israel simply because it differed from their own beliefs. This was ethnocentrism. If a New Englander with his nasal twang casts aspersions on the soft drawl of the southerner, he is being ethnocentric. We are as group-centered in our judgment when we think it is natural to read from left to right as the Arab is who thinks the natural direction for reading is right to left. Many Americans fall into the fallacy of ethnocentrism. Boxing is no more natural a sport than bullfighting. Football is not superior to soccer merely because we play the former and foreigners prefer the latter.

Because *ethnocentrism* condemns foreign customs as strange and exalts our own group values as absolutes, it is a very nonscientific way of viewing cultural diversity. In short, it is a synonym for cultural snobbery. As such, sociologists condemn ethnocentrism. Can you think of any examples of ethnocentrism in intergroup relations in the United States? In relations between religious groups? In attitudes of the dominant majority toward members of minority groups?

THE PRINCIPLE OF CULTURAL RELATIVITY

Popular anthropology books like Ruth Benedict's classic, *Patterns of Culture,* are full of examples of customs which, by our cultural standards at least, are so grotesque as to be unnatural. Benedict recounts how suspicion between husband and wife among the Dobu of New Guinea is so intense that each jealously guards his separate sweet potato garden against the evil witchcraft of the other spouse. From another group, the Kwakiutl of Vancouver Island, she depicts the custom of wasteful destruction of money and valuable property. In the status competitions one chief sought to outdo and shame his opponent by being able to destroy more property than the rival. These customs are in sharp contrast with the mutual trust between spouses and the deep concern to preserve personal goods from destruction so prevalent in our own society.

Many other weird customs can be cited. Some Plains Indians swapped wives. Michael Rockefeller lost his life while exploring a headhunting tribe in New Guinea. Missionaries attest to the prevalence of polygamy in parts of Africa. Many Eskimo adults abandon their aged and infirm relatives, leaving them to perish in the Arctic wilderness. A curious custom was brought to light in two New Guinea tribes discovered only a few years ago. From time immemorial they have engaged in periodic skirmishes of warfare. Yet, they do not look on their intertribal strife as warfare. Rather, they see it as a kind of athletic competition in which the young men give proof of their prowess and each tribe avenges its respective ancestral dead. In this athletic contest the scores were totaled in terms of the number killed!

In asking us not to judge such examples ethnocentrically, sociologists[1] appeal to a fundamental cultural principle: the principle of *cultural relativity*. Cultural relativity, the opposite of ethnocentrism, states that actions and beliefs in other societies must be judged in the context of those societies' values, not by our cultural values. Thus, for example, in America, it seems abhorrent for parents of a marriageable girl to force her, against her will, to marry a man for economic reasons. Yet, in many societies, it is thought improper for a young girl to marry for love a man who is a poor economic bargain. Which view is correct? Neither! It depends, according to the principle of cultural relativity, on how a given society views the institution of marriage: is it a free-love contract between two persons or is it also a binding economic contract between two families?

There are several parts to the principle of cultural relativity. It is first of all a simple plea for tolerance. Many modes of acting are purely arbitrary. Whether we embrace, shake hands, or rub noses upon meeting a friend will depend entirely on the society we belong to. If Americans have a preference for hotdogs and baseball, they should be tolerant of the Korean taste for fried dog meat or the British enthusiasm for rugby.

Secondly, cultural relativity goes beyond a plea for tolerance to urge us to perceive in other cultures positive values which we may lack in our own. The Mayan Indian peasant in Yucatan with his reverence for the land and sense of duty to ancestors may in many ways live a more fulfilling life than a harried New York advertising executive. Americans tend to place an absolute premium on the conveniences of modern civilization. Yet, many people find our way of life too hectic, impersonal, and mechanistic. Recently, a group of two hundred and fifty people were evacuated from the

---

[1] Throughout this chapter the terms anthropologist and sociologist are used as interchangeable. Anthropologists are more interested in the cultures of preliterate groups while sociologists study the culture of modern man. Both share the same view of cultural system.

volcano-wracked island of Tristan de Cunha in the mid-Atlantic. They had lived a simple pastoral life which was deeply infused with religious and personal qualities. After a year of internment in England they voted, to a man, to return to their idyllic life in Tristan de Cunha. Travelers to this remote island testify to the beauty of its simple life, far from the toil of modern civilization. Many anthropological reports succeed in invoking in us this same feeling of nostalgia for the simple courtesy of primitive man. Cultural relativity, therefore, bids us open our eyes to all that is good and beautiful and meaningful — although different — in communities other than our own.

Finally, cultural relativity asks us to view the seeming weird ways of other peoples in relation to *their* own standards. Just as it is not fair to evaluate a piece of folk music by the musical standards of classical symphony, so it is not right to judge preliterate societies by the model of advanced civilization. A noted anthropologist, Robert Redfield, well stated this aspect of cultural relativity. It is one thing for the highly mobile Eskimo with limited food supplies in the midst of a harsh environment, tearfully, to leave an infirm mother-in-law behind in the snow to die because she could not, perforce, travel anyway. It is quite another thing for a Milwaukee husband to abandon his crippled mother-in-law in a Wisconsin snow storm!

ETHICAL RELATIVITY

Some sociologists have overextended the principle of cultural relativity to include ethical relativity. The ethical relativist maintains that there are no actions which are, in themselves, right or wrong. He maintains that only the standards of a given community determine moral correctness. In this view, murder, infanticide, or premarital sex experimentation are morally correct for the society which approves them.

Several things can be said about ethical relativity. First, whether or not there are any moral absolutes is properly an ethical, not a sociological, question. Secondly, even if sociologists could show that there are no moral absolutes which are universally accepted, many ethical thinkers feel they can demonstrate that certain moral practices should be universally accepted. Finally, ethical relativity seems to involve us in the dilemma of justifying the Nazi slaughter of the Jews, since the prevalent Nazi value-system decreed that action.

A belief in moral absolutes does not, on the other hand, contradict the principle of cultural relativity. Even if I believe that certain practices like witchcraft, polygamy, or divorce are universal moral evils, cultural relativity directs me to seek out *reasons* these practices make more sense in a primitive society than in my own.

For example, in some societies which deny to women any real independence, women become deeply reliant on the male members of the population for food, shelter, and protection. If there is a greater ratio of women to men, many women could be left utterly destitute. Hence, such a society comes up with the institution of polygamy to spread around the limited number of male protectors. Similarly, if a group takes very literally the biblical command "Increase and multiply," viewing many progeny as the greatest possible blessing in life, a man may want to have a plurality of wives to bear him as many children as possible. Cultural relativity does not make moral judgments about polygamy. It simply attempts to show why polygamy fits in more naturally in some societies than in others.

The main distinction between ethical and cultural relativity is this: Ethical relativity is a moral principle which bids us never to make moral judgments about the behavior of other people since such judgments have no validity. Cultural relativity is a sociological principle which urges us to appreciate other peoples' actions in the setting of their own culture. It is simply a plea for real understanding. If we desire to pass judgment on actions in terms of a code of moral absolutes, that is another question, properly belonging to ethics. Because cultural relativity should be present in all sound political, educational, health, and missionary policies toward other cultures, it will be employed throughout this chapter as an accepted sociological principle.

FALSE EXPLANATIONS OF CULTURAL DIVERSITY: RACE

It would be bald ethnocentrism to ascribe the fact of cultural diversity to the perversity of non-Americans. We must seek an alternate explanation. Some thinkers have stressed innate biological or geographic or climatic variation as a satisfactory solution to the problem of cultural differences.

Theories of race are burdened with a tragic history of misuse. The folklore of racism, culminating in the Nazi doctrine of an

Aryan super race and the American myth of an interior black race has no scientific foundation. Often, also, race has been fuzzily thought of as a synonym for nationality, as in the term, "the Italian race." Only a moment's reflection will reveal, however, that nationalities include many racial types. The fair haired Lombardese of North Italy are strikingly different in physical characteristics from the more swarthy Sicilians. Americans, on the other hand, include Negroes, Chinese, American Indians, and those of European descent.

Biologists use the concept of race in a very technical sense. To the scientist, a race is a biologically inbred group possessing certain physical characteristics which tend to breed true from generation to generation. Complete inbreeding, which can be defined as mating between members of the same race only, takes place only when there is geographical isolation of a racial type, as among the Indians of Greenland, or in a perfectly segregated or isolated society. Since perfect geographical or social isolation rarely occurs in the world, most human groups are racially mixed. There is little ammunition here for the race purist! Biologists stress the term, physical characteristics, in the definition of race to make clear that except for certain superficial physical differences such as skin pigmentation, bone structure, and hair texture, we do not know how the races of mankind differ. Indeed, scientists do not agree about the number of human races. Some postulate the classic three (Negro, Caucasian, Mongolian). Others assert that there are five or more established races. Such scientific disagreement does not concern us, except inasmuch as it cautions us not to put too much credence in theories of race.

A racial interpretation of culture attempts to explain differences in temperament, intelligence, and creativity among human groups in terms of the different biological strains which characterize the races of man. In this account, Negroes, whites (technically Caucasians), and Asiatics (technically Mongolians) derive their varying customs, attitudes, and beliefs from their innate biological differences.

The evidence against a racial explanation of cultural diversity is overwhelming. Children of all racial types fully adopt the culture of the group in which they are brought up. Clyde Kluckhohn, the Harvard anthropologist, has cited the case of the young son of two American missionaries who was orphaned in China. From infancy he had been raised by a Chinese family. Several years after his parents' death, he paid his first visit to America. His complete bewilderment with the American way of life was noteworthy. His walk, gestures, and facial expression were Chinese, not American. Only his blond hair and blue eyes were clues to his Caucasian ancestry. Kluckhohn draws the conclusion that "here the point is that an individual's acts and attitudes not only failed to resemble those of his own close relatives in this country, but they resembled those of all members of an alien physical group and contrasted with all members of his own physical group."

While there are no proven innate intelligence differences due to race, the evidence indicates that some differences in intelligence are attributable to cultural background. Thus, in intelligence tests administered during World War II to all recruits into the U. S. Army, Negroes from Northern cities received higher intelligence quotient scores, on the average, than whites from southern rural areas, while Los Angeles Negroes scored notably higher in these tests than Negroes from Mississippi. Every racial group, however, had its share of geniuses and morons.

Creativity differences are hard to measure scientifically. The Caucasian race, certainly, has no monopoly on high cultural achievement. The great Chinese empire of the middle ages, the advanced societies of the Aztecs, Mayans, and Incas, and the flourishing thirteenth-century kingdom in Timbuktu are evidence that creativity has been found among all races.

Some people regard modern civilization with its large cities, developed technology, and advanced scientific and medical research, as the only standard of creativity. According to this basis of judgment, the peoples of Europe and the Americans are creatively superior to other races. This is a clear example of ethnocentrism, however, since modern man has focused his creativity in the areas of science and technology. Many so-called primitive peoples, while materially poor in technical achievement, have expressed their creativity in the poetic richness of their mythology and religious ritual, the subtle beauties of their language and art, and the complexity of their social organization.

The most convincing evidence against a racial explanation of cultural difference is the fact that peoples of very similar physical types have very dissimilar cultures, while people of very different racial stock may show striking cultural similarities. The ancient Philistine peoples, for example, while racially a non-Semitic people, adopted the Semitic culture and religion. Thus, also, the warlike Plains Indians of America were greatly dissimilar in culture from their racial brothers, the quietly ritualistic Pueblo Indians of New Mexico. Even the very same racial stock shows different culture forms over a period of time. The Mayan Indians of present day Yucatan are as fundamentally different in culture from their famed twelfth-century ancestors as Western Europeans are from their barbaric forebears who invaded Europe in the dark ages.

FALSE EXPLANATIONS OF CULTURAL
DIVERSITY: GEOGRAPHY

Geographic and climatic variations are no more satisfactory explanations of cultural diversity than race is. Hippocrates, a Greek writer, writing in his book, *Airs, Waters, Places,* asserted that "Europeans, since they live in a climate of changing seasons, are vigorous, brave, and fierce, whereas Asiatics, who enjoy a more equitable climate are calm, mild, and gentle. Where the climate is relatively unvaried, the people are uniform; where the climate changes under the influence of the seasons, the people are diversified."

A geographic explanation of culture differences would be dismissed as folklore were it not for the fact that many people still subscribe to it. Ellsworth Huntington, a Yale professor, early in our own century popularized the geographical view of culture. Huntington sees human temperament as geographically determined. He asserts that "the mountaineer is resentful and quarrelsome and much bolder than the plainsman." He also postulated that desert people would show one human culture type, seafaring people another, snowbound peoples still another.

This geographic explanation is unsatisfactory on several counts. Not all desert peoples, for example, throughout the world, have similar cultures. The Tuaregs of the Sahara are adventuresome pirates, who pillage traveling caravans. The Berbers, also a Sahara people, are herdsmen. The Hopi of the Arizona desert, unlike the Tuareg, neither engaged in armed battle nor exhibited warlike tendencies. Some peoples who dwell side by side in the selfsame New Guinea mountains have different political, religious, and economic systems.

The geographic myth is also exploded when we consider the fact that, whereas animals must totally adapt to their environment at the risk of extinction, man can control his surroundings. He can cope with a tropical environment by alternative methods: stripping to a loin cloth, sleeping out the hot hours of the day, or using air conditioners.

This much should be conceded to geographic factors. They tend to limit some of the possibilities open to culture variety. Hence, a mountain people will not maintain a navy. Perhaps also, where geographic conditions are so favorable that the population can survive by simply plucking lush fruit from trees, there will be little incentive to invent arts or the instruments of civilization. Conversely, where geographic conditions are harsh and the land arid, it is highly improbable that a great civilization will arise. Survival amidst a forbidding natural environment will require the expenditure of so much human energy, that there is none left over for inventiveness. But, if geographic conditions limit the potential directions a culture will take, they are never controlling factors. The very same lush or arid climates have nurtured peoples of widely divergent customs. We must go beyond physical factors to explain the variety of human behavior. We must understand it in terms of culture.

THE RANGE OF CULTURAL VARIATION

Although the fact of cultural diversity has already been clearly established, some examples are needed to illustrate the range of cultural variation. These examples are included not to bore the student with endless examples of culture difference, but to induce in him the conclusion that the range of cultural diversity is almost limitless.

The family is a fundamental group in every society. In our own American society, the family is a small, one generation group, consisting of parents and immediate children. Relatives of the family may be close friends but rarely intimate members of the family circle. In other societies, perhaps the majority, the family is a wider, extended kin group. All cousins of the same generation are called, and, in fact, are, brothers and sisters. In a typical extended family, as in Samoa, children may feel equally at home in the uncle or aunt's house as in their own. Indeed, they may live the major part of their lives with relatives rather than with their own parents.

In our western tradition, families have been patriarchal. The patriarchal family, centered in the father as the source of authority, traces lineage and inheritance through the father's side of the family. Although it is the type of family system we are most familiar with,

This Saudi Arabian household evidences an adaption of new Western conveniences to their Eastern traditions.

Arabian American Oil Company

it is neither universal nor "natural." Very many societies have matriarchal family systems in which lineage, inheritance, and surname are adopted from the mother's side of the family.

Matriarchal societies are found in Africa and throughout the South Seas. In the matriarchal family system, the man of family authority is not the father but the mother's brother. He it is who chastises and teaches his nephews. From him, not their father, they inherit property and titles.

Government and status systems likewise show wide variation all over the world. Some groups are democratic; others have absolute monarchy. Some rule by a council of elders; others rule through decisions of priests. All societies have government, but the form has numberless variations. Similarly, all societies confer special status and rank on select members of their group. In some tribes status belongs properly to the old. The Plains Indians, on the other hand, gave greatest prestige to the brave warrior. Still other groups honor most the mystic.

Who will receive the highest rank in a society depends on whether that society places greater value on action or contemplation, worldly success or mystical gifts, wealth or voluntary poverty, courage or quiet wisdom. Those who lack the highly honored virtues will feel out of place in their own society. Conceivably, they might have been men of great prestige, instead of outcasts, if they had chanced to be born in a different society. Thus, for example, it is hard to be in business in a society which despises merchants. It is troublesome to be talkative in a Trappist Monastery. So also, the quiet scholarly student is often out of place in the American youth culture, while the extrovert high school athlete is out of place in a rabbinic school.

THE PRINCIPLE OF CULTURAL SELECTIVITY

Almost every type of governmental, educational, economic, or family system has its virtues and defects. Courage, bravery, and activity are good things. But, so are contemplation, quiet study, and careful prudence. Unfortunately, it is almost impossible for a society to stress one virtue or way of life without slightly downgrading its opposing virtue. Foreigners admire the American spirit of enterprise while deploring our lack of reflection and intellectual life. The contemplative Brahmin, on the other hand, may lack the practical skills to make the Indian economy prosper. It is with cultures as with personality types. The busy administrator has little time for scholarly research; the soldier on active duty is a poor mystic.

The principle of cultural relativity which maintains that no society has a monopoly on all that is best in the world finds its foundation rock in an even more basic sociological principle, the principle of *cultural selectivity*. Every society must select certain definite modes of thinking and acting from a limitless array of possible ways of thinking and acting. It is as if any given human culture system only represented one limited segment of a mighty arc of possible cultural types; or, as if each culture represented one color shade in the vast technicolor spectrum of potential culture variation.

In her book, *Patterns of Culture,* Ruth Benedict compares human culture systems with human language. The comparison is worth exploring. All of us who have tried to master a foreign language are aware of the difficulties in pronunciation. There are many sounds in modern European languages which are totally lacking in English: the German *ch* sounds, the French *u,* and the Spanish trilled *r.* The German umlaut *ö* is as difficult for American students to pronounce as our lengthened vowel sounds are for the Germans. The fact that different human languages do not employ the same range of consonants is illustrated by an anecdote about the Kennedy family. The late President enjoyed playing a word game in which a phrase was given as an answer to an unknown question. The players were supposed to guess the most appropriate question to fit the phrase. For the suggested phrase, *Nine W,* one of the Kennedys volunteered the question, "Is your name spelled with a *V, Mr. Wagner?*" The German answer, of course, is *"Nein, W."*

Only a student of comparative linguistics can begin to list the endless variety of vowel and consonant sounds employed by human languages. The guttural sounds of some American Indian dialects or the tonal inflections of Chinese remain stumbling blocks for most students of these languages. Ancient Hebrew had a soft *g* sound whose pronunciation modern scholars can only approximate. A mere listing of all conceivable human language sounds would be tedious, even if it were possible. What is more significant is to know why, with so many possible sound combinations, all languages choose only a select few to build on. There is a reason. A language could employ all possible tonal variations at the cost of being utterly incomprehensible. Few humans could either pronounce or understand it. It is the need to communicate with one another, then, which dictates that members of a human language group construct their language out of a limited number of possible vowel and consonant sounds. These must be arranged in definite word-order patterns. In human language, selectivity is essential.

When we say that languages must select from the infinite variety of possible sounds, we do not intend to convey the idea that this selection process is always, or even usually, conscious. Although a few arbitrarily contrived languages like *Esperanto* do consciously select certain sounds, normally language selectivity is an unconscious process, occurring in the long history of usage.

It is not only in language that selectivity is necessary. Culture systems, also, must choose a definite group of behavior patterns from which to build meaningful social environments. It is, for example, no more natural to drive on the right side of the road than on the left. Yet, if both were equally allowed on our busy freeways, the result would be utter chaos. Greeting etiquette is likewise arbitrary. I may bow to indicate respect as the orientals do or salaam like the Arabs. I can embrace with my whole body or simply shake hands as a sign of equality. It would be very confusing, however, if all of these forms were equally appropriate. We would never know which form was the correct one to use in a standard social situation.

The set conventions of society are like rules in a game. If you could double dribble, kick the ball, make bodily contact, and take steps without dribbling, basketball would become a free-for-all. So, also, to avoid disorder every society has rules. Although the rules are sometimes arbitrary, they act as signals as to which behavior is appropriate in a given situation. Men in America know they should not wear dresses or use lipstick, except perhaps to a Halloween costume ball. Women should not smoke cigars. Men are expected to be strong and aggressive. Women are expected to be emotionally expressive.

Different culture systems choose different behavior patterns. In India, packs are often carried starpped to the head and resting on the back. In some areas of Africa, it is more common to carry a load on the head.

Marty Coyne

Society does not selectively narrow down possible behavior patterns in order to inhibit freedom. Rather, it attempts to furnish us with clues as to what behavior is expected of us, as well as what behavior we can expect of others in standard social relationships. We do not expect people to break legal contracts and simply dismiss it with the laughing remark, "I was only kidding when I signed that contract." We hope our doctor will give us medicine not just pleasant conversation. It would shock us to see people dancing or loudly laughing at a funeral. We know enough to expect different treatment from our clergyman than from our barber. These expectations are placed in us by the conventions of our society. Social life, no less than traffic, needs rules and signs if it is to be a smooth-flowing process.

The rules of society have their origin in the process of cultural selectivity. Like language selectivity, this is rarely fully conscious. There is no council of elders which legislates all of the customs in a society. Like Topsy, most social rules just grow!

From time to time, however, there have been highly reflective attempts to establish Utopias, ideal communities where all of social behavior is carefully regulated. These efforts have often been mere literary attempts, like Plato's *Republic,* designed as idealistic models of society. Most actual efforts to establish Utopian communities have met with failure. The demise of Brookdale farm in Massachusetts and the utopian New Harmony Indiana community are warnings to the would-be Utopian that culture simply cannot be legislated. The Chinese communist experiment in our own day with commune farms is a similar attempt to enact the perfect society.

HISTORY: THE SOURCE OF CULTURAL
SELECTIVITY

The question arises as to why certain beliefs and actions become part of a culture, while others are rejected. Most of cultural selectivity has its roots in the obscure happenings of history. One society may write from right to left because the first man to invent writing in that community happened to be left-handed. In a given circumstance, one way of acting is tried, found to work, and perpetuated. Thus, if the first fishermen in a group harpoon fish rather than use nets, harpooning becomes the standard way to fish. Or, an island people, living near the sea, has to journey over a steep cliff to reach the seashore. The first man from this group to accomplish the journey beats a route to the left of a huge rock at the edge of the cliff. Ever afterwards, all members of the group may travel to the shore by the same route.

Historical accident, then, is the main source of cultural selectivity. For example, one group of teachers in San Francisco has remarkably similar facial and voice characteristics in their style of teaching. It happens that each attended the same university where they shared a beloved professor whose mannerisms they have unconsciously imitated. It was a similar accident of history that King Akhenaten in 1370 B.C. was unable to convince his fellow Egyptians of the truth of monotheism. His weak and meditative personality contrasts sharply with the powerful character of Moses, who, a century later, persuaded his fellow Hebrews to leave Egypt and follow the course of monotheistic worship. Forever after, Egyptian and Israelite culture diverge in religious aspects. Fully to understand cultural selectivity, therefore, it is necessary to know the historical background of any group as well as the great historical personalities who have comprised it.

Two final reflections should be made about the comparison of cultural selectivity with the selection process involved in human languages. First, just as study of many different languages exposes us to the infinite possibilities in human phonic variation, so only a detailed study of many cultures will open up to us the numberless types of human action and belief systems. Since it is impossible in the limited space of a chapter to do more than sketch other culture systems, a fuller study of other cultures is left to the students' individual initiative. Secondly, although both cultural and language selectivity are largely unconscious, cultural selectivity necessarily will involve greater conscious reflection. Culture is concerned with important human values and behavior patterns. The choice of these can never be as arbitrary as the selection of human sound patterns. Man has always reflected on his customs in order to change them. In our own time, the civil rights revolution in America is a highly conscious effort to change certain culture values and behavior patterns, especially in the American South.

THE MEANING OF CULTURE

Two fundamental tasks remain for us in reference to the term, "cultural system." We must give the term, *culture,* a precise sociological meaning and show how cultures form patterns or systems.

We are all familiar from our study of history with the historical use of the term culture, as in the expression, "Roman culture." By culture, historians refer to the distinctive artistic, political, and religious achievements of civilized national societies. Students of history generally limit their concern to advanced nations, possessing writing and technology, whose achievements have left a permanent mark on the course of history. Although this use of the term is legitimate, sociologists feel that culture in this sense is too rigidly narrowed down for their purposes. Because the sociologist is as interested in preliterate man as in advanced civilization, he speaks as readily of the culture of a New Guinea tribe as of the culture of seventeenth-century France. Sociologists also are concerned with all human groups, not just national societies. They feel that it is proper to speak of the culture of American prisoners, the culture of prize fighters, of American Jews, etc. It is clear that, in this context, culture refers to those characteristics of a human group which set it off from all other human groups.

We are also familiar with a usage of the term, culture, in which it means the same thing as personal refinement. A cultured person is one who appreciates the fine arts. The English poet, Matthew Arnold, once defined culture, in this sense, as a knowledge of the best that has been thought and said in the world, an ability to see life steadily and see it whole. This is the culture which is the goal of a liberal education. Such an education aims to teach us to savor a Beethoven sonata, paintings by Picasso, and the philosophy of Kant. Many of your teachers, in their effort to impart a liberal education to you, will have told you to ignore rock-and-roll music because it is "uncultured." Culture in the sense of personal refinement really means a personal appreciation of the greatest artistic, political, and religious achievements of history's advanced societies.

This meaning also differs from the sociological use of the term. For the student of society, culture refers to *any* characteristic which typifies a human group. Thus, surfing music is as much a part of American culture as a composition by Aaron Copeland. A political poster may tell us more about the United States than one of Whistler's justly famous pictures. The cartoons of Al Capp and Walt Kelly are as essential to an understanding of American society as the poetry of Robert Frost. Indeed, sociologists may find a housing project or a garbage heap throws more light on trends in American society than a Frank Lloyd Wright building or the Metropolitan Museum of Art. Whereas in the other usages of the term, culture refers to the so-called higher achievements of group life in art, science, philosophy, etc., in the sociological sense culture must include *all* achievements of group life.

The classic sociological definition of culture was supplied by an English anthropologist, E. B. Tylor, in 1871. For Tylor, "culture is that complex-whole which includes knowledge, belief, art, morals, law, custom, and any other capabilities and habits acquired by man as a member of society." It is clear from the definition that culture includes more than just the higher artistic achievements of group life. Tylor's definition has been updated by a recent American sociologist, Robert Bierstedt, whose definition, with slight adaptations, we shall employ. "Culture is the complex-whole that consists of everything we think, do, *feel,* and have as members of a *particular* society."[2] Several phrases in this definition need to be underscored.

"Culture is a complex-whole." What makes something complex? Something is complex if it consists of many parts. Thus, an automobile is complex because it takes many parts like the battery, steering wheel, fan belt, spark plugs, etc. to propel it. Our American State Department is called a complex since it consists of many specialized sections, concentrating on such things as Far Eastern policy or U. S.-Russian relations. We could not even begin to list the many parts of a culture-complex like American culture. Baseball, hot dogs, the two-party system, television, a belief in the equality of man, advertising, apartment house living — all these and more belong to American culture. Even a relatively small segment of American culture, e.g., the youth culture in a certain year, would

---

[2] The italicized words have been added to Bierstedt's original definition.

Wide World

American youth culture includes such things as certain types of dress, hair styling, and dancing.

include many parts. A partial listing of items would include surfing, steady dating patterns, ivy-league clothes, special slang expressions, and hero worship for a strange group of singers.

No sociologist tries to draw up an exhaustive catalogue of culture parts because such a task would be futile. Besides, culture is not simply complex like a garbage dump, containing a multitude of unconnected parts strewn over the lot. Rather, culture is a complex-*whole*. A culture is a *whole* because the many parts or items of culture are so interconnected as to form a system. A brief illustration will be given here. Golf balls, gambling, movie theaters, and skiing are random bits of American culture. These items and actions form part of a leisure pattern, shaped by the attitude that Americans ought to enjoy their free time and summed up in the American proverb "All work and no play makes Jack a dull boy." We will say more about culture patterns in the next chapter.

THE CATEGORIES OF CULTURE

It is both impossible to list every item that forms part of a culture and unnecessary to do so, since it is the culture-whole or system in which sociologists are primarily interested. We can, however, set out general categories which will include all of the elements of culture. The fundamental elements of culture are four: ideas, norms of action, attitudes, and material things. These four elements are included in our definition by the phrase "that consists of everything we think (ideas), do (norms of action), feel (attitudes), and have (material things)."

Ideas

The category of ideas includes religious and philosophical beliefs, science, social values, folklore, and mythology. Ideas are important elements in any society. For, contrary to the Marxist belief, ideas shape history by influencing action. The idea that this world is only an illusion since reality consists in contemplation of God has given structure to Hindu society for centuries. The American idea of the fundamental equality of all men is behind the important Negro civil rights movement of our own time. The idea of the subservience of the state to the inalienable worth of the individual is a dividing idea which sets American society off from Soviet society.

Ideas may be either true or false. The sociologist is just as interested in false ideas entertained by a society as in the true ones. False ideas effect the way people act no less than true ones. For example, the belief that this world is imminently coming to an end impells many religious sectarians to lead highly abstemious lives in fear of God's judgment. Likewise, the Nazi German idea of a master Aryan race led to wholesale extermination of Jews in the greatest tragedy of modern time. Some primitive people mistakenly consider that the birth of twins is a sure sign of adultery. As a result of this belief, they mete out the punishment of death to any mother who has multiple births. The Hakka people of China have an interesting explanation of twin births. Boy-girl twins are taken to be the ideal reincarnation of a once happily married couple. Hence, among the Hakka, boy-girl twins are betrothed to each other when they reach marriageable age.

Since it would be entirely impossible to list all the ideas which prevail in any one society, the sociologist's task is to isolate those dominant ideas which typify a group's culture or form themes for action in that group.

Norms of Action

Social customs, the approved behavior patterns of a group, constitute the second major category of culture elements. No individual is expected creatively to invent new ways of acting in response to standard social situations. Society itself provides us with patterned responses appropriate to a given occasion. Thus, I know how to eat in public, address people of superior authority, act toward fellow customers in a department store, or write a standardized business letter because my society has provided me with a set of ready-made rules.

Most social conventions, like opening a car door for a lady friend, are unconscious, automatic responses. Like the air we breathe, we do not give much thought to them because they are so obvious. Wearing pants instead of lap-laps, sleeping in beds with mattresses instead of on the floor or mats, sitting at table using a knife, fork, and spoon to eat instead of squatting and using chopsticks — all these behavior patterns have become such a part of our personal habits that we take them for granted.

Indeed, social customs have their reality in the fact that many members in a group take the standardized behavior patterns of society and make them into personal habits. These personal habits become ingrained through constant repetition until they form a basic part of personality. Most of us have little routines we follow every day; a definite route to and from school, a certain time for rising in the morning, a specific ordering of events in the day to include a schedule for study and play. The importance of personal habits is that they save us the trouble of constantly thinking through the proper responses to routine situations. I swim, type, and walk without consciously rehearsing each motion of the body needed to perform these actions. So, the well-groomed, polite boy in American society who has learned the American standards of etiquette and cleanliness, need not worry about how to act in public. He has made society's standards of etiquette part of his personal habits.

Prescribed patterns of behavior are called norms. Norms are defined as patterns of behavior that regularly recur and are expected to recur among the majority of people in a group. Social behavior patterns are called *norms* to distinguish them from purely personal habits of behavior which do not serve as standards of action for all men in a group. Many examples of norms can be cited.

It is a norm in military society for soldiers to salute superior officers. Some Christian churches expect women to cover their heads while in church. It is a prime American norm for children to be procreated and educated through the institution of wedlock, and not outside of marriage. It is important to know the norms of any group in order to predict the behavior of members of that group. From a knowledge of the norms which obtain among the Hopi Indians of New Mexico, for example, we can confidently foretell that an adult Hopi living on the reservation is frugal, mild mannered, and self effacing.

Mores and Folkways

Since not all of the norms of society carry the same prescriptive force, William Graham Sumner, a noted American sociologist, distinguished between two kinds of norms: *mores* and *folkways*.

The *mores* of a society are those behavior patterns which are so respected and socially desirable that infractions of them are considered morally reprehensible. The mores include the "must" and "must not" behavior which becomes incorporated into the group's moral and legal codes. Murder, child molesting, abuse of the democratic process by violating the secret ballot, disloyalty to the American government are all examples of mores in American society. As a brief description, the phrase "everything a society considers morally or legally binding in conscience" renders a good definition of the mores.

The *folkways,* although they are also universally accepted patterns of behavior, do not carry the same obligatory stamp of the mores. They are norms in the sense that they are the "proper things to do." For example, in American folkways men wear pants and shoes. If someone insists on donning a toga and sandals, his behavior, however much at variance with American folkways, is not deemed immoral or illegal. He is simply dismissed as "odd." Whereas the penalty for violating the mores is either punishment by law or condemnation by the moral community, the sanction for disregarding the folkways is the milder, but not less effective, penalty of ridicule. So, in America, little boys who continue to play with dolls after a certain age are branded as "sissies" for their infraction of the folkways.

Some sociologists distinguish a third type of norm which has almost no prescriptive force. These are fads, styles, and usages which are widely imitated. There is no moral sanction or even ridicule visited on the person who refuses to adopt the latest custom or fashion in clothing. The only punishment, if you can call it that, is withdrawal of the positive approval given to the person who is "up on the latest trend." Since fads, styles, and usages lack a binding character, it seems improper to classify them as real standards of behavior.

Ideal Norms and Real Norms

It is sometimes customary to distinguish between the ideal norms and the real norms of a society. The ideal norms are mores which all men in the society ought to follow. Given the frailty of human nature, these ideal norms are often violated. Consequently, the term, real norms, is used to refer to the actual behavior patterns in a society. Monotheism, premarital chastity, honesty, and free speech are all ideal norms in American society. In a given American school the ideal norm of honesty may receive mere lip service while a real norm of cheating in tests prevails. There are always, of course, discrepancies between any culture's ideals and actual practices of behavior. Even if they are honored mostly in the breach, ideal norms retain their directive force so long as they remain generally accepted ideals of individual behavior. In societies undergoing rapid social change, these ideal norms may simply fall into disuse. Thus, the ideal norm of the 1920's forbidding women to smoke in public no longer obtains in the 1960's.

It is easy to see how important a role norms play in any group. They can form the basic elements of culture. For, we all act on the expectation that behavior patterns appropriate to a given social situation will be followed. The teacher in your classroom is expected to abide by the norms of acting mature, preparing class discussions, marking objectively, and keeping control in the classroom. If he or she began to dress and act like one of the students, to throw spitballs in class and play favorites, the students would become justifiably angry. For, some of the prime norms of the school classroom would have been violated.

Attitudes

Society not only teaches its young members certain ideas and norms of behavior, it also inculcates definite attitudes. *Attitudes, the third major culture category, are feelings or emotions which influence action.* They are neither as immediately observable as behavior patterns nor as capable of expression as ideas. In the study of the attitudes of various groups, we must rely on the findings of the discipline of social psychology. These are discussed more fully in Chapter 4. It should be obvious that we do learn attitudes from the groups to which we belong. A group of workers may transmit an attitude of hostility and distrust toward management to new recruits. Some societies teach respect for law and order, while others pass on to their members attitudes of disrespect for any political authority. The American school systems, public and private, try to instill in students attitudes of loyalty, patriotism, and tolerance. Could you enumerate some of the attitudes toward teachers, school authorities, rival schools, etc., which you have picked up by being a member of your particular school group?

Material Things

Our final culture category includes material objects. It would be quite impossible to list exhaustively all the material things from phonographs to pickles or automobiles to pegged pants which pertain to a given culture. The significant job of the sociologist is to itemize those material things in a culture which embody definite group attitudes or ideas. For example, the great cathedral at Chartres sheds as much light on thirteenth-century feudal society as does the philosophy of Thomas Aquinas. Similarly, the presence of veils in Arab countries indicates an attitude toward women in these societies. Finally, in the American Indian cultures, tobacco was not only a crop to be tilled, but an essential element in a friendship-ritual, the smoking of a peace pipe. It is clear that the material environment profoundly influences a group's way of life. To illustrate this point, many urban planners have pointed to the effect wide open spaces and playgrounds can have on juvenile delinquency. The simplest proof of the importance of material things for understanding a culture comes from the field of archeology. From artifacts alone, prominent archeologists have been able to reconstruct entire cultures, giving us insights into many of the ideas and values of ancient man.

Members of a Particular Society

The final phrase in our definition, "as members of a *particular* society," emphasizes the peculiar sociological stress in the study of cultural systems. There are some ideas, norms, attitudes, and material objects that pertain only to individuals and are not shared in by any group. A pathological fear that I am being followed by a group of hostile demons is an instance of this kind of individual trait. Since purely individual characteristics are the province of the study of psychology, they do not concern the sociologist unless they somehow affect the entire group.

On the other hand, some ideas, norms, attitudes, and material things characterize man wherever he is found: the need to eat, sleep, propagate the human race, and maintain order in social living. Such universal traits are studied by a general psychology, biology, geography, and a theory of society.

It is those ideas, norms, attitudes, and material objects which are shared in by members of a particular group which earn our concern in a study of cultural system. For, while all men must eat, only some men pattern their eating habits to three meals a day. Again, while all men fear danger, only some men tremble at the thought of witchcraft. Although a belief in God is shared in by most human groups, only certain monks draw from this belief the conclusion that they should become recluses in the desert. Any careful study of cultural systems will focus on that sum total of ideas, norms, attitudes, and material objects which characterize a particular human group.

We have seen, therefore, that cultures differ all over the world. Further, in trying to explain cultural diversity, we rejected racial and geographic explanations of cultural variety. The principle of cultural selectivity, rooted in history, helps to explain why no culture includes all of the humanly possible ways of thinking, doing, and acting. Finally, we have examined the definition of culture. In the next chapter, we will attempt to explore at greater depth the sense in which cultures are complex-wholes.

Major Concepts in Chapter 2

1. *Fact of Cultural Diversity:* The wide variety of human ideas, behavior patterns, social institutions, and ways of viewing life among the peoples of the earth.

2. *Ethnocentrism:* Prejudiced evaluation of the action of members of other groups, using the standards of my own group as the criterion. A judgment which rates the actions and ideas of others negatively *simply* because they differ from the ideas and actions of my own group.

3. *Principle of Cultural Relativity:* A principle of sociology which states that all cultures have good points. Actions in a society must be judged relative to the values of that society, not relative to values of my own society. Cultural relativity, founded on the need for cultural selectivity, is the opposite of ethnocentrism.

4. *Ethical Relativity:* The belief that there are no moral absolutes. Morality depends simply on what my society considers correct. Ethical relativity is not championed in this chapter.

5. *Race:* A biologically inbred group exhibiting certain physical characteristics which tend to breed true from generation to generation.

6. *The Principle of Cultural Selectivity:* A principle of sociology which states that every society must choose from the infinite variety of possible human behavior patterns and human values. The need for order and meaning in human societies demands that some possible behavior patterns be made normative and other possible patterns be rejected.

7. *Culture:* The complex-whole which consists of everything we think, do, feel, and have as members of a particular society.

8. *The Four Elements of Culture:*
   a) *Ideas:* what we think as members of a particular society.
   b) *Norms:* what we do as members of a particular society.
   c) *Attitudes:* what we feel as members of a particular society.
   d) *Material items:* things we have which characterize us as members of a particular society.

9. *Norms:* Uniformity of acting which regularly recurs and is expected to occur among the majority of people in a particular society.

10. *Mores:* Commanded or prohibited actions which are of strict obligation in a group. The mores express "must" behavior since they embody a group's moral values.

11. *Folkways:* Actions which are normative but do not carry moral or legal sanctions. The "socially approved" ways of acting.

Review Questions

1. State the problem of cultural diversity.
2. Why is the racial explanation of cultural diversity a false explanation?
3. How many races of mankind are there? Explain.
4. What is the evidence for or against the proposition that the races of mankind differ on intellectual ability?
5. Can differing geographical areas of the world adequately explain cultural diversity?
6. List some of the differences in family and government systems in the world.
7. Why must societies choose limited patterns of action and values from the infinite variety of possible culture forms?
8. What does it mean to say that history is the source of cultural selectivity?

9. What does the historian mean by the term "culture"?
10. How does the sociologist's use of the term "culture" differ from its use as a synonym for personal refinement?
11. Explain the statement: "Culture is a complex-whole."
12. Why is the sociologist just as interested in false ideas entertained by a society as in the true ones?
13. What is the main distinguishing difference between mores and folkways?
14. State the difference between ideal norms and real norms. Why is this distinction important?
15. Define attitude. What distinguishes an attitude from an idea or a norm?

Discussion Questions

1. Discuss: "The principle of cultural relativity does not necessarily involve sociologists in ethical relativism."
2. Discuss: "The set conventions of society are like rules in a game."
3. Discuss: "The adjective *primitive* when applied to preliterate people can be misleading."
4. Discuss: "Norms are the absolutely irreducible element of culture."
5. Discuss: "The material artifacts of a culture reflect the ideas and values of the culture."

Bibliography

*Benedict, Ruth, *Patterns of Culture* (Boston: Houghton Mifflin Company, 1934).

Bierstedt, Robert, *The Social Order* 2nd ed. (New York: McGraw-Hill Book Company, Inc., 1963).

Bowra, Sir Cecil M., *Primitive Song* (Cleveland: World Publishing Co., 1962).

Dobzhansky, Theodosius, "The Race Concept in Biology," *The Scientific Monthly,* 52:161–165 (February, 1941).

*Firth, Raymond, *Human Types* (New York: The New American Library, 1958).

*———— *We, The Tikopia* (London: G. Allen & Unwin, Ltd., 1957).

*Fortune, R. F., *Sorcerers of Dobu* (New York: E. P. Dutton & Company, Inc., 1932).

Goldschmidt, Walter (ed.), *Exploring the Ways of Mankind* (New York: Holt, Rinehart & Winston, Inc., 1960).

*Hall, Edward T., *The Silent Language* (Garden City, N. Y.: Doubleday & Company, Inc., 1959).

*Hoebel, Edward A., *Man in the Primitive World,* 2nd ed. (New York: Mc-Graw-Hill Book Company, Inc., 1958).

*Huntington, Ellsworth, *Principles of Human Geography,* 6th ed. (New York: John Wiley & Sons, 1951).

* Also published in paperback edition.

*Kluckhohn, Clyde, *Mirror for Man* (New York: Whittlesey House, 1949).

*Lewis, Oscar, *The Children of Sanchez* (New York: Random House, 1961).

*Linton, Ralph, *The Study of Man* (New York: Appleton-Century-Crofts, Inc., 1936).

*Malinowski, Bronislaw, *Argonauts of the Western Pacific* (New York: E. P. Dutton & Company, Inc., 1922).

*Mead, Margaret, *Coming of Age in Samoa* (New York: Random House, 1953).

Radin, Paul, *Primitive Man as Philosopher* (New York: Appleton-Century-Crofts, Inc., 1927).

*Redfield, Robert, *The Folk Culture of Yucatan* (Chicago: University of Chicago Press, 1941).

*——— *The Little Community* (Chicago: University of Chicago Press, 1955).

Sanders, Irwin T., *et al.*, *Societies Around the World*, 2 vols. (New York: Dryden Press, 1953).

Sorokin, Pitirim, *Contemporary Sociological Theories* (New York: Harper & Brothers, Publishers, 1928).

*Sumner, William Graham, *Folkways* (New York: Ginn and Company, 1940).

Chapter 3

Cultural Patterns

IN THE preceding chapter, we looked at the elements of culture. Now, these elements must, like building blocks, be fitted together to form the whole edifice of culture. For, the various parts of culture are interconnected. In short, in any society there are patterns of culture.

SOME PATTERNS OF CULTURE

In his study of Navaho life, Clyde Kluckhohn has given us a simple but brilliant example of cultural pattern. Navahos always leave part of the design in a pot, basket, or blanket unfinished.

The Navahos always leave part of the design in their craft items unfinished, an example of the fear of closure that pervades their culture.

Bureau of Indian Affairs

49

Medicine men in their instructions to their apprentices will never relate a story or cure in full. In recounting geneologies or mythology some item or detail is always left untold. Kluckhohn was able to explain these odd customs by the integrating Navaho theme, a fear of closure. This attitude, in turn, derived from the Navaho idea that if anyone finished something, it had a stamp of finality about it. Possibilities for change or improvement were closed off.

In South African society, native shanty towns and poverty of goods are material facts. Apartheid-segregation is a norm of society. Distrust of natives and fear of their dishonesty is an attitude among the politically dominant white Afrikaners. An idea which helps to explain these aspects of South African life is the peculiar Boer version of predestination. Only white Afrikaners are predestined to heaven, while all Bantu natives are predestined to hell.

Beards, old jeans, and sandals are material items. Writing in stream of consciousness style or painting only in abstraction are norms of artistic behavior. Rebellion against the values of society is an attitude. An idea which integrates all these is the belief that a person can become a real individual only by creatively expressing himself in ways that do not conform with the dominant norms of society.

As these examples make clear, a culture pattern is a characteristic *theme, value,* or *motif* which permeates an entire society. Patterns unite the four elements of culture (ideas, norms, attitudes, things) into systems. Sometimes it is very difficult to isolate culture patterns, however, because many values or attitudes of a society are not explicit. Members of the group grow up so accustomed to looking at the world in certain ways that they take their world-view for granted. The Navaho fear of closure is a case in point because the Navaho Indians do not explicitly expound this attitude although it is central to their culture.

Much of the sociologist's work, as a result of the hiddenness of many culture patterns, is a detective job — getting behind overt behavior patterns to the unstated cultural assumptions. One way of isolating the dominant theme in a group is to ask the questions, "Who is considered the ideal man, the success, in that group?" What kind of person must he be? What must his virtues be? If you asked these questions, for instance, concerning present day American youth culture what kind of answers would you receive?

A second clue to understanding culture patterns is provided by the dominant social system in a society. Every society has some prime social system around which most of its world-view revolves.

In ancient China this set of institutions was the ancestral family. In Argentina it has been the army. Medieval life centered in the church. Whereas in the Negro cultures of West Africa religion is the mainspring of society, in East Africa all of social life is oriented around the cattle economy. What do you think is the dominant social system of United States society?

CULTURE PATTERNS IN U. S. SOCIETY

It is impossible in a few paragraphs to do more than sketch an outline of American culture patterns. Because we will delve more deeply into this question in the remaining chapters of this textbook, all we attempt to do, here, is to pinpoint the most prominent culture motifs in America.

One of the curious facts of sociology is that we know much more about the culture system of an Eskimo tribe than we do about America. This is because many anthropologists, smitten with the lure of the unfamiliar, have concentrated their attentions on preliterate groups. Also, the patterns of these close-knit small tribes are easier to uncover than is the complex, highly diversified American culture system. Actually, the variables in American culture are too many to allow a controlled fieldwork study of U. S. society. As a result, much of the analysis of American culture is little more than the considered observations of sociologists. Definite proof is lacking.

A value, however, which clearly stands out in American life is our tolerance for diversity in action and belief. For, Americans pride themselves on the multinational and multireligious origins of their society. Confronted with so many varying customs in the United States, some sociologists have even denied that there is a unifying strain of culture shared by all. In effect, they view America as several cultures, coexisting in one geographic area. The more judicious view holds that, despite the diversity, America does have a consensus, a basic agreement, on certain important values and norms.

Our country has often been referred to as the nation of *cultural pluralism*. In the pluralistic society many diverse regional, religious, and group cultures are tolerated. Thus, for America, pluralism of culture becomes more than a mere fact. Rather, it is a positive ideal. To the cultural pluralist, our differences are stimulants to progress in the great forum of American life. The concern of these paragraphs is not on the patterns which divide us as a people but on those underlying culture patterns which unite all Americans.

THE CENTRAL ROLE OF BUSINESS
IN U. S. SOCIETY

Ours has been predominantly a business civilization. Both family and church have tended to be subordinated to this central institution. Consequently, the main source of leadership in our communities has been from businessmen. For example, the major contenders for the presidency in the 1964 election from both parties could justly be described as big businessmen. This pivotal role played by businessmen in American politics is unparalleled in modern European nations.

Since the business leader is the model of American success, the organizer who knows how to get things done, the structure of the successful corporation has served as an example for church, educational, and governmental organization. This fact is evidenced by the way churchmen and educators use the cliches of the business world to describe their own activities. "Selling a product" and "the academic market place" have become consecrated American expressions. Some of the ideas most central to American life are also colored with business meanings. Thus, the belief in equal opportunity for all is translated to mean equal opportunity to rise to the top rung of the ladder in the American corporate hierarchy.

Similarly, the Horatio Alger myth that any American starting at the bottom of American society can work his way up, bears the stamp of the economic success stories of nineteenth-century financiers like Rockefeller and Carnegie. It is not a mystery, therefore, that in the United States, knowledge, technology, and higher education have rarely been goals, sought in themselves, but rather means of furthering progress in the business world.

There are four key words, which, perhaps more than any others, sum up the American value system: action, newness, bigness, and youth. A careful study of magazine advertising reveals that these four terms recur in some form on practically every page of a national magazine.

Action

Americans are preeminently a practical people, interested in results. Constantly on their lips is some phrase such as "let's get

Since ours has been predominantly a business civilization, the successful corporation serves as a model for church, educational, and governmental organization.

A T & T

going" or "something should be done." Thus, knowledge is valued mainly for its utilitarian effects. For instance, it was only after the successful atom bomb tests that the name of Einstein became a household word. Even the American churches have been accused of a heresy of action which measures the effects of church work in terms of social programs, buildings, and clubs rather than by the interior peace of communicants.

Some foreign observers have deplored the American hustle-and-bustle, the busy pace of our work life, the hectic flow of traffic on the freeways. These are but symbols of an American preference for action which is linked to the fundamental conviction that there is no problem which cannot be solved by dint of unswerving human effort. Because of this belief Americans are sometimes criticized by Europeans for being unduly optimistic. Could you list some of the ideas, norms, attitudes, and material objects which fit into this American value-pattern of action?

Newness

Because we were a people of the new world with vast unexplored frontiers, constant change has been the key to our history. Americans came to equate newness or change with progress. Consequently, "traditional" was a bad word, conjuring up images of the stodginess of the old world. This preoccupation with the new not only led to progress in inventiveness and technology, it also made Americans receptive to changes in education and family values. We were, in short, a new nation in history, founded on the radically new political charter of equality and dedicated to an ideal of progress which would forever make all things new.

Our advertisements demonstrate the importance of newness to Americans when they present each product as somehow new or invite us to try Product X because it is new. Another clue to this value comes from urban living in America. For, whereas European central cities have remained intact for centuries, the American central city is dying, usually after less than a hundred years of existence, as our citizens flock to the newness of suburban life. And so, just as the value of action guarantees a hearing to any American idea which promises results, the preference for newness insures that whatever is new in America automatically tends to win favor.

Bigness and Youth

Perhaps it is the vast sprawl of American society which explains the American preoccupation with bigness. Certainly, no other nation so boasts that it has produced the biggest of everything in the world from supermarkets to the world's largest pawnshop. Not all cultures share this value with us. Some Europeans find our concern for quantitative greatness boorish, while the Japanese place a premium on small, intricate articles.

Another culture pattern in America is integrated around the value placed on youth. In no other country have so many middle-aged men and women spent so much money in a futile attempt to stay the hand of age. In a sense, Cary Grant and Marlene Dietrich personify the American ideal of perpetual youth. Probably, the American youth pattern is connected with the values of action and newness — as if an aged person has already spent all his energy for successful action and is devoid of new ideas or schemes.

Although it would be a worthwhile project to catalogue all of the ideas, norms, attitudes, and things which are integrated around these four themes of action, newness, bigness, and youth, that task lies beyond the scope of this chapter. The student can test for himself the validity of these four American patterns by an analysis of the value-colored words in advertisements and popular music. But, our job now is to show the importance of understanding culture patterns. This leads us to introduce a central concept in the study of culture system, *the principle of useful purpose.*

PRINCIPLE OF USEFUL PURPOSE

All over the world societies and culture patterns are in a state of flux as the influence of modern civilization extends to peoples from Bali to Basutoland. As every day new commonwealths and republics begin to take their place in the modern world, some primitive peoples are being asked within a generation to make the long jump from the stone age to the age of modern technology.

Small wonder, then, that this age of transitional growth is a time of hope-filled excitement! Unless, however, we naïvely equate all social change with genuine progress, it is also a time fraught with great danger. For, along with missionaries, doctors, educators, and government officials bringing the good tidings of modern civilization to preliterate peoples, have come many traders, unscrupulous adventurers, and political intriguers to unsettle the natives and breed discord.

Some native peoples, confused by the too rapid breakdown of their traditional values and grown cynical of what they consider the gross immorality of white settlers, have expressed hostility to any western influence. In some cases there have been strong nativistic reactions, attempts to throw over all the traces of colonial influences, even good ones, and to reinstate the good old days of simple tribal society. Tragically, the golden past can never be revived. In other cases where white settlers have firm political control, a breakdown of the traditional culture system has fostered cultural apathy or listlessness on the part of the natives. Denied full access to the best things of modern civilization by discrimination while cut off from their traditional rural life-ways, many primitive societies are adrift in a sea of cultural disintegration. *Culture disintegration* refers to the collapse of traditional culture patterns. When no suitable substitute system of culture is provided to take the place of the traditional ways, cultural disintegration results in apathy or drift.

Our own American Indians are classic examples of culture disintegration. When they were hemmed into reservations by the might of the American soldiers a century ago, the Plains Indians continued for a time to live their own separate lives. With the decline of the buffalo which had provided a focusing theme of their cultures and with the prohibition of intertribal war by the U. S. government, the Plains Indians' culture system simply fell apart. Today, many American Indians have lost pottery-making skills and weaving abilities which once were part of their social heritage. Nor is the American Indian an isolated example of culture disintegration in the history of culture contact between preliterate peoples and modern man. The Australian aborigines penned up in reservations similar to the American Indian have suffered much the same fate. Many South Sea people have also witnessed the total collapse of their traditional cultural system. A once proud and accomplished people became cultural half-breeds, mongrels belonging fully neither to the modern world nor to their ancient heritage. The pages of history are replete with the sad biographies of these cultural misfits, marginal men tragically cut off from the full sense of belonging to any human culture.

If missionaries, educators, health and government officials have a genuine obligation to share the best things of modern civilization with primitive peoples, they certainly have a more profound obligation to insure that other cultures of the world are not totally disoriented by their efforts. For, good will alone is not enough. It was good will which induced the missionaries on the Cook Islands in the nineteenth century to introduce European styles of dress. When, however, the Cook Islanders got caught in tropical rain storms, their soaking clothes caused many of them to contract pneumonia and die. Those missionaries had failed to inquire into the full implications of their actions. If they had seen the Cook Island culture as a complex-whole, finding out how each element fit into the pattern, they might have avoided this tragic mistake. Several case histories will be supplied to impress on the student the absolute necessity of studying other societies as culture wholes.

When the British first subdued the Ashanti tribe, a people of the west coast of Africa in what is present day Ghana, British political sovereignty seemed assured. Yet, in 1896 and again in this century inexplicable revolutions broke out which involved England in costly wars. The cause of these outbreaks remained obscure to the colonial administrators. In 1921 a third outbreak was only narrowly avoided when a British anthropologist pointed out to the officials the deep symbolic importance to the Ashanti of the Golden Stool. This historic throne of the Ashanti chiefs had mistakenly been considered by the British as a mere political symbol. To the Ashanti this was a sacred religious treasure which represented the symbolic seat of their tribal gods. Several bloody wars might have been averted if successive British officers had not arrogantly usurped this sacred stool. What the British in their ignorance of Ashanti culture regarded as political revolutions in reality were religious crusades.

It took England nearly a century of rule in Africa to learn the indispensable necessity of indirect rule. For, direct rule of colonial officials over native peoples led to misunderstanding, resentment, and resistance. Often, the subjugated natives did not recognize the legitimacy of British authority. Lacking Western concepts of private property or legal contracts, the African found Western law confusing. At first, to offset political revolution, the British deposed the paramount chiefs of the African tribes under their domain. Sometimes, they set up common-tribesmen as their legates to the people. This experiment, however, was never successful since the traditional chiefs were more than the locus of political authority. They were believed to represent the rule of gods on earth. In their person they symbolized tribal unity, historical continuity with the ancestors, and the deep connection between the tribe and its land holdings. Even after they were despoiled of political power by the British, natives continued to view these paramount chiefs as their rightful rulers, to appeal to them for decisions in disputed tribal claims, to accord to them the deepest respect. The commoner legates were despised as lackeys of the British. After World War I the British colonial officials began to realize that to ask natives to reject their chiefs was tantamount to asking them to cut themselves off from all of their historical roots. That would be cultural suicide! Hence, the British began to employ an "indirect rule" through the traditional chiefs who would apply African law and tribunals to insure law and order.

Both of these examples illustrate the failure of the British to apply a very fundamental sociological principle, *the principle of useful purpose*. Most sociologists are "functionalists," that is, they believe that every culture element has a positive job or function which helps to promote the survival of that culture. The principle of useful purpose sets forth this sociological belief by stating that any idea, custom, belief, or attitude that is widespread in a society and persists over a period of time must be assumed to have *some useful purpose for that society,* contributing to social order and promoting the survival of that culture.

Even a practice as alien to our way of life as witchcraft follows this principle of useful purpose. To Western eyes, the belief in witchcraft seems a totally negative belief which should be prohibited. Indeed, the very first impulse of civilized missionaries or government officials is to launch a campaign to stamp out the belief in witchcraft. A very careful analysis of how a belief in witchcraft operates, however, shows that in many societies this belief serves a useful purpose. In far-flung tribal societies lacking a standing police force or tribal courts, only customary belief provides law and order. In such societies, an individual is afraid to break any of the socially sanctioned customs for fear of being accused of being a witch. He is just as hesitant to display extreme anger or aggressive feelings toward a neighbor lest that neighbor attribute all his ill-fortunes to that man's evil witchcraft, as he is careful not to provoke his neighbor to anger so that his neighbor will not practice evil magic against him. It does not really matter that witchcraft is unscientific or lacks real efficacy. The point is clear. A belief in witchcraft reinforces social order and the socially approved behavior patterns in some tribes. Consequently, it serves a useful purpose for the survival of these groups.

Sometimes the useful purpose of a culture practice is not immediately apparent. Some American soldiers stationed in Greece during the war thought they were doing a great favor for the women of the tiny Greek village in which they were quartered when they laboriously built a pipe system to convey water to the middle of town. No longer would the women be forced to trek to the river to fetch water in jugs or to wash their clothes at the river bed. Now, quickly and efficiently water was available from a water pump in the middle of town. The women could wash clothes now in the privacy of their own homes. Much to the soldiers' dismay, the water pump was rarely used. The women continued to journey with their water jugs and clothes to the river bed. What the soldiers failed to realize was that the water pump would have deprived the women of one of their few legitimate pastimes: gossiping while they washed clothes together at the river or hauled water in jugs. This hidden recreation function was more important to the Greek housewives than the mechanical convenience of the water pump.

Similar cultural misunderstanding has dogged the path of a world health scheme promoting the use of latrines. The Greek government decreed that latrines be built in rural areas. Government health officials were at a loss to explain why the latrines were not being utilized. A consulting anthropologist was able to provide some explanation. The latrines had been constructed on the European raised seat model for an area in which the people customarily squatted for such purposes. The Greek peasants refused to change their motor habits to fit latrines unsuited to their culture needs. In one New Guinea tribe there was a similar reluctance to use the government sponsored latrines. These people believed that any object intimately associated with their own persons, from personal articles of clothing to excreta, was a prime object for evil witchcraft. If one of their supposed enemies should get hold of some object personally connected with them, he could breathe curses on it and cause them to fall under his evil power. Hence, these people were extremely secretive about attending to their personal needs. They would go stealthily into the bush to relieve themselves and carefully conceal their human feces. Imagine their fear when they were told to expose themselves to dangerous magic by using a public latrine. These fears were only overcome when an anthropologist suggested that latrines be equipped with shovels and a generous supply of lime. The natives were convinced that the lime would so well cover their excreta that it would be safe from the danger of evil magic. Thus, in the process, was world health promoted.

We do not need to suppose, because every widespread custom serves a useful purpose, that all customs should be immune from change. On the contrary, some practices, no matter how much they may "fit" into a given culture, seem so immoral or wasteful that Western government officials have no choice but to prohibit them. Cannibalism, infanticide, and continual intertribal warfare are a few examples. If culture disintegration is to be avoided, however, the principle of useful purpose directs us to replace a forbidden cultural practice with a suitable substitute which will serve much the same useful purpose in that culture. A few examples will illustrate the point.

In one primitive society it was believed that a death in the family totally defiled a household. The widow and children could be protected from the unpure influence of the husband's ghost only if the entire house was burned. In a society already poor in material goods, this purification rite seemed ruinously wasteful. In searching around for a suitable substitute, an anthropologist suggested to the people of this society that fumigation would serve the same cleansing purpose as burning, while avoiding the wasteful destruction of property. This cultural substitute was enthusiastically adopted.

A second example comes from two neighboring New Guinea tribes recently discovered. Since the memory of man they have been constantly at war with one another. Their battles served none of the ordinary purposes of warfare since no hostages or booty were ever taken nor did the boundary lines marking the division between the tribes ever change. Their skirmishes seemed to serve the purpose of testing the mettle of the young men who established their prowess on the field of battle. These battles also intensified tribal loyalty by appeasing the dead ancestors. The Dutch colonial officials in Netherlands' New Guinea, anxious to preserve order, outlawed these traditional battles. There are few sights more pathetic than a group of young men from a war-centered culture who have been deprived of any culturally recognized means of establishing their manhood. With time, if no substitute is found for war, such societies usually fall into cultural disintegration. Thus, since war was a central theme in the two cultures an attempt was made to avoid cultural disintegration by providing a substitute custom which would serve the same useful purposes of testing manhood, avenging the ancestors, and intensifying tribal unity. The officials proposed that a football be substituted for spears and a rigorous body-contact contest supplant the more mortally dangerous battle. While it is still too early to predict the success of this substitute, it seems to be a step in the right direction.

A final case study, illustrating the principle of useful purpose, concerns the Yir Yoront, an Australian aborigine people dwelling near the Coleman River on the west coast of tropical Cape York peninsula. These people had organized their society into a gerontarchy, i.e., the rule of the older men. The adult males were engaged in widespread trade relations with neighboring tribes, acting as middlemen in an exchange in which they traded stone from a quarry nearly four hundred miles to the south of them in return for spears produced by a tribe to their north. The main tool and utensil used by the Yir Yoront was the stone axe. Only the older men knew how to produce such axes. They would go about collecting wood, bark, gum, and the other materials used in constructing axe-handles. When they received the stone from their southern neighbors, they were able to fashion it into useful and supple stone axe-heads.

Although any member of the Yir Yoront could use the stone axes when occasion demanded, only the older men owned them. Younger men and women had to ask an older man to lend them his axe. These stone axes were much more than tools, therefore. They were symbols of a status hierarchy. Around the trade-exchanges where stone was received from southern trade partners was built a complex religious ritual. At the time of trade exchanges the young men would undergo puberty rites by which they became blood brothers to trade partners in other tribes. At the same time, religious ceremonies and fiestas were held.

When a group of missionaries opened a station near the Yir Yoront at the turn of this century, they took an intense interest in converting these aborigines to Christianity. Since the older men boycotted the mission Sunday school classes, only the women and younger boys were allowed to attend. Seeking to get a better entrance into the Yir Yoront society, the missionaries hit upon the idea of giving prizes to those women and children who attended classes. Because of the prime role axes played as utensils, the missionaries began to distribute fine steel axes to the young men and women who visited their missionary station. Besides their missionary motive, these English missionaries assumed that steel axes would be an improvement over stone ones, saving much time and effort for the Yir Yoront.

The result of their indiscriminate giving away of steel axes was disastrous. The young men and women, no longer dependent on the older men for axes, became querulous and disobedient. The rulers lost all authority. In time, there was no longer any need for stone axes. The trading relations with other tribes was discontinued. With them went the ancient puberty rites and religious ceremonies connected with trading. The traditional craft of making stone axes died out so that within a generation no Yir Yoront knew how to make them. Since they also could not make steel axe heads a new dependency on the missionaries was fostered.

The ancient social order of the Yir Yoront had been based on a belief that all social relations and culture items were exactly the same as those used by their first mythical ancestors. Since steel axes were obviously not the patrimony of the ancestors, a belief in ancestor worship broke down. When they finally agreed to enter government reservations, the Yir Yoront had suffered severe cultural disintegration. Their old self-reliance gone, their ancient world-view a matter of skepticism, the authority of the older men undermined, the Yir Yoront became apathetic and totally dependent on the white man.

If those missionaries had foreseen the far-reaching effects of their distribution of steel axe heads, they would have, undoubtedly, hesitated before acting. Perhaps, they would have altogether avoided introducing steel axes. Maybe they would have seen to it that only the older men in the tribe received them. Their mistake lay in a failure to see Yir Yoront culture as a whole system integrated around the material item of stone axes. They likewise neglected to apply the principle of useful purpose, mistakenly supposing that axe handles were merely utensils. We will restate the principle of useful purpose in full as a summary of this section of the chapter. There are three parts to this principle:

1. The principle of useful purpose states that any belief, custom, attitude, or other culture element which is widespread in use and persists in time serves a useful purpose for the survival of that society's cultural system.
2. Often the useful purpose is hidden or not totally apparent.
3. Any attempt to suppress a widespread custom or belief may lead to cultural disintegration unless a suitable substitute for the suppressed custom is found which will fulfill the same useful purpose for the society's cultural system.

SOME AUXILIARY CULTURE CONCEPTS

We will complete our treatment of cultural system by adding, as a kind of appendix, a brief discussion of three important culture concepts: subculture, acculturation, and culture lag.

Subculture

The idea of a subculture is a relatively straightforward concept. While it is comparatively easy to draw up an outline of culture patterns which obtain for small preliterate societies, it is a much more difficult task to indicate the culture patterns of a large, complex, culturally pluralistic society like the United States. Do the same religious patterns of behavior which prevail among American Catholics also characterize United States' Protestants? Are the customs of our industrial Northeast the same as those of the rural Southwest? Obviously, if there is such a thing as American culture, certain culture patterns will cut across regional, religious, and occupational groupings. But, in order to deal intelligently with those ideas, attitudes, and norms which set off groups within a larger society and which are at variance with the pattern of the dominant society, sociologists employ the term *subculture*. A subculture is simply the culture of smaller units or groups within a culture.

Examples of subcultures in United States society are the regional subculture of New England society, the age subculture of American youth, the racial subculture of the American Negro, the occupa-

The Negro could be said to have a racial subculture in America.

Children's Bureau

tional subculture of American doctors. It is possible to analyze subcultures as isolated units so long as we bear in mind that any subculture is in constant interaction with the dominant values of the larger society. For example, it might be argued that the American Catholic family system has norms and values sufficiently different from those of the general American family system as to form a subculture. Yet, the Catholic family system feels pressure to conform to the general American family system regarding norms of divorce, contraception, type of education given to children, etc.

Acculturation

Cultures are rarely static. Rather, they are constantly undergoing changes. The fact of cultural change necessitates the introduction of two concepts, acculturation and culture lag.

All over the world different cultures come in contact with one another. Culture contact almost always leads to borrowing of elements from the alien culture and incorporation of these elements into one's own culture. If the native East Africans of Kenya are not the same as their ancestors were before the coming of the white man, the white settlers, also, are different in significant ways from their European forebears. Through a century of contact, both cultures have adapted customs from one another. Sociologists use the term, *acculturation,* to refer to the process by which members of one society divest themselves of some of their own culture elements and take on elements from a foreign culture.

Several aspects of acculturation need to be emphasized. In the process of culture contact, both cultures change. Because of political or economic dominance, one culture may be much more selective in adopting foreign culture elements. But, even the most devotedly purist Britisher in the African tropics eventually, in some ways, goes native, if only in the matter of food preferences. Secondly, acculturation is always selective. A culture does not indiscriminately take over all culture elements from an invading culture. Rather, it adapts those elements which are most congenial to its own cultural values. For example, as foreign missionaries attest, a polygamous tribe in Africa may accept Christian notions of baptism and salvation while rejecting the Christian dogma of monogamy. An interesting study has been done by a Calvinist minister in South Africa showing how certain Bantu nativist Christian sects have used traditional Christian symbols to perpetuate ancestor worship and the ancient craft of their witch doctors. So also, after the American occupation, Japanese society selectively adapted certain American business values and the ethos of materialistic success without notably accepting the values of the American family system.

The successive waves of immigrants to the United States have provided sociologists with a unique laboratory for studying acculturation. At first, the migrants formed separate ethnic ghettoes designed to protect them from the influence of Americanization and to perpetuate Old World culture. But, even after a relatively short time in America and despite the protecting buffer of the ghetto, when the first generation immigrant returned home to Europe for a visit to the mother country many of his culture values had significantly changed. He was often surprised to find himself described as a "Yank" in his country of origin. Within several generations most immigrant families become totally assimilated to the dominant United States culture.

The immigrants to the United States were not the only ones to experience change in the culture contact situation. The dominant original Anglo-Saxon American culture has also profoundly changed because of its contact with the foreign immigrants. In the process of acculturation the original English-based American culture became a melting pot so that the polka, spaghetti, and beer and pretzels have become as much a part of American culture as the Anglo-Saxon concept of law and the two-party system.

Culture Lag

Sociologists use the concept of culture lag to refer to the fact that in the process of culture change not all of the elements of a culture change at the same rate. There are always culture elements which are holdovers from a previous era. Thus, for example, the political and moral values of a frontier rural society are very much alive today, despite the fact that the United States has become a highly urbanized society. The construction of highway systems and freeways has seriously lagged behind the rapidly increasing number of automobiles that use these highways. A recent supreme court decision calling for redistricting of congressional districts for the United States Congress and of state senate districts was based on the fact that a culture lag existed between present political arrangements and demographic population, changes which have brought the majority of Americans to urban areas. The laws in the 1920's lagged behind style changes which allowed women to wear bathing suits which were above the knee. Some economists have argued that economic theories based on scarcity are anachronisms in the American society of abundance.

Although culture lag is a very useful concept we must beware of making value judgments in our use of it. We cannot expect morality, family values or our political system to change at the same rapid speeds as technology. Unfortunately, there are some who have a cult of progress who think that all values in society must be constantly in flux. This is a species of ethical relativity. But, as the examples of culture lag in the foregoing paragraph illustrate, we need not deny all moral absolutes in order to employ the concept of culture lag.

Major Concepts in Chapter 3

1. *Culture Pattern:* A dominant value, theme, or motif which threads its way throughout an entire society. Patterns are the themes which unite the four elements of culture into systems.

2. *Culture Disintegration:* The collapse of the dominant values of a culture without suitable substitutes for them.

3. *The Principle of Useful Purpose:* A sociological principle which states that every widespread custom or belief in a society which endures over a period of time serves a useful purpose for the survival of that

society's cultural system. Two corollaries to this principle must be noted. (1) Often the useful purpose is hidden or not apparent. (2) Any attempt to suppress a widespread custom or belief must find a suitable substitute custom or belief which will fulfill the same useful purpose for the society's cultural system. If this corollary principle is not adhered to, cultural disintegration may take place.

4. *Subculture:* A group within a larger society having its own culture pattern of ideas, norms, attitudes, and material things at variance with the pattern of the larger society. Subculture can never be studied in total isolation from the culture of the larger society.

5. *Acculturation:* The process by which members of one society divest themselves of their own culture values and take on the culture elements of another society. Partial acculturation is going all the time. Full acculturation or total assimilation of the culture of a new society takes a long time.

6. *Culture Lag:* The theory that when a culture is changing, some elements (e.g., material things) change at different rates than other elements (e.g., ideas).

Review Questions

1. How does the sociologist discover culture patterns?
2. What is the central institution in American society? Explain your answer.
3. What are the main values of American culture?
4. Give some examples of the process of cultural disintegration.
5. What is meant by the British Colonial policy of "indirect rule"?
6. Explain how witchcraft can serve a useful purpose in preliterate societies.
7. Why is it important to find suitable substitutes for legally forbidden culture practices such as polygamy or cannibalism?
8. What is meant by a gerontarchy?
9. Using the Yir Yiront tribe as an example, show how a material artifact reflected the ideas and values of the culture of the Yir Yiront.
10. What is the relation of a subculture to the whole culture of a society?
11. List ten subcultures in American society.
12. How does the concept of acculturation differ from cultural disintegration?
13. What is meant by the statement: "Acculturation is always selective"?
14. When two cultures come into continuing contact, which culture changes? Explain.
15. Do all elements in a culture change at the same rate? Explain.

Discussion Questions

1. Discuss: "The useful purpose of a culture practice is not immediately apparent."
2. Discuss: "Much of the sociologist's work is a detective job."
3. Discuss: "The United States is several cultures, coexisting in one geographical area."
4. Discuss: "Cultural disintegration is inevitable when preliterate societies come in contact with industrial civilizations."
5. Discuss: "Good will is not enough when missionaries, educators, health, and government officials attempt to change culture patterns in preliterate societies."

Bibliography

*Benedict, Ruth, *Patterns of Culture* (Boston: Houghton Mifflin Company, 1934).

Bierstedt, Robert, *The Social Order,* 2nd ed. (New York: McGraw-Hill Book Company, Inc., 1963).

*Gluckman, Max, *Custom and Conflict in Africa* (Glencoe, Ill.: The Free Press, 1959).

Hogbin, Herbert Ian, *Social Change,* Josiah Mason Lectures, 1957 (London: Watts, 1959).

*Kluckhohn, Clyde, *Mirror for Man* (New York: Whittlesey House, 1949).

*Mead, Margaret (ed.), *Cultural Patterns and Technical Change,* World Federation for Mental Health (Paris: UNESCO, 1953).

Ogburn, William F., *Social Change with Respect to Culture and Original Nature* (New York: Viking Press, 1922).

*Paton, Alan, *Cry, The Beloved Country* (New York: Charles Scribner's Sons, 1948).

*Spicer, Edward H. (ed.), *Human Problems in Technological Changes* (New York: Russell Sage Foundation, 1952).

*Turnbull, Colin, *The Lonely African* (New York: Simon & Schuster, 1962).

Williams, Robin M. Jr., *American Society,* 2nd ed. (New York: Alfred A. Knopf, 1951).

Wilson, Godfrey, and Monica Hunter Wilson, *The Analysis of Social Change* (Cambridge: Cambridge University Press, 1945).

---

* Also published in paperback edition.

Chapter 4

Personality System

IN THIS chapter we shall be concerned with a behavioral system which has long been of great interest to philosophers, psychologists, dramatists, novelists, and poets — the human personality. We shall be concerned with personality as it is possessed by all human beings, with the particular ways in which Americans acquire their personalities, and in the concluding part we shall treat of the distinctively American personality. We shall discuss some of the more penetrating analyses of American character which have been attempted.

PERSONALITY

Yet before we begin this task it becomes imperative to specify exactly what we mean by the term "personality." To the philosopher the term means one thing; to the psychologist another; to the layman still another. None of these conceptions quite suit the sociologist. But let us look at them closely so that you will understand why sociology needs its special concept of personality.

Philosophy and the Person

Personna is a Latin word which comes from a Greek dramatic convention which the Romans adopted. Originally the word meant "mask"; and if you have ever seen a Greek play, you will understand why the word person (from *personna*) has come to be used to signify the identity of an individual in the world. In Greek drama the actors wore masks which symbolized the actor's part in the drama. And the classical Greek plays were intended to dramatize man's plight in the world. Hence the exterior of any man, his "mask," is the way in which others see him. The Latin word *personna* may be derived from *personare,* "to sound through," the sound that comes from behind a mask.

As philosophy developed a fuller conception of the individual it *looked within* the individual and discovered the soul. The principle of life in the body, inside the "mask" was the soul. But what kind of soul? Other animals have life, even vegetation has a kind of life. Hence, philosophers tried to narrow their quest even further: the true identity of a human being as a rational entity. "Person," then, refers to everything about a man. Human personality, in the philosophical sense, cuts across the boundaries of psychology, sociology, theology, and philosophy.

Social sciences are confined to empiric research and theory based on such research. Do you remember this from Chapter 1? Such generalizations of "total personality" are obviously outside the scope of empiric science. This is true for psychology as well as sociology. Beware the psychologist or sociologist, who in the name of his science, tries to pronounce on the total personality of man!

Psychology and Personality

You will remember from Chapter 1 that psychology is concerned with the behavior of the individual. In contrast, sociology is concerned with any given individual only insofar as his group identifications and social behavior are concerned.

Consequently, it is to be expected that psychology would look upon personality as it does. The individual, in psychology, is viewed as *an organism in environment.* His personality is viewed by psychologists as the *totality of his disposition to behave.*

Both the philosophical concept of total human nature and the psychological concept of total dispositions to behave are more than we need for sociology's purposes. But before we get more specific about a sociological definition, there is a concept of personality in social lore which you should not confuse with our sociological concept.

Personality in Social Lore

It is common in social lore to speak of personality as something that some people possess in greater amounts than others. "Mary has a great deal more personality than the other girls in her class." It is obvious that we have here a term that is used in varied senses and one which we cannot trust to mean the same thing every time it is used. Since this present book is a *sociological* analysis of American society, you should keep in mind that sociology has a special way of looking at the individual. This way serves the purpose of linking the individual to the groups in which he participates. In this sense everyone has a personality, not just the people with charm.

Social Personality

So we can use the term personality throughout this book if you will not confuse it with the way it is used in social lore, in psychology, or in philosophy. Just what, then, distinguishes our concept of social personality? There are two essential features of our definition. These are *role attitudes* and *self attitudes.* Together they comprise what we call the personality system, the social personality, or simply, the personality.

The simplest way to learn this conception of personality is to ask a few questions of yourself. Ask yourself how you are prepared to act. After mulling this over, you will arrive at another question. Act with whom? I am not prepared to discuss dating, rock and roll, or home difficulties with my teacher. The ways I act around my teachers are not suitable around my friends. Nor are they the same as the ways in which I act around the house. You must introduce the concept of *role* to make meaningful the question of how you are prepared to act. This makes your question more specific. Once you think of role you can think of the ways in which you are prepared to act when you are the student in a student-teacher relationship. How about the role of friend in a friend-to-friend relationship? Or as a teen-age son or daughter in relationship to father or mother. These are all role relationships. These *predispositions to act* are role attitudes. They are part of your personality.

Do you remember our discussion of the Greek mask? It seems that role attitudes have a lot in common with the Greek actor. This is true if we look at personality solely from the viewpoint of role attitudes. The individual is behaving toward others like an actor in a play. This "acting" is only a part of his personality. Yet it is an important part. Shakespeare, in his *As You Like It,* has one of his characters, Jaques, pronounce on this aspect of personality.

> All the world's a stage,
> And all the men and women merely players.
> They have their exits and their entrances;
> And one man in his time plays many parts.

There is an astounding similarity between Shakespeare's comments and our discussion of roles. This is not because Shakespeare was a sociologist or that sociology has followed Shakespeare. It is simply that one aspect of every man's life is his *role playing,* with him as the *actor.* The "whole person" is obviously much more than the role playing actor, but it is enough for sociological analysis to develop a construct or theoretical view of "personality" which does not mean the same as "the total human being" but is nevertheless adequate for our purposes. The actor possesses a *total complex or system of attitudes.* This complex includes on the one hand his more or less enduring conception of himself (self attitudes) and on the other hand, his predispositions to act (role attitudes). This total system is what the sociologist considers to be personality.

You should remind yourself again that this construct is for analytical convenience. Notice that *roles,* which link people together in social systems, are in this definition, linked to something inside the individual, the *self,* which governs the course of the individual's participation in society.

You Have Something to Say About It!

But there is a big difference between being an actor in a play and being an actor in social life. You have something to say (or do) about it. If people want you to do something that you do not wish to do, you are free to act or not to act. For example, if others expect you to be a cutup on a public bus you may choose to behave more appropriately. You do not see yourself as a cutup. This is simply moral character as we commonly understand it. In sociological language it is the self-concept which helps us to predict the behavior of individuals. If course of action *A* (being a cutup) is seen by the individual as inconsistent with his conception of himself and if course of action *B* (behaving properly) is seen to be quite consistent with his self conception, then we can predict that the individual will follow course of action *B.* What happens in real life, of course, is usually much more complex, but we can see by this simple illustration that the sociologist does not "surrender the individual to society" as the misinformed believe, but rather that, via the concept of personality, sociology gives full sway to individual differences in social participation.

THE VARIABLES IN PERSONALITY DEVELOPMENT

But it might be protested that the sociological conception of personality is oversimplified. What about heredity? it might be asked. What about environment? What about the body and its role in the behavior of the man? It would seem that "attitudes" are not enough to explain social behavior. This problem begins to clear itself up when we consider that attitudes are "outcomes" of three interactive variables, *physiological constitution, unique life experiences,* and *culture.* Each of these contributes to the development of personality, yet each is separate from personality. The physiological constitution is the foundation of personality. Who could conceive of a personality floating around without a body? Efforts to explain social behavior in terms of the body (the equal and opposite fallacy) have been historically, and are currently, tirelessly advanced.

Social behavior is also explained in terms of the life experiences of the individual. It is becoming increasingly fashionable among laymen and professionals, not without some justification, to speak of deviant behavior such as criminality or mental illness as consequences of a poor background. Thus, inadequate parents, improper companions, unfortunate economic situations, and the like are advanced as reasons for deviant behavior. Others are more alert to culture and its influences upon behavior. They point to cultural differences between dominant and minority groups as the source of misunderstanding, prejudice, and deviant behavior on the part of members of minority groups. None of these interpretations is without foundation, but sociological analysis of personality cannot rest upon any of these alone.

Personality — Passive or Active?

The complex interplay of these three variables as they operate to shape attitudes cannot be ignored or treated one-sidedly if the actor's behavior is to be understood. Further, there is a danger, even if the complexity of the interrelationship of these three interactive variables is taken into consideration, that the actor will be viewed as the mere passive agent of these variables. From birth, the human infant is an ongoing concern, with needs and wants imposed by the structure of his body and its biochemistry. From these needs there soon emerge other needs for affectional relations and, as the mind develops, needs to know and to find meaning in life and human relationships develop. Hence it is necessary as a minimum to understand something of the way the body, life experiences, and culture interrelate. But you know from your own life that you are not just a relationship of body, life experiences, and culture. You are *yourself.* What happens to you has *meaning* for you as a special individual. Don't we all tend to talk too much about ourselves? This is precisely because everything that happens has a special significance for us as selves.

The rest of the chapter is organized to accomplish your progression in the understanding of the way in which the actor comes to find meaning in his social participation. First we shall examine the broader aspects of his biological nature, the significance of his unique life experiences, the molding influence of culture, and finally the interrelationship of these in the context of the self and the social nature of the actor.

BIOLOGICAL NATURE

Biologists separate the development of an organism into two broad aspects, that class or race of which it is a specimen and that of the individual. From the broader point of view the human organism is a specimen of his subrace (Alpine, Mediterranean, Nordic, etc.), his race, (Caucasoid, Mongoloid, Negroid), his species (Sapiens), his genus (Homo) or the order of primates, the phylum of chordates and finally, simply, of the animal kingdom.

The Race Fallacy

The biologistically minded have, therefore, simply related the actor's behavior to his racial inheritance. After all, they reasoned, man is linked to the other animals through heredity. The single fertilized cell with which the individual begins life contains hereditary traits which science demonstrates can be traced back through the individual's parents, grandparents, his more remote ancestors, and presumably to his subrace, race, and far back into the animal kingdom. Thus, since the behavior of animals runs true to species, the behavior of man must in some way be related to his heredity as an animal.

This kind of reasoning led to racial psychologies which, because of their simplistic nature created a great deal of confusion in the behavioral sciences and contributed to a great deal of prejudice in relations between the races. The fallacy in such reasoning lies in mistaking constitutional or bodily traits for behavioral traits. Later in this chapter we shall discuss behavioral traits in more detail, but at this point the distinction between the way in which the body is put together and the way the social actor participates in his society should readily be seen. Traits such as the physical and skeletal structure, certain basic reflexes, which are constitutional or hereditary can easily be distinguished from personality traits such as promptness for social engagements, honesty, conformity, gregariousness or aloofness, and the like. Hence, the importance of the body as it "carries around" the personality, as that which contains the personality and conditions its operation cannot be underestimated. But the biologistic explanation cannot be advanced as the cause of the actor's social behavior.

The Body and Behavior

Individual biological variation, on the other hand, refers not to the fact that, in general, men by virtue of their species possess the same body characteristics, but rather to the fact of individual differences. Despite racial differences the fact is that an individual member of the Negroid race may be lighter than a member of the white race; members of the same race many range in body build from the tiny and frail to the large and tall. Thus, many who would reject the racial psychologies would accept an explanation of behavior based upon body build and physical constitution. The same fundamental fallacy exists in this reasoning as in the racial psychologies, viz., the assumption that the actor's attitudes are *caused* by his body structure. Attitudes, as we saw in our definition of personality, are conceptions of self and predispositions to behave, which are the outcome of learning. Hence, the important factor to consider is the actor's self conception and his role attitudes rather than his body build if we are to understand his behavior.

To illustrate the different ways in which body build and self conception operate, let us point to a simple example. In a rural high school a boy who is a good student and wishes to prepare himself for college may find himself under a great deal of pressure to play football because of his body build. His splendid physique prompts many people whose opinions mean a great deal to him to comment on the fact that he should utilize his talents for the good of the team. Others, perhaps including the teacher who first noted his college potential urge that he devote himself to his studies. He is torn between these alternatives. To the extent that he has achieved a social self, a perceived social identity as a potential scholar, he resists the challenge to seek another social role as a high school hero. The resulting behavior will then be understood best in terms of his self attitudes rather than in terms of his body build. Needless to say, however, a tiny physique would have removed the difficulty in making the decision. It is not that the physique does not enter into social behavior, which it most assuredly does, but rather that it enters into social relations *through the attitudes of those around him and through his own self attitudes.* This point will be developed later in the chapter as we explore the interrelationships between the three variables which enter into the development of attitudes.

UNIQUE LIFE EXPERIENCES

Beginning at birth, life circumstances begin to shape and influence the personality. The child is born into an ongoing system, the family. The family is, in turn, related intimately to the other social systems in the society of which it is a part. Rather a staggering confrontation for a six to eight pound infant to be thrown into American society with its enormous political and economic machinery, its richly diverse religious and social classes! Obviously a period of preparation is needed during which the child may "grow up" and grow into political, religious, economic, and other roles. This period can conveniently be broken into stages of social development. These stages are to some extent imposed by human nature itself. Obviously every human must at some time be an infant. And if he survives he will become a young adult; if he survives that he will become an old or (more politely) a mature adult. But some of the stages we are going to describe here are matters of cultural difference. Adolescence, for example, is not a life stage for the young in some societies where there is a smooth transition from childhood to adulthood. In American society the life cycle is as follows:

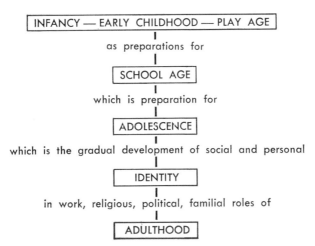

It is currently quite popular to speak glibly of personality adjustment, or in troubled times to overwork the notion of "maladjustment." Since the time of Freud and others it has also become a popular sport to blame one's parents for shortcomings or emotional problems of adjustment that we might have. As with most fads, this type of thinking is quite shallow and superficial. To speak of adjustment or maladjustment as general terms is, practically speaking, meaningless. The more meaningful question is, "Adjustment to what?" Life as a Watusi dancer? As a South Sea shell diver? Obviously, for you, at least, adjustments to work and marital roles in modern American society are more real and personally relevant. You should keep in mind that the following discussion of unique life experiences is considerably specialized so as to be relevant to the American culture, the final topic of the chapter.

Preschool Childhood

Infancy, early childhood, and play age are, from the sociological point of view, a series of progressions in social relations. The infant's whole world is the mother. Then as the thrust of humanness carries the infant to a greater horizon of consciousness, his social relationships grow in a widening circle to include his father, his brothers and sisters (siblings), his grandparents, and others in the home and family circle.

Early childhood solidifies these relationships. The child even develops relationships which can be called social roles. He learns to do things that bring satisfactions (statuses) to himself. He is little concerned with the satisfactions of others. In most American homes he is a "little king."

Ordinal Position in the Family

Now a variety of things can occur. The little king can be dethroned by the simple fact of a new baby in the family and a consequent curtailing of the previously unbounded homage that had been paid to him. Social psychologists have stressed the importance of ordinal position in the family, first-born, second, middle, last (the "baby"), in affecting the unique life circumstances of the infant and child. Has your ordinal position affected your family roles? Infant and child training philosophies differ also among different cultures and subcultures. But most students of personality agree that despite these variations, the infant and young child in America are much loved and cared for — even to the point where books

Play brings the child into contact with various systems of morality.

on infant and child care are among the top ten best sellers on any book list!

The Urgency of Growth

The situation is not without its hazards, however, for the urgency of growth begins to set up a tension which works against the child's desires simply to be adored and cared for. He ventures, he is helped, or he is pushed into play relationships with other children. Regardless of his mode of entry into the world of play and its fascinating games, a whole new world of social relationships will have its effects upon his personality. The problem is simple — the solution difficult. The problem is that the most meaningful play for him is play with his peers (those of this own age), but they also consider themselves in the same light as he — wanting to have their own way, not wanting to experience any personal unpleasantness, and demanding the center of the stage. It is the first major social crisis for the child outside the family.

To stay and suffer the indignities of the playmates or to run home and be safe and secure (and bored) — that is the behavioral crisis. Successful resolution of this crisis involves experimentation (doing some of both) with the final outcome of learning to accept the give and take of group play. The significance of this outcome for personality is twofold: it is the first exposure to morality (rules of the game) outside the family and ordinarily invokes much more give and take (accent on "take") than the child has previously experienced.

This exposure to the world outside the family and the personal toughening it involves can prepare the child for the greater degree of autonomy (standing on one's own feet) that will be needed in school. If his previous experiences have prepared him well he can become absorbed into the play and work of school without excessive fantasy (day dreaming) about how nice it is at home where none of these demands are made upon him. In a word, he can grow.

School Age

Successful experience in school leads to more successful experience in school. Setbacks can and do occur even for the most successful school child, but a record of successful achievement gives him confidence which in turn prods him toward intellectual curiosity and academic achievement. His world continues to expand. He simply cannot seem to grow as fast as he would like. He imagines himself an adult and begins to dream of a career and marriage. At first, as a child his dreams are bizarre and unrealistic. There is no immediacy nor urgency in his plans. When they begin to be immediate, in the sense that he must begin planning his school courses in preparation for academic specialization or dating as a prelude to future mate selection, things indeed become more urgent for him. In fact, in America, one of the societies that has this problem, this crisis has a name. It is called adolescence.

Adolescence

Adolescence is the bridge between childhood and adulthood. It is a time when American parents and their teen-age children typically bring a number of unnecessary problems upon themselves. These problems are most successfully resolved when something of a moratorium (holding off for awhile) is declared on parent-child conflict. The most effective role attitudes for the parent are supportive assurance and understanding. This supportive assurance and understanding of the parent should take place within the well-defined boundaries of the family's social and moral roles. For the teen-ager the most effective adjustment is productive schoolwork and reasonable attitudes toward sex and dating. To be avoided emphatically is *identity foreclosure* — premature commitments to marriage and premature commitments to unfulfilling or unsuitable career plans.

Identity

The successful outcome of adolescence is ego identity. The young person in today's specialized society achieves his identity much earlier than he achieves the social roles of adulthood. He does so through *anticipatory socialization,* a sociological term which means that he sees ahead to the positions in life which he wishes to hold and that he is training himself formally and informally for ultimate occupancy of those roles. Before turning to a consideration of the desirable social roles in American culture, let us turn back to our discussion of the transition from infancy through childhood in order that we may consider the concept of the self and its relationship to social experience and identity.

The Rise of the Self

Sociologists, following George Herbert Mead, say that the self arises when the person becomes an object in experience to himself. Further, they contend that one's attitudes toward one's self occur when we see ourselves in interaction with other people. This is the problem that we are considering here. How do we come to view ourselves as we do? This is the social and psychological aspect of moral character. We can see ourselves as being good or bad in various aspects of our behavior. Objectively, it can happen that we feel good while doing badly and that we can feel badly while doing something good. On the basis of our own experience we cannot argue this. Hence, it is well to remember the difference between objective morality and subjective feeling states. This is the difference between how we ought to feel and what we actually do.

Self and Role

Nevertheless a well-integrated personality is one in which the attitudes toward self are related to the behavior which others expect of us. Using the sociological conception of "role-set" we can illustrate this point. Imagine a situation where you are interacting with a group of your friends. The others expect you to behave in certain ways. These expectations are what sociologists call "roles." Suppose the situation is the classroom. As one of the students you have a role to perform and the role obligations include being reasonably quiet and studious. Your role-set consists of the teacher and your fellow students. Now imagine that the teacher wishes to leave the room in order to discuss something with another teacher. The teacher asks you to take charge, in effect, changing the role-set that now you are asked to assume some aspect of the teacher's role. There is a great deal of commotion while the teacher is absent. When the teacher returns what would you say? Don't feel too badly if you are tempted to gloss over the problem and get off the hook with your fellow students. It is a situation in which you have the choices of meeting the expectations of the other students or meeting the expectations of the teacher. In a word it is a problem of roles and its purpose at this point in our discussion is to illustrate the part which self attitudes play in role performance.

If one sees himself as needing the approval of his peers (and what teen-ager does not?) we can see one motive for conformity. If one sees himself as respectful of adults and authority, another strong motive exists to complicate the picture. Thus, when we speak of motivation, the reasons *why* we do what we do, we must look to self-attitudes. On the one hand then, roles are composed of what others expect of us and on the other hand, self-attitudes are what we think about ourselves and what we expect of ourselves. Before turning to American role patterns let us seek to uncover the sources of the *self,* the patterns of self-feeling and self-expectations that motivate us. This can best be accomplished by going over the life stages of the individual again. We can focus our attention on the crisis each stage involves for the developing self.

The Infant Has No Social Self

Psychologists tell us that we have no developed sense of self before age two, or until we have developed some use of language. Before that time the self of the infant is submerged in a total identification with the mother or the mothering person. During this period the crisis is learning to trust others, to rely upon them; it is a period of complete dependency. When something troubles him the infant blames the mother. If he could use words he would call such times the "bad mama." When he feels comfortable and full of warm food (which for most babies is most of the time) he would, if he had the use of words, call these times the "good mama." He experiences global (all-encompassing) feelings of comfort with alternating periods of global discomfort. These are his first self-feeling states. They are not yet a system of attitudes; they are the foundations for such a system.

Language and Self

As the infant becomes the child, he uses language to manipulate the people in his growing social world. "Good" and "bad" are the commonest of the words he uses. Now he has the words, but instead of using them exclusively for his mother he often applies them to himself and to others. At first "good Johnny" and "bad Johnny" as applied to himself are meaningless. But he gradually begins to distinguish himself. He develops the ability to see himself through the eyes of others. Language is an important part of this process.

Looking-Glass Self

Sociologists call this "taking the role of the other." And, following Charles H. Cooley, they call the self-system a "looking-glass" self. This is the process by which we imagine how we appear to others, how we evaluate that image which we think they have of us and finally, how we feel about what they are thinking. These feelings of pride or shame (related, of course, to Good-Mama — Good-Johnny and Bad-Johnny — Bad-Mama in earlier personality development) are not just figments of our imaginations. Other people, by their words, gestures, facial expressions, and other means do give us clues as to how they really feel.

Little girls and boys often give us a clear picture of this process of self-evaluation when they imagine themselves as parents and their toys and dolls as themselves. "You be good now or Mama will have to spank you" when said to a doll has great meaning for the child. Now she knows more about herself and her relationship with her mother. She is "taking the role of the other," putting herself, in imagination, in her mother's place.

Conceptions of Good and Bad Self

Gradually the child's world has important overtones of good

and bad. Western movies, animated cartoons and other creations for children are amply peopled with clear-cut heroes and villains. Finer distinctions come with maturity. If healthy self-satisfactions come with group identification, then success and self-esteem ("good" feelings) accompany play activity and later school work. The path from infancy to childhood and young adulthood is a progression in social roles which is accompanied by a series of self-adjustments which fit or misfit the individual for these roles. As we have seen, good and bad feeling states, especially with the self as the object, are crucial in the development of the self.

The Maturing Self

Childhood ends when the life-goals of the individual are no longer make-believe; when identification of self with cowboys gives way to identification with the real world and the adults in it; when self-esteem depends upon making a place in the social world of adults.

Adolescence is the stage of life in America which connects childhood and adulthood. We have seen that it is the period during which *ego identity* is forged. Now let us proceed to clarify this notion. We have discussed the childhood experiences which lead to the adolescent identity "crisis," as the psychiatrist Erik Erikson styles it. But we have hitherto treated the rise of the self only as it relates to the personality of the child and his immediate social environment. By considering the family, the play group, and the school as the child's social environment, we achieved our purpose of showing the influence of these social groupings on the developing personality.

CULTURE AND PERSONALITY

Now, in order to show the influence of the larger environment upon the child it is necessary to see some of the relationships between the larger environment, American society (and its way of life or culture) and the immediate environment of the developing personality.

In other words, the immediate environment is responsible to a larger environment of social systems. The infant will be cared for in terms of a philosophy of child care which varies importantly from social class to social class. From the beginnings of personality the child confronts the larger society as represented by his parents who, in turn, represent religious, economic, political and other systems in which they participate and whose values they subscribe to. Now

STAGE OF DEVELOPMENT	IMMEDIATE ENVIRONMENT	SOCIAL SYSTEMS
INFANCY	**Family** — related through social roles of the parents to ⎯⎯⎯⎯⎯⟶	Stratification Systems Economic Systems
CHILDHOOD	**Family** (as above)	
	Play groups — children of other families which are related through social roles relate them to ⎯⟶	Political Systems Religious Systems
	Schools — whose children are related through families (as above) and through teachers whose roles related them to ⎯⟶	Educational Systems Recreational Systems

since these systems vary strikingly from society to society because of their *cultural* differences, it is a different thing to grow up in American society than in some other network of social systems held together by a different culture.

While it may seem that we have digressed from the subject of adolescence, nothing could be farther from the truth, because unlike earlier periods of socialization, adolescence is the stage of development where the child is being prepared for *direct* involvement with the broader social environment with decreasing reliance upon adults to mediate between himself and American social systems. We ask what special adjustments are required for the transition from childhood to adulthood in America? Or, put another way, what is involved in achieving ego identity in America?

In Chapter 2 we learned that there are a handful of values (conceptions of the good life) which dominate American social systems. One American value is that of *pluralism;* as Americans we cherish our right to be different from each other and we tolerate *diversity* in action and belief. We have multinational, multiracial, and multireligious origins. In order to live together we have had to tolerate one another's differences. But our diversity is not merely a hodgepodge. All immigrant groups (and all Americans have immigrant origins no matter how remote) have succumbed to the American dream of prosperity. Consequently, business, the means of achieving this prosperity, has been our dominant social system. In turn, the businessman has become the archetype or model of American success. The political system is not an end in itself, but has been the means or the instrument by which the individual is enabled to achieve his success and, again, the means of protecting the individual from unfair encroachment by those who would unfairly hamper his activities toward success. Above all, the American cultural system stresses *action* toward success goals and individual responsibility for *active* pursuit of those goals.

American adults, then, have two major sets of expectations of the adolescent: that he progress toward capability in a job role and toward the selection of a marital partner. They often create problems by ambivalence in their expectations: they may want conflicting things, like popularity in dating but no "involvement," or wanting the adolescent to choose an occupation or profession which they, the adults, have chosen. With the ever-spiraling standards of occupational competence in American society come increased adult expectations of adolescent accomplishment.

Before turning to the adult person in our society, it may be well to set down a norm of adjustment for the adolescent. There are various kinds of norms, like statistical averages, which would tell us what most adolescents feel (information that we do not have) or like abstract norms of conduct such as we learn from ethics or religion. However a sociological analysis calls for *social* norms, i.e., the expectations of others in society which are or are not being met. The "normal" adolescent in this socially relative measure is one whose self-system corresponds roughly to the social personality which he has. Thus his inner self is geared to his outer self.

This diagram defines a process, not a condition. The thrust of human consciousness and thought make it possible for the adolescent to be the best (or the worst) of what others and he expect of him. Some of the problems of adolescence which we have suggested here and which are greatly distorted and magnified in the popular literature are quite functional in preparing the adolescent for the modern American social world. When you work at these problems, you are working toward adulthood in a society which expects its members to work at their problems.

The Adult in American Society

Not because we wish to gloss over the very real difficulties which adolescents experience in preparing for adulthood but precisely because American adult life requires adaptability and flexibility, we treat adolescence as an indispensable stage of preparation for life in *the kind of society* that America is. Anthropologists have been extremely impressed by the fact that children in primitive societies usually progress directly to adulthood without undergoing adolescence. The difference between a primitive society and a modern, urban, industrial society is, above all, a difference of complexity of social life. Hence, adolescence is a period in which adaptability to complex social life is learned as a matter of course in the process of achieving ego identity.

American adulthood is, then, an achievement. In a society which stresses action taken toward success goals, it is a continuing achievement. Each day's, week's, month's activities count or do not count toward successful outcomes of marital, career, or other goals. Difficulties presented by ill-fortune or even difficulties placed in the path by the system itself are to be overcome within the boundaries imposed by the rules of the game, by institutionalized norms. Deviants accept the success goals even while violating the rules. Robbing a bank may lead to financial success, but few Americans accept the means of achieving it. Unscrupulous business dealings may meet with secret acceptance, at least by those who are engaged in them. Others may secretly reject the success goal and publicly emphasize how hard they work. Still others may reject both the American goals and the American standard of hard work to achieve the goals. The much publicized beatniks are cases in point. Finally, there are a handful of rebels who would destroy the system and build a new social structure; they are, characteristically, hazy about the details of such rebuilding.

But for better or worse, the modal (the most frequently found) American accepts the strains of modern industrial society, absorbs the tensions of such a complex work life through leisure time spent with his wife and children in whatever pursuits their capacities permit them. While it cannot be said, against the evidence supplied by a high divorce rate, that marriage and family life are completely satisfying, Americans have always been the most married (proportionately) of the world's peoples. For the American who plays the game of working toward success through legitimate means, marriage and a family are far and away the most complementary roles in sustaining him along his course.

Major Concepts in Chapter 4

1. *Personality:* The system of self and role attitudes possessed by an individual.

2. *Attitudes:* Tendencies to act according to self and role conceptions of an individual.

3. *Role playing:* Acting according to role prescriptions.

4. *Role:* Norm prescribing expected behavior.

5. *Self:* The organizing system of personality. The consciousness of one's social identity, including person and body as affecting and being affected by others.

6. *Looking-glass self:* Consists of three elements: (1) an imagination of one's self in the eyes of another; (2) an evaluation of the other's perception; (3) a subjective reaction such as pleasure or shame.

7. *Adjustment:* Integrity of self and role which involves similarity of self and "other" (role) expectations.

8. *Maladjustment:* May be subjective in the sense of self-adequacy or may involve conflicts in behavior because of conflicting expectations by others. Neither adjustment nor maladjustment should be confused with morality or immorality.

9. *Identity:* A sense of integrated self even in the presence of conflicting external expectations.

10. *Taking the role of the other:* Through play or imagination performing the role of another which results in insights into the other's role problems.

11. *Socialization:* Learning, in a social context, which results in more effective functioning in social systems.

Review Questions

1. What are the different ways in which philosophers, playwrights, novelists, poets, psychologists, and sociologists treat the human personality?
2. Why do sociologists confine themselves to such a narrow view of personality?
3. Compare social roles and roles in a play.

4. Social lore and sociology are not contradictory on the subject of personality. Defend this position.
5. What is the organizing element of the personality system?
6. How do roles link the individual to the group?
7. Criticize the notion that sociology surrenders the individual to the group.
8. What do we mean when we say that experience has a meaning for the individual?
9. What are the variables in personality development? Which is the most important?
10. What minority groups in your city or state are sometimes (even in social lore) thought to have a certain kind of personality because of their biological background? Can you demonstrate the fallacy in this thinking?
11. Are fat people jolly and lean ones shy? Do you know people who may act in these ways because it is expected of them?
12. Do you know of anyone whose unique life experiences have given them a distinctive personality? Can you think of one from literature?
13. What is meant by "life cycle"? Is it the same for everyone?
14. Do you know any preschool children? Describe their behavior, especially the beginnings of "self."
15. Can you see the importance of ordinal position in the family in the development of your personality? Do you know someone for whom ordinal position has been especially important?
16. Using the chapter as a guide prepare an outline of a case history.
17. From watching television programs on Saturday mornings can you tell which characters a child would identify with? Are any of them realistic?
18. What are the problems of identity during adolescence?
19. What is "identity foreclosure"?
20. Can you find data on identity foreclosure in your community?
21. What is "anticipatory socialization"?
22. Is a person born with a "self" in the sociological sense?
23. In our ethical and legal codes do we employ the sociological concept of self as a definition of the human person?
24. How many role sets do you have? Diagram them.
25. Contrast the identity crisis of the individual in American society with that of individuals in other societies. The chapters on culture may be of some help.

Discussion Questions

1. Discuss: "All the world's a stage."
2. Describe a complete "personality"?
3. Does the personality of a hero end with his death? John F. Kennedy and Winston Churchill can be used as examples.

4. Discuss infantile determinism.
5. Is abortion justified on the grounds that the unborn infant has no personality?

Bibliography

Brody, Sylvia, *Patterns of Mothering* (New York: International Universities Press, 1956).

*Elkin, Frederick, *The Child and Society: The Process of Socialization* (New York: Random House, 1960).

*Erikson, Erik H., *Childhood and Society* (New York: W. W. Norton & Co., Inc., 1963).

Iscoe, Ira, and Harold Stevenson (eds.), *Personality Development in Children* (Austin, Texas: University of Texas Press, 1959).

*La Barre, Weston, *The Human Animal* (Chicago: University of Chicago Press, 1954).

Miller, Daniel R., and Guy E. Swanson (eds.), *Inner Conflict and Defense* (New York: Holt, Rinehart & Winston, 1960).

Munn, Norman, *The Evolution and Growth of Human Behavior,* 2nd ed. (Boston: Houghton Mifflin Company, 1965).

McCord, William, and Joan McCord, *The Origins of Crime* (New York: Columbia University Press, 1959).

Sears, Robert, *et al., Patterns of Child Rearing* (Evanston, Ill: Row, Peterson, 1957).

Shibutani, Tomatsu, *Society and Personality: An Interactionist Approach to Social Psychology* (Englewood Cliffs, N. J.: Prentice-Hall, Inc., 1963).

Stouffer, Samuel, *et al., The American Soldier,* 2 vols. (Princeton, N. J.: Princeton University Press, 1949).

*Valdes, Donald M., and Dwight G. Dean (eds.), *Sociology in Use: Selected Readings for the Introductory Course* (New York: The Macmillan Company, 1965).

*Watson, Robert L., *Psychology of the Child* (New York: John Wiley & Sons, Inc., 1959).

*Whyte, William F., Jr., *The Organization Man* (New York: Simon & Schuster, Inc., 1956).

———— *Street Corner Society: The Social Structure of an Italian Slum,* rev. ed. (Chicago: University of Chicago Press, 1955).

Winch, Robert F., *Identification and Its Familial Determinants* (Indianapolis, Ind.: Bobbs-Merrill Co., Inc., 1962).

* Also published in paperback edition.

PART TWO

AMERICAN SOCIAL ORGANIZATION

Chapter 5

The Social System

So FAR you have been dealing with two kinds of systems. Do you remember that the key notion in analyzing culture was the concept of *pattern?* In that chapter you saw that pattern referred to the way the parts of culture hang together. There is an American way of life, not just an unrelated number of American ways of doing things.

In the chapter on personality you saw that a person does not just have a number of attitudes, but that the self *organizes* the attitudes into a coherent whole. Your personality is you, as you see yourself and as others see you.

In this chapter we want to show you more about social systems. Think of a football team, a baseball team, or a choir, any number (aggregate) of individuals who are working together as a team. This is what we mean by a social system. There is a way in which the members of the system hang together like the parts of culture, and a way in which they are organized like a personality. When you see this, you will know more about social systems.

The basic concept of sociology is that the sum of the individuals who make up an aggregate adds up to more than the sum of its individual parts! While this seems impossible on the face of it, this proposition is quite solid. Some scholars have scoffed at the idea that any aggregate can have an identity of its own. "Take away the individual and you have nothing left." On this basis many have accused sociologists of advocating a false "group mind" which can somehow think apart from the minds of the individuals who make up the group. Some sociologists, especially those who have been influenced by Émile Durkheim, the great French sociologist of the late nineteenth and early twentieth centuries, have provided critics of sociology with ammunition for their attacks. They sometimes write of groups and societies as if there were no individuals in them.

After we examine the concept of system in this present chapter, you will be able to see that the criticism is not valid. The reason is that the idea of system links the individual to other individuals in a web of relationships. The *web of relationships* is what adds up to more than the sum of the individuals. Of course, we freely concede that without individuals no group could exist. What we are saying is that, for example, your school existed before you arrived, it existed on the days you were absent, and it will exist after you graduate. In other words, as a web of human relationships it is free of complete dependence upon a given individual.

The concept of system was taken over by sociologists from the natural sciences. As we shall see below, the basic elements of a system are present throughout nature. The human body is a system as are other biological organisms. The body is an orderly arrangement of parts. Sociologists have long noted the interrelatedness of the various parts of the social body. As we observed in Chapter 1, preoccupation with social problems and social disorganization can blind us to the nature of society. If we confine our attention to *disorders,* our attention is distracted from social *order.* When we understand the systems that unite individual people into social systems, we can then better understand social problems. It is this understanding, *insight,* into social order which the sociologists seek in studying the systems of society. Armed with this insight, we are then provided with a powerful tool for correcting the ills of social systems.

Our objections now are clarified. In a series of steps we can progress from an understanding of systems of whatever kind to an increased understanding of the special kinds of systems that sociologists study in their attempts to provide insight into social behavior.

Our first task looks more difficult than it really is. The simple mechanical example of a system provided by Lawrence J. Henderson, the physiologist, is shown in Figure 1. If you are one of the many students who likes the social sciences because they study people instead of things, the idea of using a mechanical diagram to explain human behavior may be repugnant. If you prefer the methods of natural science, however, do not make the mistake of assuming that human systems can be understood without considerable modification, which, of course, we shall discuss soon. Whatever your preferences, however, Henderson's model is simple to understand and provides a convenient starting place for our discussion.

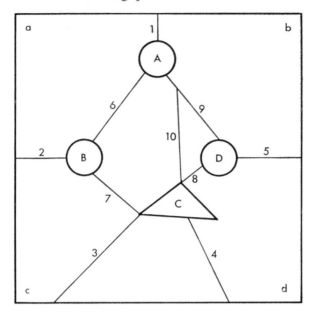

The four rigid bodies can be metal hoops (A, B, D) or a metal triangle (C). They are fastened to a rigid frame (which could be four small pieces of pipe) joined at points a, b, c, and d. The four rigid bodies are connected to this outside frame by rubber bands $(1, 2, 3, 4, 5)$. But that is only the way the rigid bodies (A, B, C, D) are connected to the frame. They are connected to *each other* by elastic bands 6, 7, 8, 9, and 10, in such a way as to give a form or order to all of the parts in the diagram. Now, keeping in mind these relationships of the normal arrangement of the diagram, you are asked to imagine what would happen if you were to apply pressure to any of the rigid bodies (A, B, C, D) or to any of the rubber bands $(1, 2, 3, 4, 5, 6, 7, 8, 9, 10)$. Would it not be true that this system would be out of balance not merely at the point where the elastic, the hoop, or the triangle was pulled or pushed? Would it not also be true that another diagram would have to be drawn to illustrate the new relationships that would exist in the model? And, of course, if you quit tugging or pressing any of the elements of the system it would return to its original form.

From this simple exercise we can see that systems can be defined by three major characteristics:

1. Systems are made up of parts.
2. These parts are mutually interdependent; each part influences and is influenced by the other parts.
3. The parts make up a whole (the system) which is something distinct from the mere summation of the parts.

Once this becomes clear the problems discussed at the beginning of the chapter take on more meaning. Can a group, a high school, a community, or a nation be considered as something distinct from all of the individuals who comprise it? The idea of system provides us with a first answer in the affirmative. But, of course, we must develop the idea of system further in order to make it applicable to humans and social life. Many systems which can be illustrated by Henderson's model do not concern us in a sociology course. The direct concern of sociology is the *social system,* which we shall consider in the remainder of this chapter. In earlier chapters we have already considered the personality system and the culture system.

THE SOCIAL SYSTEM

Since *social* means "shared," the key feature of a social system, which sets it apart from others, is an element which the individuals have in common. In a word, this element is the social *norm,* or, more simply, norm. There are two main kinds of norms that govern the conduct of the members of a social system. There are *relational* norms and *regulative* norms. Now let us pause to absorb these concepts, since they are crucial for understanding the illustrations of social systems which lie ahead. The most pervasive of all social systems is the family. What are the norms which regulate family life? First, the relational norms govern the behavior of individual members of the family *according to their position in the system.*

In the simple diagram 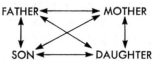 the positions of individual members in relation to each other are governed by norms. Who has not been told "that's no way to treat your mother"? What father is not expected to treat his wife in one way, his sons in another way, and his daughters in still another? Relational norms, then, constitute expectations of behavior of the individual. Family life (and all social life) is something like a play, in which the script is held by the other actors while the individual performs the role assigned to him.

In fact, sociology has taken over the term *role* to describe just that — the expectations of behavior which go with his position in the system, in this case, the family. So the son is expected to behave toward the daughter as a brother *should. Sanctions* are imposed to insure proper role behavior. The actors are rewarded or punished according to whether they meet or do not meet the expectations of others in the system. This description of relational norms is, of course, only part of the whole story of human social behavior. The individuals in a social system are not mere robots who *must* do what is expected of them. For one thing, individuals may derive a great deal of satisfaction from performing the roles appropriate to their positions in the social system. Obviously, when roles are well understood by all participants and satisfactions are obtained through role performances, the system will run more smoothly. These satisfactions are called *statuses.* So the holder of a given position is provided with two sets of expectations.

In contrast to relational norms, regulative norms govern the behavior of everyone in the system. Standards of behavior are, of course, not all relative to social position. Cheating, lying, swearing, and lack of modesty are but a few examples of violations of regulative norms. While violations may and do occur they are regarded by members of the system as violations of general rules rather than of specific rules governing the behavior of a father, a son, a daughter, or a mother.

These, then, are the main elements of a social *interaction* system: position, status, and role. Recalling the definition of a system which was suggested by Henderson's diagram — parts, interdependence, and a system-as-a-whole — we can see that the actions of the individuals are *interdependent.* From the *inter* (dependent) *actions* of the members we derive the term *interaction.* Not all social systems are interaction systems and we shall discuss these others at the conclusion of this chapter.

But first, let us consider a social interaction system in more detail. The Bank Wiring Room Group study is one of the most informative of sociological research projects yet done on this subject. Secondly, we can place the Bank Wiring Group (interaction system) in the larger perspective of American social systems as a whole. This will help us to get a first perspective of the way in which systemic analysis enables sociology students to reach from the smallest systems such as the family or a work group to American society as a social system in itself.

THE BANK WIRING ROOM

In order to study a small interaction system some Harvard sociologists placed a trained observer in an actual work situation in a Western Electric Company factory. What they wanted to study was precisely the question we are considering in this chapter. To what extent can the work of a group be explained in terms of individual contributions? The other side of this question, of course, is, to what extent can the work output of a number of individuals be considered a product of the group as a group? Put more simply, what are the effects of an interaction system upon the performance of workers?

Since the Bank Wiring Room (from which the study derived its name) had four walls which closed it off from the larger factory, it was ideal for examining the work situation inside it. Sociologists know that boundaries like these are predisposing factors for the creation of social systems within them. So the conditions were right for the experiments they wished to conduct.

The management of the Western Electric Company assumed that they were dealing directly with the individual worker. They offered incentives for individual work performance. Consequently, they expected each person to work as hard as he could, even to the point of total fatigue each day. "Obviously," they thought, "if a man does only 400 units of work when he could receive twice as much pay for doing 800 units, he will strive to do 800." The assumption is that they were dealing with individuals *as* individuals. As the sociologists expected, however, the social system which developed had more to do with workers' production than did individual financial aspirations.

The workers were indeed governed by the regulative norms of "doing a fair day's work for a fair day's pay." To this extent they shared the norms of management. But, the observer noted, the workers developed a social system out of their workday relationships. And this social system seemed to generate norms which changed the norms which management expected them to have.

They developed friendship cliques which had a great deal to do with the statuses and roles of their relative positions. Their original positions were of the following kinds:

wireman   solderer   inspector

The intention of management was that their statuses and roles would be as follows:

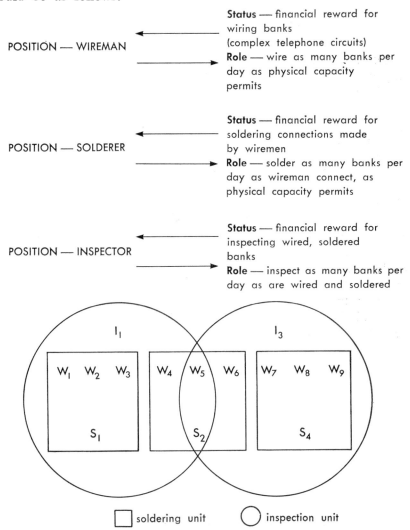

POSITION — WIREMAN

Status — financial reward for wiring banks (complex telephone circuits)
Role — wire as many banks per day as physical capacity permits

POSITION — SOLDERER

Status — financial reward for soldering connections made by wiremen
Role — solder as many banks per day as wireman connect, as physical capacity permits

POSITION — INSPECTOR

Status — financial reward for inspecting wired, soldered banks
Role — inspect as many banks per day as are wired and soldered

I_1 I_3

W_1 W_2 W_3 W_4 W_5 W_6 W_7 W_8 W_9

S_1 S_2 S_4

☐ soldering unit   ◯ inspection unit

The soldering and inspection system of relationship planned by Western Electric Company for the Bank Wiring Room.

Obviously the wireman would be expected to produce as many banks as possible in a day's time, and it seems equally logical that the solderers and inspectors would encourage maximum production. However, the friendship cliques produced other leaders than those designated by management. Group norms arose *within* the system. Sanctions for these norms also arose. Sentiments and opinions about a fair day's work gave rise to the norm of a set number of banks to be produced by a wireman, a solderer, and an inspector in a given day. Rewards for conforming and the punishments for not conforming, which we have already defined as "sanctions" came into existence. The norm of "a fair day's work" came to be a basis for judging those who violated the norm.

The management-workers' originally shared norms of a fair day's work for a fair day's pay came to be importantly modified by the norms developed in the interactions of the workers. They set the daily norm. Those who did not do enough work to meet this norm were *chiselers*. Those who did more work than the norm prescribed were *ratebusters*. A feeling of comradeship developed among the men. They looked down upon their fellows who associated with supervisors. Those who disclosed any information to supervisors were considered *squealers*. Those who did not identify with the friendship cliques were regarded as standoffish and peculiar.

The sanctions imposed to protect these norms resulted in new kinds of statuses for the worker. Now, much of what he "got out of" his position had to do with the psychological satisfactions of being accepted, admired, and respected by his fellow workers. Being excluded from lunch bull-sessions or being ostracized, served as negative sanctions; attempts to bring the deviant back into line.

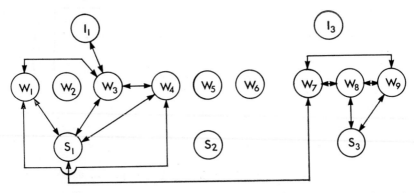

Informal pattern of friendship which modified the company's formal plan for the Bank Wiring Room.

The roles of the workers, since status and role are always connected, inevitably changed. Their work production corresponded
far more to the norms of the social system than to the goals which
management assumed each individual worker would establish for
himself. Through changes in role behavior produced by status changes,
the production of the men in the Bank Wiring Room become a function of the social system rather than of individual striving.

What Is Illustrated by the Bank Wiring Room?

Let us pause here to reflect upon what the Bank Wiring Room
interaction system teaches us. First, we must understand that the
interaction system is a universal feature of human life. In primitive
societies and in modern, the most significant human relationships
that people have are those that have their setting in small interaction systems. In the family, in the play group, the classroom,
friendship groups, and work settings, human individuals form their
deepest sentiments and loyalties. In later chapters all of these individual group relationships will be developed further. At this point,
however, our primary objective is not to demonstrate the psychological, i.e., effects on the personality, but rather the social significance of the interaction system.

The interactional system, whose members meet face to face,
have intimate knowledge of each other, and are most deeply involved, is called a *primary* group. If society were just a connected
string of such primary groups our lives would be simple, indeed.
If life were just a matter of being a member of a family, a member
of the senior class, a member of a crowd that enjoys recreating
together, it would be an extremely uncomplicated matter. But common sense tells us that "out there" in the larger society there are
major human activities so large in scope as to defy analysis in such
simplified terms as "small groups" or "interaction system."

The adult worlds of work, religion, education, recreation, politics, and other organized life activities are vast and complicated.
Size is not the only difference between your school and United States
Steel. If your school is small, it may be possible to add up all of
the interaction systems in it and achieve a fairly good understanding
of "what goes on there." But suppose it is extremely large and its
interaction systems so numerous and complex and so rapidly changing as apparently to defy analysis. This is what sociologists have
faced in analyzing modern society. The concept of systems has
helped them deal with the size and complexity of modern society.

The concept of system works, of course, only because there is an organization in society. If there were nothing out there in the social world that conforms to what we call a system, we would only be engaging in a mental exercise. The usefulness of the concept of system, then, is that it explains what is going on in society. But obviously Henderson's model of a system helps us only in getting started. The Bank Wiring Room interaction system helps us progress a little further. But we shall have to go further yet in our quest for a broader concept which will fit society.

What are the similarities between Henderson's model of a system and the Bank Wiring Room? What are the differences? Finally, to achieve our present purpose, what can we carry over from our comparisons that will enable us to analyze the broader organization of American society? The answer to our questions must, of course, deal only with the main elements of comparison, rather than with distracting minor differences. Hence:

1. The similarities between Henderson's model and the Bank Wiring Room interaction systems are:

   a) *Both systems had boundaries* (iron pipes in the Henderson model and walls in the Bank Wiring Room).

   b) *Both systems were made up of parts* (hoops and a triangle in the Henderson model, individual workers in the Bank Wiring Room).

   c) *In both systems, the parts were interconnected.* (The parts of the Henderson model were connected by rubber bands, the "parts" of the Bank Wiring Room by statuses and roles.)

   d) *In both models, the system as a whole worked as a system rather than the sum of individual parts.* (A change in the rubber bands affected the whole of the Henderson model's parts; a change in statuses and roles affected the Bank Wiring Group's productivity as a whole.)

2. The differences between Henderson's model and the Bank Wiring Room interaction systems are:

   a) *There is a significant difference in the kinds of boundaries* of the two systems. (The Henderson model was self-contained; the Bank Wiring Room, as a system, was organically connected to a larger system, the Western Electric Company.)

   b) *The parts of the two systems are essentially different.*

(The capacity of human individuals to change their minds makes it possible for change to come from within the system, as in the Bank Wiring Room. Obviously, metal hoops, triangles, and rubber bands depend upon external manipulation for change.)

c) *The interconnection of parts is essentially different in the two systems.* (Norms bind the members of the interaction system, while only rubber bands bind the parts of the physical model.)

d) *The "wholeness" of both systems is not the same.* (Since norms can and do change, depending upon attitude changes of individuals, interaction systems are action systems while mechanical systems are static or passive systems.)

In summary, many of the elements of system are present in social interactional systems, but, of course, they are present in ways that reflect the pressure of human beings within them. The give and take of social interaction makes human face-to-face encounters and interacting a rewarding aspect of sociology and its quest for understanding human social life. But what of the larger society outside, say, of the Bank Wiring Room? We still have the task of extending our concept of social systems into the broader social world. Sociologists have come to agreement that it is better to start with the broadest conceivable social system. For reasons we shall soon discuss, sociological consensus is that a *society,* is, at present, the largest human aggregate that can be considered a social system. But since it seems to be too great a jump from a small room in a Western Electric factory to American society as a whole, perhaps it would be better to achieve the transition in manageable stages.

The Bank Wiring Room and the Larger Community

First, let us simply relate the Bank Wiring Room to the Western Electric Company. As a smaller system the Bank Wiring Room is relative to the larger systems that contain it like the human hand is related to the total body. Just as interdependence exists within a system, so interdependence exists between such larger systems and the smaller systems contained within them. Your hand not only *does* something in itself, it also does something for the rest of your body. You grasp something, like bread, and you use your hand to place it in your mouth. From this point on the other systems of the body each perform their appropriate *function,* like digestion, circulation, or elimination. This "something" which your hand does is called its function, which is roughly what your hand "does."

Now, what is it that the Bank Wiring Room does for the Western Electric Company? It provides a daily quota of banks and these are necessary for what the Western Electric Company does. In turn, Western Electric's function is to provide telephone companies with necessary equipment for maintaining a vast, intricate, and complex network of communication in America. Diagramatically, the relationship can be traced something like this:

AMERICAN SOCIETY

which function for
AMERICAN ECONOMIC SYSTEMS

which function for
AMERICAN INDUSTRIAL SYSTEMS

which function for
AMERICAN TELEPHONE SYSTEMS

which functions for
WESTERN ELECTRIC COMPANY

functions for
THE BANK WIRING ROOM

The diagram must be read from the bottom to the top in order to make sense. This principle of hierarchy must be maintained in functional analysis of systems. The reasons for this will be made clear later in the chapter.

AMERICAN SOCIETY AS A SOCIAL SYSTEM

Having worked up to American society from the Bank Wiring Room about all we have shown is that a relationship of interdependency from one to the other can be traced. All that is asked of you for the moment is that you see the relationship. In the remainder of the chapter we shall expand and clarify the relationship much more fully. And, of course, we have only scratched the surface of functional system analysis.

The first question that needs to be clarified is the manner in which we find it possible to conceive of American Society as a social system. Everything we read may lead us to believe otherwise. Perhaps the commonest error in thinking of American Society is to think of it as "the Government." This perspective leads down the path of error very readily. We read in the paper that "the Government" is instituting legal proceedings against certain large corporations. The same newspaper may carry stories about conflicts between farmers and the secretary of labor. Or perhaps your father grumbles about the way taxes are "bleeding" him. He is probably especially irritated when "the Government" takes his money and spends it in ways of which he does not approve. This superficial impression of a society divided against itself is only a small part of the real truth about the American social order. A more penetrating analysis reveals that American society is as much an organized system as Henderson's model or the Bank Wiring Room group.

1. American society is made up of parts.
2. These parts are mutually interdependent; each part influences and is influenced by the other parts.
3. The parts make up a whole (the system).

You might think we are stretching the concept of system too far. We think that objection will be cleared up before this chapter is finished. On the other hand, you might also think that the concept of system may be carried further. For example, the United Nations is made up of parts. Nations belonging to the UN are interdependent, they influence one another. And they all make up a whole which is the United Nations Assembly. But these nations do not function as a system of the type we shall describe below.

Hence, at least at present, sociologists do not consider the UN a social system in the full sense. The largest working system that sociologists consider a system is, as we have said, a society. The United States is a society. It has the distinguishing characteristics which enable us to define it as such. It is a group which has (1) a definite territory; (2) sexual reproduction; (3) comprehensive culture; and (4) independence. Let us consider these characteristics one at a time.

A society has a definite territory, i.e., it has boundaries. You will recall the emphasis which was placed upon boundaries in our discussions of system. A necessary condition for people to consider themselves as belonging to one society instead of another is, at least at present, their awareness of sharing a territory with others. Even nomadic people who move around a great deal do so within broad territorial limits which they consider theirs.

A society must reproduce itself sexually. This is by no means the only way to recruit members. A society can recruit immigrants, enslave others, and even adopt people from other societies. But the overwhelming majority of a society's members are biological progeny of the preceding generation of the society's members. Within societies, families, towns, cities, require sexual reproduction in order to provide themselves with new members. As we shall soon see, these subunits function for the society as a whole, their members are society's members.

"Comprehensive culture" is such an important concept that it receives special attention in a full chapter. But in order to define a society as a system we need to recall something about culture at this point in our discussion. As already pointed out in Chapter 2, culture is, according to the English anthropologist Tylor, "that complex whole which includes knowledge, belief, art, morals, law, custom, and other capabilities acquired by man as a member of society."

Every group, no matter how small, must have a culture. The two examples of small interaction systems that we have used for illustration purposes in this chapter were a family, which we discussed very briefly, and the Bank Wiring Room group, which we discussed in more detail. Both groups rely for their existence upon culture. In an American family each position is related to every other position in a peculiarly American way. Mom and Dad most likely speak English (culture) in teaching their sons and daughters the right (culture) ways to act. This way of life is what social scientists mean by culture. The Bank Wiring Room group could not have functioned without a great deal of technical knowledge about wiring and soldering, without language, and without norms.

Returning to American society, the concept of comprehensive culture that we are analyzing, means not only that all the cultural elements present in American families are part of American culture. The cultural elements found in industrial groups like the Bank Wiring Room, and all other groups in American society are, indeed, substantively a part of the American culture. In this sense, American culture does comprehend or contain these cultural elements. But comprehensive culture also means much more which is extremely significant for considering American society as a *system*. In its fullest sense, comprehensive culture means that a society which possesses it has worked out ways for enabling *its members as a whole to meet all of the requirements of social life.*

You should keep in mind that we are defining a society. We are doing this at this point primarily to enable us to conceptualize American society as a social system. So far we have considered three of the four characteristics of a society: definite territory, sexual reproduction, and comprehensive culture. The last of the four characteristics is independence. Independence is equally crucial for considering America as a society. To be independent, the people of a definite territory and possessing a comprehensive culture must also *not be a part (subgroup* or *subsociety) of any other group of people.* And, of course, America meets this qualification. Now that we have seen that America qualifies as a society, let us examine its workings as a system.

THE FIVE MAJOR SYSTEMS OF A SOCIETY

While we have seen that American society has the properties of a system — parts, interdependence of parts, and functioning as a whole — we have paid little attention to the differences between the parts of a mechanical model like Henderson's and the human parts of social systems. We saw in the Bank Wiring Room that the hoops and triangle of Henderson's model can be compared to live human beings in an interaction system. And we saw in that interaction system that the rubber bands which relate the hoops and the triangle to each other could be compared to the statuses and roles which relate the workers' positions to one another. The thing to keep in mind here is that such statuses and roles are *norms.* This is the key concept which will help you to gain insight into American society as a social system. Obviously all Americans do not interact with one another. In our daily lives we do not and could not come into contact with more than one one-millionth of America's population. What are the rubber bands that bind this vast multitude of people from the Atlantic Ocean to the Pacific, from the Canadian border to the tips of the Southern states? And don't forget Hawaii and Alaska. The answer, again, is that we all share systems of norms, but since we are not all interacting, this system of norms must be broader and more encompassing than merely statuses and roles. These are called *institutional norms* or, simply, institutions.

All of your acts are not normative, but you would be surprised at the number which are. *Undefined acts* are, as the term suggests, acts which you can do as you please. When you get up in the morning you can put on your left shoe first, or perhaps your right. During the summer you may decide not to wear any shoes at all on a given day. If anyone turns around to look at you it is probably because, barefooted, you are not observing the *folkways*. Folkways are accustomed ways of doing things. They can be violated with no more sanction than perhaps running the risk of being considered eccentric. But now suppose that you decide not to wear any clothing at all. You will probably land in jail! In this case, society has imposed a sanction, just as did the Bank Wiring Room group, for deviation from the norms. And the graver consequences are due to a violation of the norms, which are, like folkways, accustomed ways of doing things, but norms are accustomed ways of doing things which a society judges essential for its well being. In rewarding or punishing (sanctioning) observance or violation of the norms, a society is reacting to what its members consider a vital threat to their common welfare.

Of course, the most penetrating question to ask at this point is, "What standards does a society use to judge by?" How can the members of a society decide what is good for them and what is not? The answer is that human beings have *needs*. To insure that these needs will be met, the members of a society develop *institutions. These are systems of norms (folkways and mores) which have grown up around a major social function.* The major social functions are the things which the institutions *do* for people. Since people have needs for affection and response, societies have institutions which provide for their needs. We have institutions of marriage, inheritance, responsibilities to children, and responsibilities of children to parents. All of these institutions form a *family system,* which is the basic system of all societies.

Other social systems are made necessary by human needs. We need protection from those within and without our society. We need regulations of property and of behavior which threatens social order. The multitude of institutions which make our laws and enforce them, which protect our rights and defend them, comprise the *political system.*

The complexity of our society has made necessary an elaborate *economic system.* Institutions for facilitating trade and commerce, manufacture of goods, agriculture, marketing, and banking — all are economic institutions. The need of the human, like all biological organisms, to make a living in the environment necessitates the economic system. Unlike the animals who are engaged in a direct ecological relationship with the physical environment, men have developed economic institutions which mediate between the individual and the physical environment.

Since man is helpless at birth, knows nothing of the folkways, mores, and institutions so vital to society, he must be taught. Like the other social systems, the *educational system* grew out of the family and came to supplement the learning which takes place in the family interaction system. As the other social systems developed to their present high level of complexity the educational system had to keep pace. A complex sophisticated society requires well educated men and women to occupy positions in all of its major social systems. Role performance becomes increasingly exacting.

While there are many other social systems in American society we are considering only the major systems in our analysis.

Of the five major systems of any society we have thus far mentioned only four, the family, the political, the economic, and the educational systems. The last is to many people the most important of all. This is the *religious system*. All of the major systems can be traced historically back to primitive man. The family huddled by the fire is the first known unit of social organization. The economic system can be traced (at least in imagination) back to the primitive food-quest. The political system can also be seen in "turning back to nature." Men banded together for protection. The educational system can be traced back to a relatively recent point in history, when it became an appendage to family training. But religious systems can be traced to no such "natural" beginnings. Universal in human societies, the human need that gives rise to religious systems is man's quest for the meaning of his existence. "Man does not live by bread alone." He elaborates much of his culture and main institutions to provide meaning to the whole of life and society.

One question remains for us to deal with in this chapter. We have seen that America has five major social systems and many others with which we have not dealt. But what we started out to accomplish was to show that American society is viewed by sociologists as *one* social system. Thus far, in dealing with norms, culminating in a discussion of institutions, we have worked from the ground up. That is, we have dealt with institutions as historically developed responses to the needs of men. This is quite valid, but we have yet to consider the fact that *once men create a society, the society itself has needs*. Sociologists have attacked this problem by viewing society as a system with problems that have to be met if the society is to survive effectively. Intensive study of many societies has led to the conclusion that every social system, small as well as large, has four major problems. By analyzing the four major problems of American society, then, we can see American society as on ongoing system.

THE FOUR FUNCTIONAL PROBLEMS
OF A SOCIAL SYSTEM

The four problems of any system, which must be met in order for the system to survive, are: (1) the problem of replacing worn out parts for the system; (2) the problem of making a living from the environment for the system; (3) the problem of achieving the goals of the system and, (4) the holding together of the parts of the system.

The best example for you to think of is an automobile. When the parts of the automobile wear out they are replaced with new parts. When the parts of society age and wear out they are replaced by new parts, younger people who have been supplied by the family and trained by the family and the schools to assume their place in the system. The function of replacing parts by the family is called the *pattern-maintenance* function.

The problem of making a living from the environment is met by the economy. All of the activity which goes into production and distribution of goods forms a system which meets the *adaptive problem* of American society.

The problem of achieving the goals of the system is met by the political system. Governmental machinery meets the *goal attainment* problem. It performs the goal attainment function.

The problem of the holding together of the parts of the social system is called the *integrative problem*. On an automobile this is easily achieved. You just bolt or weld the different parts of the automobile together! Things are vastly more complicated in a social system with millions of individual parts, each capable of going its own way. What holds them together? Morale is one answer. Beliefs and values in common tend to produce morale, a sense of identity with the social system, and the feeling of having a personal stake in the outcome of the system. Religious systems share this function with other systems. Political, economic, and familial systems all serve in varying degree to urge loyalty to the larger society by the individual. But when we think of the integrative problem sociologists usually associate it with the religious system because integration is the chief social function of most religions.

So if you think of American society as a system, the social

systems which serve it (family, economy, political, religious) can be thought of as subsystems each performing functions for the whole. The family system can be seen as the subsystem which performs many of the pattern-maintenance functions for American society. The economic system can be seen as the subsystem which performs many adaptive functions for American society. The political system can be seen as the subsystem which performs many goal attainment functions for American society. The religious system can be seen as the subsystem which performs many integrative functions for American society.

It would be well to memorize these functional relationships between each of the social systems and the larger society. In the next few chapters we shall be examining the systems individually and much would be lost if you were to think of each system as standing by itself rather than in the larger perspective of its functions for the total society. This is especially true of the family, so we shall begin our treatment of the individual social systems in the next chapter with the family system.

Major Concepts in Chapter 5

1. *System:* An aggregate of identifiable parts which are mutually *interdependent* and which form a whole which can be viewed as an entity in its own right.

2. *Social organization:* The organization of society into subgroups, or parts, and the pattern formed by these parts.

3. *Social disorganization:* Disharmonious social patterning. Disruption of stable social organization. Often (but not always) called "social problems," e.g., disruptions of family system.

4. *Social system:* Systems in which the elements of cohesion are social norms. They are dynamic rather than static since they are made up of the interactions of humans.

5. *Social norm:* Any socially sanctioned mode or condition of behavior.

6. *Relational norm:* Norms governing the obligations of individuals which apply only to their position in a system.

7. *Regulative norm:* Norms governing the behavior of all participants in a system.

8. *Position:* The location of a given individual within a social system.

9. *Status:* Rights and privileges associated with a position in a system.

10. *Role:* Expectations of behavior associated with a position in a system.

11. *Interaction:* Refers to two or more people in a condition of inter-dependence, relationship, and interstimulation.

12. *System boundary:* The limits of a system. In a social system boundaries may be self evident, e.g., who belongs in a family and who does not is usually determined by residence. In more complicated cases the boundaries must be established logically: who (or what) belongs in the system and who (or what) does not belong in the system?

13. *Sanction:* Any threat of penalty or promise of reward set up by a group to induce conformity to norms.

14. *Group:* Two or more people who form an interactional system. Properly, the people are a group, while their interactions make up a system.

15. *Primary group:* Group characterized by intimate, face-to-face association.

16. *Society:* Largest conceivable group. Characterized by (1) a definite territory; (2) sexual reproduction; (3) comprehensive culture; (4) independence.

17. *Function:* Activities carried on by persons in a group or society for the benefit of the members.

18. *Functional analysis:* The analysis of the particular social benefits which parts of the society perform for the whole.

19. *Folkways:* Accustomed (normative) ways of doing things in a group or society.

20. *Mores:* Accustomed (normative) ways of doing things in a group or society which are accompanied by strong sanctions, since they are judged essential to the welfare of the group or society.

21. *Institutions:* Patterns of norms built up around a strong interest (need) of the group or society.

22. *Pattern maintenance:* Renewal of the units in a system. In a social system individuals must learn the patterns and invest them with the appropriate attitude of respect. The family's function in this regard is obvious as is the school's.

23. *Adaptation:* Sustaining and promoting the material welfare of a system. The social system which performs this function for a society is called the *economy*.

24. *Integration:* The interrelations of units (or members) in a system

and the function of pulling them together. In social systems this refers to morale, or group cohesion. The willingness of individual members to work together.

25. *Goal attainment:* The regulation of the units (or members) of a system in order to achieve its main objectives. The polity, or government, performs this function for a society.

Review Questions

1. How can a culture be considered a system?
2. How can a personality be considered a system? In what ways are personality and cultural systems radically different?
3. How valid is the concept of a "group mind"?
4. What is the "web of relationships"?
5. Did sociologists invent the concept of system?
6. What is the relationship between social organization, social disorganization, and social problems?
7. What are the main features of Henderson's model of a system?
8. Where is a norm — in the reality outside the mind or in the mind itself?
9. What are some sanctions of one of your own family, work, or friendship groups?
10. Do sociologists use the term status the same way it is used in social lore?
11. Have you ever worked or participated in a group that could be analyzed in much the same way as the Bank Wiring Room group?
12. What is the difference between the system planned by the Western Electric Company and the system created by the workers?
13. What is wrong in thinking about the system of the Bank Wiring Room group as a model for American society?
14. Without memorizing the similarities and differences between a physical system and a social system can you infer them logically?
15. Can you relate the Bank Wiring Room system to American society? (Work "up.")
16. Can you think of American society as a system having four functional problems and place the Bank Wiring Room in the proper subsystem addressed to one of these problems? (Work "down.")
17. Why is the United Nations not considered a society by sociologists?
18. Is Poland a society?
19. Can you construct a continuum, or yardstick of undefined acts, folkways, and mores? What are you measuring on your yardstick?
20. Is a family institution the same as a family system?
21. What is the primary function of the political system for American society? The economic system? The family system?
22. What other social systems are there that are not mentioned in the chapter?

23. Can you think of functions other than integrative that the religious system performs? Should religion always be integrative?

Discussion Questions

1. Do the representatives to the U.N. and its staff constitute a social system?
2. Discuss: "In a human group the whole is more than the sum of the parts."
3. Is society an organism?
4. Are beatniks separate from the system they are rejecting?
5. Discuss: "The morale of the soldier in World War II was his loyalty to his buddies."

Bibliography

*Barron, Milton L., *Contemporary Sociology: An Introductory Textbook of Readings* (New York: Dodd, Mead & Company, 1964).

Blau, Peter M., and E. Richard Scott, *Formal Organizations: A Comparative Approach* (San Francisco: Chandler Publishing Company, 1962).

Cartwright, Dorwin, and Alvin Zander (eds.), *Group Dynamics,* 2nd ed. (Evanston, Ill.: Row, Peterson, 1960).

Hare, A. Paul, *et al.* (eds.), *Small Groups: Studies in Social Interaction* (New York: Alfred A. Knopf, 1955).

Hertzler, J. O., *American Social Institutions: A Sociological Analysis* (Boston: Allyn and Bacon, Inc., 1961).

Hollander, E. P., *Leaders, Groups and Influence* (New York: Oxford University Press, 1964).

Homans, George C., *The Human Group* (New York: Harcourt, Brace and Company, 1950).

Johnson, Harry M., *Sociology: A Systematic Introduction* (New York: Harcourt, Brace & World, Inc., 1960).

*Lasswell, Thomas E., *et al.* (eds.), *Life in Society: Introductory Readings in Sociology* (Chicago: Scott, Foresman and Company, 1965).

O'Brien, Robert W., *et. al.* (eds.), *Readings in General Sociology,* 3rd ed. (Boston: Houghton Mifflin Company, 1964).

*Parsons, Talcott, *The Social System* (New York: The Free Press of Glencoe, Inc., 1951).

Riley, Matilda White, *A Case Approach,* Vol. I of *Sociological Research,* 2 vols. (New York: Brace & World, Inc., 1963).

*Shepherd, Clovis R., *Small Groups: Some Sociological Perspective* (San Francisco: Chandler Publishing Company, 1964).

*Valdes, Donald M., and Dwight G. Dean (eds.), *Sociology in Use: Selected Readings for the Introductory Course* (New York: The Macmillan Company, 1965).

* Also published in paperback edition.

Chapter 6

The Family System

By now you will have absorbed enough of family sociology to know something about it. From the first part of the book you will have gleaned the facts that (1) the family is one of the major social systems of any society; (2) that family life is expected to meet the needs of individuals and certain needs of society. In the discussion of culture you saw that popular conceptions of love, romance, and sex are often distortions of the true facts about American family life and the functions it performs. In the discussion of personality you saw the crucial importance of the family in personality and attitude development. This provides you with some background for the present chapter, not to mention the experience you have had as a family member yourself. This "head start" should be of great help in mastering the chapter.

But we are not going to omit any material on the grounds that you already know it. Our main purpose will be to organize what you know and what you may not already know into a unified sociological perspective on the family. This unified perspective begins on a note which may be new to you. At the beginning of human history all of social life was family life! The family as we know it today is the product of a long process of evolution. It is important that you not be misled by those who misunderstand this evolution and see it as the "falling apart" of the family. So it is appropriate that we begin here.

THE EVOLUTION OF THE MODERN FAMILY

The primitive society was small, isolated, and as you saw in the chapter on culture, it was culturally homogeneous. Do you remember that this meant that its members had pretty much the same ideas and beliefs about things? This cultural homogeneity of the primitive society was contrasted with the cultural complexity of modern American society. A moment's reflection will show the relationship of cultural homogeneity and cultural complexity to the family systems of primitive and modern societies. There are more different kinds of families today.

A primitive society typically had fewer than ten *clans* while modern societies have literally millions of *families*. So the modern society is not only immensely greater in sheer size than the primitive society. It is also vastly more "atomistic." This means that it is made up of vastly more units than primitive societies. For our purposes here, this means that the basic unity of society, the family, is much smaller than it was in primitive society. It is also doing less than in the past, as we shall see. And we shall also see that what the family is doing, while less in scope, is of even greater importance in the modern world.

The Clan

The clan is the basic kinship group of primitive societies. We distinguished it from the modern family above, but in a broad sense, the clan was also a family. When we speak of kinship we moderns immediately think of the family. We think of father, mother, brother, sister, aunt, cousin, and grandparent. How many kin do you have? The term "kin" itself is old fashioned and if it were not for folk songs you probably would not even have heard of the term. The point here is that your range of kinship, the number of kin you can count, will doubtless be much smaller than that of your parents. You could ask them to count their kin and then compare their answers to this question with your own.

Whether or not the experiment would work in your case, the point is that, generally speaking, there has been a long evolution in the family which is still going on. In the beginning of the history of the modern world, according to Fustel de Coulanges, in his *Ancient City*, the father of the clan was priest, judge, police, and general boss of everything that went on in his small farm-settlement. This, of course, was in the general area of what later was to become Greece and Italy. Hundreds of years before the Greeks and Romans that we study as "the ancients," these primitive societies were made up of single clans with a single patriarch. In other words, in the beginning of the Western world the "family" was the same as the "society."

The history of the Western family, then, has been a history of loss of functions by the family. The evolution of other social systems one by one replaced the family as a religious system, an economic system, a political system, and even to some extent as an educational system. By the time of the Greek and Italian city-states some of this transition had already occurred.

The clan and its leader, the father (pater), in order to band together with other clans for protection and economic advantages surrendered some of their powers to the city-state. Religious and political leaders with powers over family heads had to come into existence. Heads of important families still retained some power. "Patricians" are good examples of such a class. Can you see the relationships between the *patrician* and the *pater* from the words themselves?

After the fall of Rome and the development of cities in Europe, the Medieval Church completed the transfer of the religious function from the clan to the established Church. Political power went the same way — from the family to the monarch and the nobility. The medieval family retained its economic function in one major sense. The family made its living as a family, but a great deal of economic control had already passed to the gentry and to some extent to the Church.

With the rise of a merchant middle class a new element was introduced into the medieval social system. This meant that a family with money became a power to be reckoned with in contrast to the power of the titled nobility. The great religious cleavage called the Reformation evolved with religious and political changes for the family. By the time of the settling of the northeastern seaboard of the United States by the Puritans, control of the family by the Church had already lessened. From this time forward there is a clear historical picture of the family "standing on its own feet."

The Transition From Clan to Modern Family

This being on its own was not the same thing as the self-sufficiency of the primitive clan. Churches, the state, the economy, and later, the public school now supplemented the family. The Industrial Revolution had the further effect of narrowing down families' activities and control over their members' activities. Now the family members had to go outside the family to work. Factories and commercial enterprises took fathers and even children out of the family's control during long working hours.

In the early years of the Industrial Revolution, the family

remained somewhat clannish. Some families, even today, have managed to retain their clannishness. You can probably think of families that are clannish and families that are not. But even the most clannish families of today are smaller than the families in America around the turn of the century. It was not unusual for a single family household to contain several generations. Surviving grandparents, old maid aunts, and bachelor uncles were a normal part of the household give and take. Imagine the help that parents received in rearing their children! And the children themselves were more numerous. Families with ten to fifteen children were not uncommon.

The Crisis of the Early Modern Family

But certain of the influences that we have mentioned began to take their toll upon the family. Churches began to lose their control of family life. The Industrial Revolution also influenced the family. Jobs outside the house drew single aunts and uncles away from it. Children began to leave the home when they achieved economic independence. The number of children per family decreased. Birth control became increasingly effective and widely used. In general, the industrial society favors the individual, rather than the family. Mobility became the rule rather than the exception. Moving out of the house is one thing; moving to another part of the country (in pursuit of a job) is another. Families are strengthened by "get togethers" on work holidays. This is impossible, of course, when great distances separate them.

The final blow for the old family form came as the romantic love theme became a part of American culture. Romantic love stresses the satisfactions of the individual with marriage, not the responsibilities. Divorce was a natural consequence. Freed of the constraints of the churches, marriage lost its sacred nature and became increasingly a matter for individual decision.

Sociologists of the 1930's viewed the situation with great alarm. The decrease in birth rates, the rising tide of divorce and drastic changes in sexual standards provided strong evidence for very gloomy predictions for the future of the American family.

Sociologists of that era noted, as we have in preceding paragraphs of this chapter, that the history of civilization had been, for the family, a history of losing functions to other social systems. There had gradually come to be fewer links between husband and wife due to the fact that the activities performed by them have been taken over by the Church, the school, the playground, and other extra-familial agencies. Some sociologists held that companionship would, in a lonely society, provide some basis for a relatively stable association between the sexes. The family seemed at the end of the line as far as its usefulness was concerned.

Industrial Revolution and Divorce

In summary, the industrial revolution and other historical developments had produced a high divorce rate by the 1930's in America. Some of the main factors contributing to this high divorce rate were:

1. A decline in the influence of religion upon the family.
2. More and more legal and social toleration of divorce.
3. Emancipation of women through jobs outside the home (industrialization).
4. Less control by neighbors over one another's conduct (urbanization).
5. Birth control, resulting from the economic devaluation of children.
6. Greater mobility (both geographic and social) which loosens family ties.
7. More mixed marriages (urbanization produces heterogeneity of population).
8. The emphasis on romance which placed too much demand on the intimate, affectional side of marriage.

This, then, was the crisis of the early modern American family.

Has almost forty years of history made the situation better or has it been merely aggravated? Let us view the facts about the family of today.

The Modern Family

Nothing could be more stupid than to say that everything is all right with the modern family of the late 1960's. But nothing could be further from the truth than some of the early gloomy predictions for the family. From the vantage point of today's outlook for the American family we can discount the "total disorganization" point of view completely.

In the first place, the disorganization of the family in the early period of industrialization was an initial reaction to a crisis. The family had to adapt itself to the new work conditions that were thrust upon it. As you will see in the chapter on the modern community (Chap. 10), city life brought strains to the old *extended* (larger) family. The new, *nuclear* (smaller) family of husband, wife, and three or four children has survived the crisis and by all evidence is stronger than ever.

What is this evidence? In the first place, the divorce rate has leveled off. While still too high for our own societal stability, its upward spiral has been checked. Examining the divorce rates to see *who get divorces,* we find further evidence. Two categories of people contribute a great share of the divorces — the recently wed and the childless (more than fifty percent of those applying for divorce are childless). Can you see why this means that marriage is for many people still an unstable arrangement? If so, can you also see that the family is not as disorganized as the divorce rates would lead us to believe?

But there are also many broken families and we must not be overly satisfied with the situation. At present there are between two and three hundred thousand children each year whose homes are broken by divorce. Many of the disturbing statistics on juvenile delinquency and emotional maladjustments have been traced to broken homes, although it can be argued that in some cases a broken home is a better environment than the existing one. Both in the chapter on personality and in later sections of this chapter, evidence of the family's role in personality development illustrates the serious facts that the broken or unstable home provides a poor start for personality and that this poor start is related to all kinds of social maladjustments.

Perhaps, in the light of these serious facts about American family life, you are still not convinced of the stability of the family. There are still more facts to be weighed. For one thing, Americans are the most "married" people in the world. By this we mean that the present ratio of married people to the total population is the highest in the world. Also, proportionately more people in America have chosen marriage than ever before. Look at the suburbs of your city. They may be "ticky-tacky" to the ballad singer but they are the overwhelming choice for male and female in modern society.

But statistics do not tell the whole story. In the remainder of this chapter we shall examine in detail the functions that can be performed by the family and only by the family. If you will remember that "functions" means what the family *does* for society, parents, and children, you will see the strongest argument for the family. To rephrase the argument, there are certain functions that can be performed by the family and only by the family. So it is a much stronger argument to point up the *essential* place of the family rather than family disorganization in our society.

Recreation and other
emotional releases are
part of the family's
tension-management
function.

Bell & Howell

WHAT THE FAMILY DOES FOR SOCIETY

The larger society is dependent upon the family in so many different ways that it is difficult to summarize them all. The basic relationship is simple. Society depends upon the family to maintain its pattern of social systems from one generation to the next. Sociologists call this the *pattern maintenance* function. Since each of these systems is necessary for the survival of society, it follows that society itself requires the family for survival. It is obvious that the political, the religious, the economic, and other social systems need a constant source of supply of new members. This is true simply because of the loss through death of older adult members of the systems. What is not so obvious is that new members of social systems cannot be of just any kind. They must be prepared to fit into the society and to carry it along its course. So procreation and education of children are essential pattern maintenance functions of the family.

But the family also functions for the society in more subtle ways. As the tensions of modern society increased, the role of the family in *tension-management* became more apparent. As your education progresses you may have become aware that society is expecting you to reach a higher level of achievement. This means that the competition for grades increases! This may seem at times like the whole world is simply applying the screws to get more work out of you. Perhaps, but a modern society that has an increasingly specialized economy has great need of trained and disciplined workers. A democratic society has great need for educated voters. The pattern-maintenance function of the family is shared by the school and you are feeling its effects. The tension-management function of the family is to help the individual handle the psychological problems that come from role performance. Recreation and other emotional releases are part of the family's function for society. What are the tension-management activities of your family? Can you see the importance of the family and its role as a haven for the worker in our society? When we discuss what the family does for its individual members you will probably get some new insights into its psychological functioning. Society itself is aware of the pattern-maintenance and tension-management functions of the family. While much improvement is still needed, American society shows its vital concern that these functions are performed effectively. Proofs of this concern include:

1. Legal control of the family.
2. Family guidance services.
3. Support of the family by other social systems.

Legal Control of the Family

Each of the fifty states has laws pertaining to marriage, divorce, and protection of family members. These legal controls are an expression of societal concern for pattern-maintenance and tension-management. A great deal of reform is needed. The laws are such that what is legal in one state can be illegal in another. Requirements for marriage vary. Regulations about divorce are so variable that people "escape" from one jurisdiction to obtain a divorce in another. Do you know of any cities or states where impetuous couples can go to escape what they consider to be irksome marriage restrictions? Do you know of states near you where quick divorces are possible? If you do, it is an interesting sociological study to obtain statistics on the success of marriages contracted there.

It is equally interesting to examine the remarriages of those who obtain "quickie" divorces. The high incidence of failures of such marriages and remarriage creates grave societal concern about more uniform protection of the family throughout the fifty states.

But you should not get the impression that American society has completely ineffective legal control over the family because of varying state regulations. Needful of even more uniformity, the states as a whole do have some common family legislation. Each state has some laws requiring permission to marry. Varying age requirements do occur, but all states have them. All states do have regulations concerning prohibition against marriage for the insane and others not considered suitable for marriage.

Once a couple has received state permission (license) to marry, all states have regulations governing relations of the marriage partner to each other and to any children that might result from the marriage. These include financial and moral obligations such as inheritance rights, obligation for support of dependent children, and the like. Further, each state does regulate divorce even though some are lax in this regard, as we noted earlier.

Many states and other political systems such as cities and counties have gone beyond mere legal control of family behavior. Their reasoning is that prevention of difficulties is more effective for society than waiting for troubles to develop. One form of this prevention approach is the establishment of family guidance and counseling service to families in trouble.

Family Guidance Service

In a later chapter on community, a more comprehensive treatment of the family in the modern community is undertaken. At this point of the discussion you are being asked to consider what the family does for society. As a demonstration of society's awareness of its dependence upon the family we have discussed some of the legal protection which it supplies to the family. Most of the legal protection which is supplied is negative in character. For example, those who are unfit or below a certain age may not get married. The provision of family guidance services is a more positive step. How to stay married and how to provide a wholesome environment for children? These are more positive approaches than merely setting up negative road blocks to marriage or divorce. The general legal trend is toward family reconciliation services. Here, typically, a judge may insist that a couple be counseled and advised before further consideration of their divorce proposal will be entertained. Does your city have such a legal service for married couples verging on divorce?

The social service agencies of the community usually have some legal backing to help them with couples in trouble or with children in a disrupted family situation. But you may not be aware that all of the social systems, whether possessing legal authority or not, have some awareness and are doing something about the crucial importance of the family for society.

Support of the Family by Other Social Systems

In the religious systems the churches are becoming involved in special services for the family. Traditionally the churches have been the "port of call" for the members of the marriage or the family in trouble. Rabbis, priests, and ministers are increasingly clamoring for more training in psychology and sociology so that they can assist more effectively in family counseling. It is quite common for clergymen, psychiatrists, and other helping professionals to conduct training sessions for each other to offer a fully rounded psychological, social, and religious dimension to the family counseling process.

In the educational system two general directions of family support have developed. In university research, studies of marriage itself have been fruitful. The main emphasis of such studies has been upon *marriage prediction* studies. We shall consider the results of these studies later in the chapter. The second direction is a logical extension of the first. Once research has enabled sociologists and psychologists to predict success in marriage, the logical outcome is the offering of courses which inform students about what factors predict a successful marriage and which do not. As we mentioned earlier in the chapter, Americans are greatly interested in marriage and such courses are enormously popular among college undergraduates. Presumably these courses strengthen the family in America. Certainly they do illustrate the awareness of people in the educational system that society depends upon the family.

Marriage and the family have always been important to the economic systems which cannot flourish without workers who are well motivated. Prosperous families are vitally necessary to buy and consume the products of the economy. But until recently the economic system did not recognize the full significance of its dependence upon the family. Absenteeism, alcoholism, poor incentive, and such related problems gradually came to be recognized as family problems. Unions and management are both casting around for effective ways to contribute to family stability. Don't be surprised when a hard-boiled union official or plant manager employs a social worker! This is an increasingly occurring phenomenon and signifies a growing awareness of the need for stabilizing all social systems through stabilizing the family.

While we have not exhausted the subject, about which many whole books could be written, we have at least indicated many of the ways in which the social systems of society are acknowledging their dependence upon the family. But, if you will recall, we wish to relate this societal dependence upon the family to two other kinds of dependence — the dependence of adults and the dependence of children upon the family. Do you think of dependence in the sense of perhaps "leaning" on something? When you lean on a table you would fall down if the table were moved. Many people do lean on their families. But we mean by dependence that people have needs and meet these needs in and through the family. Just as society has needs for pattern-maintenance and tension-management so do adults and children have needs which are met (or not met) in the family.

WHAT THE FAMILY DOES FOR ADULTS

In the chapter on personality we emphasized that adolescence is the bridge between childhood and adulthood in our society. Do you remember that "anticipatory socialization" (preparing for and looking forward to) into marriage and work roles was considered the identity problem of adolescents? Then you should not be surprised to see that our discussion of adults and the family begins with adolescence.

Sociologists agree that, for the adults, the family consists of five stages, sometimes called the *family cycle*. These are:

1. The stage of marital partner selection.
2. The honeymoon era.
3. The nursery stage.
4. The transitional stage.
5. The empty nest.

Before considering each of these stages separately you will want to have an overall idea about what the family cycle is as a whole. Certain aspects of the stages may puzzle you otherwise. The premarital stage is included as part of the family cycle because sociologists have come to see that *success or lack of success* in marriage begins here — in the dating and courtship years of the adult's life. The honeymoon era lasts from the day of marriage until the day the first child is born! By now you will have decided that sociologists view things differently from the way they are seen in popular American culture. This is true. Sociologists do not look down on marriage but the transition from single to married is not as critical as the transition from young *married* to young *parent*. The difference lies in the social role of parenthood, which involves more personal adjustment and social responsibility. By now you will have grasped the essential feature of the family cycle. *It is the life cycle of a system* in which the stages are the selection of elements (mates) in the system, the stabilizing of relations between the elements (honeymoon era) and the expansion of the system to include new members (nursery stage). The transitional stage follows. This is the stage where the new members are trained for membership in their own families. When this has been achieved the system gradually contracts (reducing size) back to the original members. The family system thus has performed its function for society. This sounds more like a discussion of what the family does for society than what the family does for its adult members. But it is a necessary background for that discussion. The family does something different for the adult member at each stage. What is it that the family does for individuals who are not yet married?

The stage of marital partner selection does a great deal for the young people who are not yet married. By looking forward to marriage an important aspect of personal maturity is achieved. Most teenagers look aghast when they read that sociologists view dating as preparation for marriage. "Marry that creep?" This question is often raised when the teenager is asked to think of the last (or the next) date as a marital prospect. But the question is extremely revealing. While, perhaps, lacking in charity, the question nevertheless reveals the presence of an important *self-attitude.* Do you remember this concept from the chapter on personality? In context here it refers to the fact that teenagers are building up a composite *conception of the ideal mate.* It is a self-attitude in that it is of a mate appropriate for *me.* It is an ideal in the sense of being a standard. How else do we judge a "creep" if not by such a standard?

Studies show that conceptions of the ideal mate are built up from fragments of admiration for parents, from romantic attachments of various sorts, and even from negative feelings toward parents and others. For example, if a parent is a spendthrift one may "build-in" the notion of financial responsibility in the conception of the ideal mate.

The realistic elements in the conception of the ideal mate have been separated from the unrealistic ones by the patient studies of sociologists and psychologists. These are the marriage prediction studies mentioned earlier in the chapter. The method of these studies is simple although carrying them out is complicated. The basic method is to find two groups of subjects one of which is "happy" and the other is "not happy" with their marriage. Then the subjects in each group fill out a questionnaire which covers such areas as background factors (e.g., relations with parents, personality factors), economic factors, in-law relationships, children and sexual adjustment, religious factors, friends, and recreational interests. The findings are very revealing. The actual ideal mate in these studies is someone who is like one's self in social background factors — social class, religion, and culture. But the ideal mate is often unlike one's self in personality factors. In brief, one's mate may supply a need for something which one lacks. Psychologists call this *personality complementarity*. A dependent person may mate best with a more independent one, for example. Does this scientific approach do violence to your conception of the ideal mate?

So the stage of marital partner selection serves the purpose of refining the conception of the ideal mate. Two other secondary functions should be mentioned. Dating is fun, it is often involved, and much is learned about the opposite sex. These constitute a positive function of dating. On the negative side, there is a great deal of ego-bruising that occurs. The "picking over" in the dating and the rating of dates inevitably bruises even the most fortunate. Nevertheless, some psychological gain occurs as the teenager learns — the hard way — to cope with disappointments in interpersonal relationships.

The next stage in the family cycle also involves its learning problems but, in general, it is a more settling period of life.

The Honeymoon Era

While the popular literature stresses the stormy upheaval of this stage — the bride burns the toast and the husband develops indigestion — many important and desirable personality changes occur in the people whose marriages survive this stage. On the one hand it is the stage which produces most divorces, as we have already shown. On the other hand, this crucial period in the family cycle does more for the people who enter it with proper attitudes than is popularly believed. The engagement period should be of sufficient length for the couple to know each other well enough to be realistic about each other's limitations and strengths. Sociologists have found that *poor adjustment* in this stage is more characteristic of those who were engaged under six months, *good adjustment* is more characteristic of those who were engaged from six months, and *excellent adjustment* is characteristic of those who have been engaged for two years and up.

What does good adjustment involve? Married persons who are adjusted become more interested in tranquil satisfactions than in seeking thrills. The curbing of self-indulgence and the learning of self-denial are notable in the well-adjusted married person. His social world changes. Instead of many social relationships he now has fewer, but

The responsibility of
providing and caring
for children is a test
of the emotional
stability and flexibility
of the parent.

they mean more. Marriage involves an even greater commitment to moral order and to society. The loss of self is transformed into an other-regarding emotion. Daydreams tend to disappear. Instead of living vicariously through fantasy, the happily married tend to live more in the real world. There is a growth in the married person's ability to participate in joint decision making.

All of this may sound heroic to the as yet unmarried. Does it seem like something of a "drag"? Nevertheless, the persons who put up with the necessary conflicts of adjustment at this stage of marriage do not see it that way. They find a new sense of meaning in life. Above all, it can be an important period of settling, of getting used to the demands of married life. From the standpoint of the next stage, the nursery stage, the honeymoon era serves the valuable function of preparing the married adult for the further personality growth that this next stage can produce.

The Nursery Stage

Some element of crisis is present in the child-bearing stage as there is in all situations where personality growth occurs. For the new parents the problem of adjustment to *the role* of parent rests squarely upon their readiness to accept *responsibility*. In the chapter on culture and personality it was emphasized that ours is an activist culture. Do you remember what this means for the individual? The successful individual is one who initiates and carries out activities. Above all the valued individual in our society is one who bears responsibility. In a word, the new parent has crossed an important threshold in his life cycle. As a responsible parent he is an *adult* as our society defines one.

This new social role is, for most, a satisfying one. The satisfactions of having the baby as a pet are numerous and pleasant. But the responsibility of providing and caring for children defines a role for the individual which will be with him for as long as his children are dependent. It is a test of emotional stability and of the flexibility of the couple. The requirements of the infant take right-of-way over the feelings of the couple toward each other.

If the honeymoon era brings the individual out of himself to a concern for the couple, the nursery stage brings the couple out of themselves to a concern for a family.

The Transitional Stage

In the final section of this chapter we shall discuss what the parents do for the children of a family. Has it ever occurred to you that very little is written about what having children does for parents? The very dependence of the children serves an important psychological function for the parents. Adult needs for protecting and loving are gratified in serving children. As we said above, the honeymoon is over when the first child is born; conjugal love, a love built out of sacrifice and service, is not a thrilling love but is a much more stabilizing one which has worked amazing transformations in people. Many people who would have been stunted otherwise in their emotional growth, have grown up as a result of enacting parental roles.

The parents relive their lives through their children; the parent-child relations of their own childhood are recreated, only this time they are on the controlling side. There are basic needs of *belonging, response,* and *security;* and needs to be important to someone.

Watching the miracles of growth and development of children offsets boredom and forces one to grow and develop instead of becoming stagnant. You may not approve of all the gratifications which people derive from the parent role. Sometimes these gratifications may become neurotic, as when a parent becomes overbearing or demanding.

Standard Oil Co.

Older couples who have raised their children may still find their lives happy and creative.

But whether wholesome or neurotic these satisfactions often exist only as memories when the home has become an empty nest. Still, there are compensations besides memories for the parents whose children have grown up and left the parental home.

The Empty Nest

When the children have formed families of their own, the mother and father of the original family are left to their own resources. Often they baby sit, visit their children, and if the family is at all clannish, the old family home can be the gathering place on holidays and special family occasions. The family link is not destroyed in such cases. The older family serves as a link to religious, social class, or perhaps to Italian, Polish, Irish, or other ethnic groups. In a word, the adults may find a great deal of meaning in providing *a link in a social heritage* for their children and their children's families.

It may not seem to you that providing identity to generations is not a sufficient purpose in life for older people. Perhaps so. There is a great deal of maladjustment among the aged. Individuals vary greatly in their personality resources. Sociologists and psychologists find many people who are creative and happy in the older years. They are people who have *identity-integrity*. This is a difficult concept for a young person to grasp. It means that an older person lives with a self-image which is a summation of his life experiences. He either feels that it has all been worthwhile or that it has not. Disgust and despair are opposites of identity-integrity.

Before proceeding to a discussion of what the family does for the children there is a social and psychological study which can be cited here to illustrate all that we have discussed previously in this chapter. The conclusion from this study should help you evaluate whether or not it is "worthwhile" from a social and psychological point of view for an American to go through the family cycle.

Earlier in the chapter we noticed the effects upon the family of modern conditions of urbanization and industrialization. The Midtown Manhattan Survey was a study by sociologists, anthropologists, psychologists, and psychiatrists of the people of Manhattan Island, the most industrialized, urbanized district in America. The purpose of this study was to ascertain how well or how impaired individuals are who live in modern society. A sample was drawn and individuals in the sample were interviewed, tested, and evaluated for psychological wellness or impairment.

Young people were least impaired; the middle-aged were moderately impaired, and the older people studied were characterized as the most impaired. This may seem gloomy on the face of it. The longer we live the more impaired we are! But there are some comparisons which throw light on the success of the modern family in serving the needs of adults. At each level *the single, the divorced,* and *the widowed* were the most impaired.

From this and other research evidence it seems safe to conclude that whatever the problems of adjustment of the individual to modern society, participating in the family cycle must be reckoned a strong positive factor for psychological maturity!

WHAT THE FAMILY DOES FOR CHILDREN

Do you recall the overall problem of this chapter? First we discussed the crisis of the modern family. Then we began our analysis of the strength of the family in terms of (a) what the family does for society; (b) what the family does for adults and (c) what the family does for children. By now you should have developed a deeper understanding of the essential nature of the family for American individuals and their social systems. In this concluding section we hope to illustrate the importance of the family in developing human nature itself. What the family does for children has a great deal to do with personality, of course. You may wish to review the chapter on personality as a supplement to this discussion.

Sociologists have a great deal of information on the relationship between the family and the child. It can be summarized most concisely as five major relationships:

1. The family affects the child first.
2. Family experiences build habits.
3. The family transmits the culture to the child.
4. Family life has special emotional effects on the child.
5. The family confers social status.

The Family Affects the Child First

Without the family, society would necessarily have to become a vast network of nursery and training schools. Many societies have attempted to assume the responsibility for the shaping of the child's personality during the early formulative years. Can you see why totalitarian governments usually experiment with schemes for influencing the child during this flexible time of personality development? Even the state of Israel, experimental though not totalitarian, has attempted to modify the customary family arrangement in the *kibbutzim*. When it comes to child care and training such experiments are limited in their success.

The basic reason why society has been and will be wary of interfering with the family-child relationship is that all five of the relationships we have listed above *are also related to each other*. For example, the family affects the child first, but the family has a special emotional quality which other agencies would find it difficult or impossible to provide. The family provides for the needs of the infant and teaches him so that he develops patterns with which he will meet life situations. But the teaching function cannot be separated from the emotional contact of the home. The mother's love and the father's love and discipline are necessary requisites for personality formation. And as we have seen in this chapter, mothering and fathering meet the needs of adults.

Hence the groundwork for personality is laid in the family and is accomplished by people who are highly motivated to do the work involved in it.

Family Experiences are Repetitive

The family persists through time. Many extremely important formative agencies outside the family could rival the importance of the family, were it not for the factor of time. How many teachers have you had? How many best friends? In a modern society like ours school districts and church boundaries are frequently subject to change. If you lived in one residence all during childhood, would you attend the same school all of that time? Most families move on the average of once every five years. Can you see why sociologists stress the *continuity* of family experience in a mobile society?

Thus habits are developed in the family through the continuous influence of parents and family members upon the child. With all of the conflicting pulls upon the child from outside the family it remains the main steadying influence in the child's life. Here again is a reason why societies have been unsuccessful in replacing the family as a habit-builder of the child.

The Family Is a Major Agent in Transmitting Culture

When you read the chapter on culture, you were probably surprised to find that there was so much of American culture that you accepted unconsciously. You may also have discovered that there are elements of American culture that you do not accept in the same way that others do. This is due to the fact that the family presents the culture to the child in its own individual way and without emphasizing the fact that what is being learned is culture.

Hence the child comes to regard as natural what sociologists and anthropologists know to be the American middle-class way of life. The family puts its own stamp on the culture so that it has a great deal of personal meaning. If one's father is more competitive than most, the impression that success is paramount may be the result in the child. Parents also vary in their attitudes toward romantic love. Standards are maintained by the parents. Who has not heard (or voiced) the complaint that "my parents won't let me do anything"? Many parents resist mass culture and impose their censorship upon the exposure of the child to movies and other mass media.

Family Conditioning and Emotion

Basic needs to love and be loved are met in the family. Even when necessary restraints are imposed upon the child the bitterness which he may experience is tempered by the love of parents which he feels. Family emotions have been described by sociologists as bittersweet. It has been observed that families which are "close" emotionally have more conflicts and more successful love relationships than families which are not so close. Psychologists emphasize that effective learning takes place in an emotional context. Simply doing something over and over again will make it easier for us to know how to do that something in the future. But something which has an emotional meaning for us is learned much more quickly and remains with us much longer. Little wonder that family life is irreplaceable as a learning situation!

In former years when homes were broken through divorce or death, the common practice was to place the children in institutions. There are still many circumstances which require institutions for children, but the common practice in modern times is to place children in foster-homes wherever possible. Thus they will have access to foster parents who can provide the emotional warmth in which human learning flourishes.

The Family Confers Social Status

This is the most subtle of the things which the family does for the child. We do not often think about this gift which the child receives when he is born into a family. Perhaps you have looked up socially and dreamed about what it would mean if you had been born into a richer or more socially prominent family. Have you ever looked down and been grateful for being where you are on the socioeconomic ladder?

Family members share a social identity. In modern urban communities the family derives its social standing from the occupation of the father. The interdependence of the family's members means that parents will wish to see their sons and daughters start life at least at their own social level. This means that they will be motivated to educate and to keep their children to maintain this social level or move higher.

Conclusion

In this chapter we saw that the small modern family is an adaptation to the demands of modern society. While the family was undergoing the adaptation from the larger, extended family to its present form many gloomy predictions were made about its future. Divorce rates and other signs of family disorganization certainly provided a basis for alarm. But the problems of the early modern family, while still with us to some extent, were seen to be abating somewhat. We analyzed what the family does for society and what protections for the family are provided as recognition of society's dependence upon the family, then we analyzed what the family does for adult members and finally what the family does for children. Without laboring the point further the only conclusion consistent with the facts that have been presented is that no matter what problems the modern family faces, it is an irreplaceable system in modern society. Arrived at through sociological analysis, our conclusion is also supported by the fact that all societies have had the family system in some form. This is strong evidence that it is rooted in human nature.

Major Concepts in Chapter 6

1. *Atomistic:* Social condition in which larger social groups or patterns have been broken into fragments or reduced to smaller units.

2. *Clan:* A kin-group based upon traditional common descent. Consists of all adult members, their spouses, and children.

3. *Marriage:* The social institution for entering matrimony or setting up a family unit.

4. *Nuclear family:* A man and a woman joined in a socially recognized union and their children.

5. *Extended family:* Any grouping related by descent, marriage, or adoption that is broader than the nuclear family.

6. *Kinship:* A relationship between two or more persons on the basis of officially recognized common ancestry.

7. *Divorce:* The legal dissolution of an officially recognized marriage relationship.

8. *Divorce rate:* The ratio between the number of divorces and the number of marriages performed in a year.

9 *Birth rate:* The number of births per year per thousand population.

10. *Industrialization:* The process of technological development by the use of applied science and the expansion of large-scale production.

11. *Urbanization:* The movement of people to urban areas and the increase of urban areas and their populations. Characterized by large size, density of population, heterogeneity, and impersonality.

12. *Mixed marriage:* Marriage across social barriers. Applied to marriages between persons of different ethnic backgrounds, races, or religions.

13. *Romantic love:* An attitude which exalts feeling and considers im-

pulse to be self-justifying. In its extreme it is individualistic rather than social, the attitudes toward the one loved being self-satisfying rather than other-regarding.

14. *Companionate marriage:* Proposed form of marriage for people not yet ready for the responsibility of family life. Would be tentative marriage with absolute control of births of children until the couple was mature enough to want them.

15. *Tension management:* The people in any social system are subject to emotional disturbances and distractions which must be managed if they are to function effectively. Relieving anxiety and providing encouragement are examples of tension management.

16. *Patriarch:* The father and ruler in a type of social organization (patriarchate) characterized by absolute authority of the father, by patrilineal descent, inheritance, and succession, and by legal subordination of women and children.

17. *Social evolution:* Continuous orderly social change in a given direction, involving adaptation to an environment and increasing complexity of social structure for greater functional effectiveness.

18. *Family cycle:* The span of the lifetime of a given nuclear family marked by crises, episodes, and stages.

19. *Personality complementarity:* In marriage, the situation where the role playing of one mate meets the needs of the other mate and vice versa. For example, a dependent mate plays a childish role while the other mate enacts parental roles and a personality balance results.

20. *Kibbutzim:* Plural of kibbutz, a collective farm in Israel where the somewhat socialistic life permits a married couple sexual relations and regular cohabitation but precludes the usual marital arrangement of economic cooperation.

Review Questions

1. Robert Redfield called the clan "primitive man's social security." What did he mean by this?
2. Are there any ethnic groups in your community which are clannish?
3. How clannish is your family compared to other families in your community?
4. In Western civilization, when did the chiefs of clans begin to surrender some of their power?
5. Explain "the history of the Western family has been a history of loss of functions by the family." Was this bad?
6. Relate Patricians (Rome) and Eupatrides (Greece) to the family.

7. How did the rise of a merchant middle class affect the family?
8. How did the Reformation affect the family?
9. Is the family in the United States controlled by the religious system?
10. What were some effects of the Industrial Revolution upon the family?
11. Is romantic love functional for the family in America?
12. What do you think of companionship as a basis for marriage?
13. What are some of the causes of divorce, sociologically speaking?
14. What do we learn from divorce rates about the dissolution of families in America?
15. Can you conceive of a home situation where even a broken home would be better for the children?
16. Explain: "Americans are the most married people in the world."
17. What functions are left to the modern family?
18. What is the justification for legal control of the family?
19. What family guidance services are there in your community?
20. How do other social systems support the family?
21. What are marriage prediction studies?
22. What is the family cycle? What are its stages?
23. What is accomplished (hopefully) for the individual marriage partner at each stage?
24. What is the conception of the ideal mate?
25. What is personality complementarity?
26. How long should a couple be engaged?
27. What does the Midtown Manhattan Survey tell us (indirectly) about marriage?
28. What does the family do for the child?
29. Has there been any change in your outlook on marriage and the family as a result of reading this chapter?

Discussion Questions

1. Discuss: "There would not be any juvenile delinquency if parents would only do their jobs as parents."
2. What modifications in the family can the state bring about?
3. Is a broken home sometimes more desirable than a home with both parents?
4. Discuss: "American family life is the cult of momism."
5. What is the relationship between the family and mental illness?

Bibliography

Anshen, Ruth N. (ed.), *The Family: Its Function and Destiny*, rev. ed. (New York: Harper & Row, Publishers, 1959).
Blood, Robert O., *Marriage* (New York: The Free Press of Glencoe, Inc., 1962).

Blood, Robert O., and Donald M. Wolfe, *Husbands and Wives: The Dynamics of Married Living* (Glencoe, Ill.: The Free Press, 1960).

Bowman, Henry A., *Marriage for Moderns,* 5th ed. (New York: McGraw-Hill Book Company, 1965).

Burgess, Ernest, and Paul Wallin, *Engagement and Marriage* (Philadelphia: J. P. Lippincott, Co., 1953).

Burgess, Ernest, and Leonard S. Cottrell, *Predicting Success or Failure in Marriage* (Englewood Cliffs, N. J.: Prentice-Hall, Inc., 1939).

*Coser, Rose L. (ed.), *The Family: Its Structure and Functions* (New York: St. Martin's Press, 1964).

Duvall, Evelyn M., and Reuben Hill, *Being Married* (Boston: D. C. Heath & Co., 1960).

Farber, Bernard, *Family: Organization and Interaction* (San Francisco: Chandler Publishing Company, 1964).

Goode, William J. (ed.), *Readings on the Family and Society* (Englewood Cliffs, N. J.: Prentice-Hall, Inc., 1964).

Hertzler, J. O., *American Social Institutions: A Sociological Analysis* (Boston: Allyn and Bacon, Inc., 1961).

Kephart, William M., *The Family, Society, and the Individual,* 2nd ed. (Boston: Houghton Mifflin Company, 1966).

Landis, Judson T., and Mary G. Landis, *Building a Successful Marriage,* 4th ed. (Englewood Cliffs, N. J.: Prentice-Hall, Inc., 1963).

Locke, Harvey J., *Predicting Adjustment in Marriage: A Comparison of a Divorced and a Happily Married Group* (New York: Henry Holt & Company, 1950).

Miller, Daniel R., and Guy E. Swanson, *The Changing American Parent* (New York: John Wiley & Sons, Inc., 1958).

Nimkoff, M. F. (ed.), *Comparative Family Systems* (Boston: Houghton Mifflin Company, 1965).

Spiro, Melford E., *Kibbutz — Venture in Utopia* (Cambridge, Mass.: Harvard University Press, 1956).

Srole, Leo, *et al., Mental Health in the Metropolis* (New York: McGraw-Hill Book Company, Inc., 1962).

Stephens, William A., *The Family in Cross-Cultural Perspective* (New York: Holt, Rinehart & Winston, 1963).

Terman, Lewis M., *et al., Psychological Factors in Marital Happiness* (New York: McGraw-Hill Book Company, 1938).

Zimmerman, Carle C., *The Family of Tomorrow: The Cultural Crisis and the Way Out* (New York: Harper & Brothers, Publishers, 1949).

---

* Also published in paperback edition.

Chapter 7

The Religious System

THE SOCIOLOGY OF RELIGION — WHAT IS IT?

ALL over the world, religion, whether organized or not, has important effects on society. We are told that we cannot understand political and cultural problems in Southeast Asia without some insight into Buddhism. Similarly, many conflicts in the Middle East can only be explained in terms of the religion of Islam. Social structure in India reflects a Hindu religious belief in *Karma* or fate which dictates that men remain in the caste into which they are born since their caste position is determined by the will of God. A leading authority on European history, Christopher Dawson, has stated that we can equate Western Europe and Christianity. It is clear, therefore, that religion has social effects. These effects are studied by the sociology of religion.

What is the sociology of religion? How does it differ from theology? To begin with, it is important to recall what sociology of religion is not. It is not some "no man's land" between science and religion which combines theology and sociology into a unified synthesis or world-view, subordinating theology to sociology or vice versa. Sociology of religion is neither a substitute for nor an opponent of religion. *It is a scientific discipline which views religious organizations and practices as part of culture and society, studying the interrelations between religion and other institutions of society such as economics, the family, and the state.* Both the theologian and the sociologist tend to agree that there will be no unsolvable conflicts between sociology and theology so long as each is faithful to its own method of achieving knowledge or truth. Whereas the theologian sees his faith as a reality to be experienced and lived, the sociologist views any one faith

Head of Krishna, a Hindu god. An empirical definition of religion must embrace a wide variety of religious and quasi-religious movements.

Metropolitan Museum of Art

as a fact to be studied and analyzed. Theology analyzes faith by systematically interpreting and explaining one particular faith. Sociology of religion describes how different faiths affect society.

An Empirical Definition of Religion

Since it is not enough for the sociologist to take any one religion's definition of what religion should be, his first problem is how to define religion empirically. His definition must be broad enough to include both individual experiences (private prayer, mysticism, individual belief) and collective experiences (a church, worship services, group attitudes). Some religions stress the individual experience — for example, Zen Buddhism in Japan — while others, such as Judaism and Christianity, lay great weight on the community of faith. You can imagine the difficulty in formulating a definition wide enough to include revival meetings, rain dances, the solemn liturgy of Eastern Orthodox churches, and the sober vesper services of an Episcopalian cathedral.

The problem of defining religion empirically is complicated by the fact that Western and Middle Eastern religions think of God as a personal, loving being while many Asiatic faiths think of God as an impersonal, all-embracing state of existence. Then, again, even atheistic movements such as communism, humanitarian existentialism, or secular nationalism have religious aspects. They use religious-like rituals, speak of conversion and salvation, have their own secular saints such as Lenin. Hence, an empirical definition of religion must include a rich variety of religious or quasi-religious movements.

One such definition — adopted by many American sociologists of religion — is that of the late Paul Tillich, a Protestant theologian: "religion is that which concerns man ultimately." For Tillich, religion is man's attempt to relate himself to what is beyond him and of ultimate concern for him. What is this "beyond"? It may be the personal creator God of Christianity, Judaism, and Islam, or the goal of history (Marxist communism), the betterment of humanity (atheistic humanitarianism), or the national genius of a people (Japanese Shintoism). We may conclude, therefore, with Tillich, that wherever we find an experience, group, or system of belief which lends dignity to life, makes suffering more tolerable, and gives an ultimate system of values to a group in society, there we find religion.

Religion and Magic

Although the major emphasis in this chapter lies with the great organized religions of mankind, especially Judaism and the branches of Christianity, since these latter are the religious systems which influence our American society, illustrative examples from other religions will be given. When these examples deal with primitive religion, we will need to keep in mind a distinction between magic and religion drawn by anthropologist Bronislaw Malinowski. Magic is believed to be a source of power or control over God. Magical words or ceremonies force God to grant what a man desires — good crops, more children, health, death to personal enemies. Magic either wards off evil influences or wins favors. Religion does not control God but tries to worship him. As Joachim Wach, an eminent sociologist of religion, put it, "religion . . . means submission to and worship of the divine power upon which man feels dependent."

Sociology of Religion Defined

We are now ready for a formal definition of sociology of religion, a definition based on the work of sociologist J. Milton Yinger in his book, *Sociology Looks at Religion*. The sociology of religion is the scientific study of the ways in which society and culture influence religion — its origins, its practices, and its doctrine. It is the scientific study of the types of groups and kinds of leadership which express religious experience. It is also the study of ways in which religious groups affect society and culture. It is the analysis of social change or social conservatism caused by religion. It studies the structure of religious norms and attitudes as well as the ways in which religion either frustrates or satisfies personality needs.

THREE METHODS OF APPROACHING THE SCIENTIFIC STUDY OF RELIGION

There are three principal methods of approaching the scientific study of religion — the descriptive, the typological, and the theoretical. Of course, in many studies there is an overlap of methods used.

Description

The first approach is purely descriptive. Like the proverbial police investigator, this approach is interested in "just the facts." Thus, for instance, whole sections of libraries contain books about the social history of Catholicism, Lutheranism, or Mormonism. There are many purely descriptive studies of primitive religions in Asia or Australia. Again, there are innumerable fact-finding surveys dealing with who goes to church and why, as well as census characteristics of major religious groups in the United States, Europe, or Asia. Attitude scales have been devised to test the differences between religious believers and nonbelievers on items such as public morality, racial attitudes, and orientation to change or nonchange in society.

What is the main value of social histories of religion or fact-finding surveys for understanding sociology of religion? They make two contributions to our knowledge of religion in society, one positive, the other, corrective. The positive value of such studies is that they provide pertinent data for understanding the nature of religious systems. Their corrective function lies in the fact that the more we know about the wide range of religious expression the less likely are we to define religion too narrowly or equate religion with our own system of religious belief. Yet, purely descriptive studies of religion in society are presociological in the sense that they do not, of themselves, give us insight into or explanation of the facts which they uncover. That is why sociology of religion must pass beyond description to typology and theory.

Typology

The sociologist is much in the same boat as the botanist or biologist. After he carefully describes social facts about religion, he is in need of categories or typologies for understanding these facts. He looks for family resemblances between the founders of great religious movements such as Mohammed, Buddha, or Moses. He seeks for identities between religious practices in ancient Roman and Greek religion and present-day American or European forms of belief. He wonders if, underneath the individual differences between primitive circumcision rites and Christian confirmation, for instance, there might not be underlying similarities. Thus, the second approach to a scientific study of religion is the construction of typologies or categories which point to similar processes in different religions.

Theory

The third approach to a scientific study of religion in society is the construction of theories which attempt to go beyond description or understanding to explanation. What theory in sociology of religion tries to explain is the social origins and effects of religion. It tries to explain why religion is found to flourish in almost every culture and society. It is especially interested in finding out what positive role religion performs in strengthening the social bonds which bind society together. The next section of this chapter takes up an historical review of sociological theory about the religious system in society.

HISTORICAL REVIEW OF SOCIOLOGICAL
THEORY CONCERNING RELIGION

It would be impossible to present all the major contributions of sociologists in formulating a theory about religion and society. Hence, we will single out six men who have, more than others, left their impact on the sociological study of religious system.

Auguste Comte

A French philosopher, Auguste Comte, often referred to as "the father of sociology," published his *Treatise on Sociology* in 1854. This book bore the subtitle, "Religion." While most present-day sociologists reject his rather arbitrary reading of history, his work was influential for many years. Traces of his "evolutionary" theory of religion are found even today in works on sociology of religion.

Comte pictured all of history as a three-stage evolutionary process. The first stage, beginning with the dawn of history and reaching to the European Middle Ages, was characterized by a *religious* understanding of man, the world, and society. Ancient man, in Comte's view, responded with awe and wonder to a world he could not understand. He saw nature as under the control of supernatural spirits who must be placated. Since he could not understand the world or society, he attributed to "fate" or "the gods" everything that happened. When he tried to explain his life he used myth and symbolic theology.

Medieval man, according to Comte's theory, came one step closer to the modern world. He abandoned religious language of explanation for more abstract, *philosophical* categories. Instead of a pantheon of gods he substituted terms like *nature of things* and *substances* as ways of understanding reality.

Finally, since the seventeenth century, modern man has discovered *science*. He must abandon religious or philosophic ways of talking about the universe. Whatever of religion or philosophy which remain in the modern world are, like the human appendix, vestigial remnants from man's historic past. Comte predicted that religion based on God or the mystery of life would yield to a secular religion of humanity founded in science.

Historians criticize Comte's theory of religion because it does not do justice to historical facts. Anthropologists reject his implication that religious belief follows an evolutionary pattern. Sociologists point to the fact that his theory neither explains the persistent continuance of religion in modern society nor helps us to understand the relation between religion and society. A few sociologists who write about religion agree with Comte that religion is only one stage in man's social evolution which he will some day outgrow. They are forced to employ psychological explanations to account for the survival of religion in modern society which they attribute to superstition or the failure of nerve of some contemporary men who cannot face up to a world based entirely on science. Most sociologists reject Comte's evolutionary theory, however, because it is more a type of theology-in-reverse than a scientific theory of sociology of religion. The student should recognize that Comte's theory cannot adequately explain two social facts about religion: many scientists believe in God; religion not only survives but grows in importance in modern industrial societies.

Karl Marx

Another nineteenth-century social thinker, Karl Marx, is well known for his dictum, "religion is the opiate of the people." Like

Comte, Marx thought that religion was only one stage in social evolution. He predicted that in the communist utopia religion would wither away. It is instructive to note that students of contemporary Soviet society have not found Marx's predictions to have come true. Despite persecution and antireligious propaganda by the government, organized and underground religion survives in the Soviet Union.

By calling religion, "the opiate of the people," Marx was objecting to the preaching of business-oriented ministers of religion who told the laboring classes that their poverty was the will of God, and stressed that the poor should accept their lot in life as unchangeable. The poor would get their reward in the afterlife. As the slogan puts it, the hungry poor would finally get their "pie in the sky." Like opium or alcohol, pie-in-the-sky religion dulled the sensibilities of the poor to the injustices they suffered from greedy capitalists and made them inert about doing anything to better their social position.

Marx's conclusion was that religion always reflected the values and interests of the ruling class in society. The ruling classes used religion as a weapon of social control over the multitude. Religion was essentially conservative, not revolutionary — that is why Marx had little use for it in his revolutionary communist society. He claimed that the history of religion proved his theory true. "Thou shalt not steal" — the seventh commandment of the Mosaic decalogue — invoked supernatural sanction against any of the poor who stole from men of property. "Blessed are the poor" was a statement calculated to keep the poor content with their social environment. When asked, "What function does religion play in society?" Marx's theory replied: religion is a mechanism of social control which justifies the economic interests of the ruling class and prevents dissatisfaction among the poor by diverting their eyes from the problems of this life to the rewards of the afterlife.

While Marx's theory of religion contains obvious flaws, it retains usefullness in helping sociologists understand some aspects of religion in society. The major defects of his theory flow from a distorted reading of history. Marx overlooks the fact that the biblical prophets from Amos to Jeremiah preached a gospel against the rich of Israel. He does not stress that Jesus, besides saying "Blessed are the poor," also reminded us how difficult it is for a rich man to enter the kingdom of heaven. It is simply not true that all religious movements are conservative. As Dr. Martin Luther King's leadership in the Negro Civil Rights movement reminds us, religion can be a revolutionary force to change society, going against the interests of the ruling class. Marx's theory has permanent sociological value, however, because it shows that religion can be one means of social control in society. Marx was probably correct in his emphasis that religion is usually a conservative force. There is also sociological merit in his suggestion that some religious movements among the poor and disinherited classes, like alcohol or opium, serve as escape devices from the harsh face of the reality of poverty. Several contemporary studies of sects and store-front churches in urban slums seem to have corroborated Marx on this point.

Émile Durkheim

Émile Durkheim, the best-known French sociologist in the early part of this century, introduced in his book, *The Elementary Forms of the Religious Life,* a distinction between *sacred* and *profane* areas of life. In profane areas of living, man uses rational techniques, such as science and industry, to control his environment. Even primitive man tries to use the best methods for fishing, hunting, or harvesting crops. The sacred, according to Durkheim, is characterized by an attitude of respect or awe which men take toward certain objects, places, times, and religious legends. Durkheim's central question was: "What is the source of this attitude of respect toward the sacred?" Drawing most of his conclusions from anthropological studies of primitive religion, Durkheim examined those objects which men in primitive societies consider sacred: special totem animals, sacred trees or waterholes, carved idols, specially holy people such as a tribal chieftain or witch doctor. All of these things, concluded Durkheim, are not sacred in themselves but symbols of the sacred. What, then, is the sacred? Durkheim saw a similarity between the attitude of respect which primitive man has toward sacred objects and his attitude of respect toward moral authority in law and society. Hence, he concluded that religion was a symbolic expression of the moral authority of society. It was by this line of reasoning that Durkheim arrived at his famous proposition that society is always the real object of religious belief and worship. Religion is the social means of expressing and reenforcing those sentiments which are most essential to preserving a society: respect for law, a sense of group-solidarity in times of crisis such as death.

It is a real weakness in Durkheim's theory that he restricted his study to religion among primitive tribes. There are some radical differences between primitive religion and the great monotheistic religions of Judaism, Christianity, and Islam. Again, Durkheim's theory does not do sufficient justice to purely individual religious expressions such as private prayer and mysticism. Finally, he seems oblivious to the fact that religion can revolt against society as well as preserve it. For, far from always approving the socially accepted values, religion often condemns the actions of a major portion of society as immoral. Both Christianity and Islam began as religions of social revolt. Few men of religion accept Durkheim's contention that they are really worshiping society not God.

Max Weber

A contemporary of Durkheim, German sociologist Max Weber, has made the most significant contributions to sociological studies of religion. Against Karl Marx, Weber contended in his classic study, *The Protestant Ethic and the Spirit of Capitalism,* that religion does not always reflect and justify current economic arrangements in society. He reminds us in this book that religion is not always a conservative force in society. We will consider the argument of this book of Weber later in the chapter. In opposition to Durkheim, Weber reminded sociologists that religion was not restricted to an explanation of ultimate crises and frustrations such as war, famine, or death, by pointing out the obvious fact that religion often influences the everyday choices and attitudes of men. This is the only way we can explain such a universal religious custom as blessings and thanksgivings before and after daily meals.

In another important study, *The Social Psychology of the World Religions,* Weber drew on his wide knowledge of various world religions to illustrate his method of "ideal types" in sociology. An ideal type is a category which sets out the essential characteristics of a social phenomenon. Nothing in real life perfectly corresponds to the ideal type. For example, if you drew up the essential traits of the modern political tyrant, your portrait should include characteristics which are typical of real political tyrants such as Hitler, Stalin, Mussolini. None of these men, perhaps, perfectly fits the ideal type. All, more or less, have the traits of the "ideal modern political tyrant." Weber used his method of ideal types to categorize religious authorities such as the priest, the prophet, and the founder of religion. We will employ his method of ideal types later in this chapter under "Typologies in Sociology of Religion."

The Twentieth Century: Freud and Parsons

The twentieth century produced major contributions from a psychologist and a sociologist for an empirical study of religion.

Sigmund Freud counteracted Durkheim by stressing individual psychological aspects of religion. He pointed out the key role of family upbringing in determining religious attitudes. Freud tried to explain the origin of religion in his book *Totem and Taboo* by appealing to the guilt feelings of some primeval men who killed their father. Most modern sociologists of religion reject the quest for finding the historical origins of religion in society. Sociologists know that because historical records do not go back that far theories such as Freud's are primarily hypothetical. They also point out that an attempt to discover the historical origin of religion presupposes that there was a time when man, as we know him, did not have any religion. There is no evidence to support such a supposition. Freud and some of his followers tend to define religion as a psychological delusion. Many extremists of this school of thinking describe religion as "a psychological response for which there is no stimulus." Probably, a majority of students of psychology maintain that religion is helpful for human personality.

Talcott Parsons, a student of Max Weber, espouses what is called "the functionalist" theory of religion. We already saw in Chapter 3 a statement of the "functionalist" theory of society which we called there, the principle of useful purpose. In Chapter 3 we defined this principle as the belief that "any idea, custom, belief, or attitude that is widespread in a society and persists over a period of time *must be assumed to have some useful purpose for that society,* contributing to social order and promoting the survival of that culture."

Functionalist theory maintains that religion interacts with other parts of the social or cultural system. Sometimes religion acts as a cause of changes in other areas of society. It is also affected by these and other changes in culture and society. Religion must somehow contribute to the preservation of society — otherwise it would not survive. Talcott Parsons and his followers wish to keep the best insights of both Weber and Durkheim as they try to uncover how religion contributes to social cohesion. Since the functionalist theory of religion as set forth by Parsons is the most widely accepted theory in contemporary sociological studies of religion, we will test this theory in the following section of the chapter by asking how functionalists explain the role of religion in our own society. We will examine their answer to the question, what function does religion perform in promoting the survival of American society?

THE TEST OF FUNCTIONALISM —WHAT FUNCTION DOES RELIGION PLAY IN AMERICAN SOCIETY?

The United States of America is a good candidate to test the functionalist theory because, as Robin Williams of Cornell University pointed out in his book, *American Society: A Sociological Analysis,* "In no other modern industrial state does organized religion play a greater role than it does in the United States." In choosing to focus attention on religion in America, we limit the discussion, practically, to Protestantism, Roman Catholicism, and Judaism.

At first glance, the size and prosperity of religious organizations in America is impressive. Foreign visitors to America who have commented on social life in the United States from their European vantage point, almost to a man, emphasize the impact of religion on American society. Over a century ago, Alexis de Tocqueville in his book, *Democracy in America,* stated that religion in the United States was more vital and influential than in Europe. A century later, British political analyst, Denis Brogan, echoed his sentiments. As Mister Justice Douglas wrote in a decision of the United States Supreme Court, "We are a religious people whose institutions presuppose a supreme being."

The religious statistics, indeed, seem to verify these men's statements. *The Yearbook for American Churches* estimates that, at the last census, there were 62,544,000 Protestants, 40,871,000 Catholics, and 5,500,000 Jewish religious adherents in the United States. Nearly 1,500,000 Americans affiliate themselves with Greek or Russian Orthodox churches. The largest nine denominations in America worship in a total of 210,499 churches. During the past forty years, as Table 1 indicates, the percentage of Americans who claim allegiance to organized religion has steadily increased. This trend is predicted to continue through the next decennial census in 1970.

TABLE 1	
Year	Percentage of Americans claiming allegiance to some organized religion
1920	43.0
1930	47.0
1940	49.0
1950	57.0
1960	63.0

So impressive is the size and influence of religion in America that some social analysts have argued that, despite the "no established religion" clause of the first amendment of the constitution, we have a religious establishment in the United States. What is meant by a religious establishment? Usually, the term refers to one church which is the official faith of the nation. In this sense, Lutheranism is the established religion for Sweden, The Church of England for England, and Roman Catholicism for Spain. In these countries the established religion enjoys special privileges and tax support from the government. Usually, the prime minister must, at least nominally, belong to the established religion. While other religious beliefs may be tolerated, they do not receive direct tax subsidy from the government. Of course, an established religion in this sense does not exist in America. When, therefore, sociologists such as Peter Berger and Will Herberg refer to a religious establishment in America, they cite the fact that in the United States *all religions* (but, especially, Catholicism, Protestantism, and Judaism) enjoy special privileges and government support. What is some of the evidence Berger and Herberg point to in order to substantiate their claim that there is a religious establishment in America?

In our country elected officials swear their oath of office on the Bible. Congress retains a paid chaplain who opens congressional sessions with a prayer. Both our system of coins and the oath of allegiance to the flag remind us that Americans believe that this nation is "under God." In one of the stanzas of the National Anthem, we ask God's blessing on the country. Religious organizations do not enjoy direct tax support. Nevertheless, there are hidden financial benefits such as the exemption of all church-owned property — including income-producing property — from property taxes. Ministers, priests, and rabbis are exempted from military service.

Politicians in our country are fond of using religious vocabulary to support their own political programs. How often have you heard religious terms such as "God," "faith," or "crusade" used in political speeches? God is cited by politicians to endorse their views on war, foreign policy, taxes, segregation, and integration. Former President Dwight Eisenhower voiced his approval of the establishment of religion-in-general in America when he stated, "Our government makes no sense unless it is founded in a deeply felt religious faith — and I don't care what it is." So strongly do most Americans agree with President Eisenhower that it is nearly impossible for an avowed atheist to win elective office in the United States.

Many religious leaders and social scientists, however, have noted that this prominence of organized religion in America is counterbalanced by an increased *secularization* in American society. By secularization they mean an isolation of religion from influence on the important decisions of national and everyday life. These men argue that religion has had only minimal influence on the revolutionary social forces which have transformed the social and political face of America since 1900 — the industrial revolution, the decline of the small farm, increased automation, the growth of large cities, a mass media explosion connected with the invention of radio, movies, and television. There is an apparent paradox that as organized religion has grown in public support and number of adherents, what it has to say has become increasingly irrelevant to the complex political and social problems of our society. America has become secularized, they argue, by relegating religion to Sunday worship and state occasions.

If organized religion, despite its flourishing condition, has very little direct impact on society, what function does religion perform in American life? Social scientists who accept the functional theory submit that religion in America serves society by offering *a symbolic integration* of those values which characterize American culture. Religious groups lend their theological support and prestige to ratify and sanctify values already prevalent in the general community. Believers do not hold views different from those of nonbelievers; they simply hold the common American values more intensely, supporting them through the theological aura of religious language. If Americans in general are patriotic, religious men are super-patriotic in the name of God. If Americans believe in success, religious men endorse this value even more strongly by seeing success as a sign of God's favor. Many social scientists have underscored this function of religion as the symbolic integrator of American values.

Thus, Robert and Helen Lynd, in their famous study of Muncie, Indiana, in the 1930's — a town they disguise in their report by the fictitious name, Middletown — conclude that "To Middletown, the role of religion is not to raise troublesome questions and to force attention to disparities between values and current practice." A more recent study of a small rural community in upstate New York, Springdale, emphasizes the same point. The two sociologists who studied religion in Springdale comment that "Religion serves to accentuate and emphasize the public values within a framework of church activity which further accentuates participation in and commitment to those public values."

What are some of the cultural values to which religion lends the sanctity of its symbols? In Chapter 3 when discussing culture patterns in United States society, we singled out the following key values: a tolerance of diversity, the central role of the business institution, and a stress on action and bigness. Are these values reflected in American religious life?

Tolerance of diversity is a central tenet of American religious faith. We have already seen President Eisenhower's remark to this point. Because Americans of different faiths are often next-door neighbors, the United States could not afford to countenance religious intolerance. "Attend the church of your choice," reads the billboard advertisement, and it reflects the sentiments of most Americans.

Most American clergymen are vitally aware of their businessmen role. This role puts the clergy in touch with the business values of efficiency, organization, and rational planning. Not a few pastors in America, like the character in Henry Morton Robinson's novel *The Cardinal* who won the nickname, "Dollar Bill Monaghan," have had to concern themselves with their fund raising task. More often than not the successful minister, priest, or rabbi is judged more by the size of the church he builds than by his pastoral work among members of the congregation. His success is measured by his efficiency in the businessman role.

How do the values of action and bigness affect American religious institutions? European churchmen have often underscored the effect of these two values on American religious life. Thus, European ecclesiastics are often unimpressed by the sheer numbers of Americans who attend church or by the extent of church property holdings. They claim that the quality of Jewish or Christian religious life is a better index of religious success than statistics pointing to percentage increases in church attendance, number of baptisms, or conversions. They also claim that the American churchmen are so engrossed in action programs connected with the "social gospel" and church recreational programs that they do not devote enough time to instructing their faithful in prayer, meditation on scripture, and the interior life of holiness. Indeed, a recent book by a French churchman speaks of the heresy of Americanism which is equated with the heresy of action. It is not the sociologist's job to pass judgment on the religious value of stressing bigness or action. He can simply relate the fact that many observers see these values as integral parts of American religious life.

Perhaps sociologist Peter Berger in *The Noise of Solemn Assemblies* best sums up the view of those who hold the functional theory. He claims that "religion in America affirms the legitimacy of national symbols and integrates them into a sacred whole." The slogan

"For God and Country" typifies what he means by calling religion in America a culture-religion. The two terms *God* and *country* are simply reversible since God stands for whatever the national society does. As he states it in his book on religion in America, "The social irrelevance of the religious establishment is its functionality. If organized religion in this society were highly relevant to the major social institutions, it would not be functional in the way it is now. It is functional precisely to the degree in which it is passive rather than active, acted upon rather than acting." For Berger and those who write from his viewpoint of functional theory, religion in America is a conservative force which inhibits social change by lending sanctity to American culture values just as they are.

An impressive array of facts seems to lend credence to the functionalist theory that religion in American society only serves as the symbolic integrator of our culture's values. Some sociologists, however, cannot help asking whether the functional theory of religion does justice to *all* of the facts. We must concede to the functionalists that religious leaders often simply mirror the predominant values of the community. We can even admit that this may be the most usual role played by religion in our society. It cannot be denied, for instance, that many Christians and Jews in this country support racial and economic practices which deny the historic beliefs of their religious groups.

Nevertheless, religious leaders sometimes espouse unpopular social causes. Consider the example of the political issue concerning the renewal of a contract between the United States and Mexico to allow Mexican farm laborers — braceros — to migrate to those states bordering on Mexico. Although public opinion polls in California, Texas, and Arizona consistently showed that a majority of citizens in these states supported a continuation of the bracero program, religious leaders in those states were among the most vocal opponents of the policy. Clearly, in this case religious spokesmen were not "symbolic integrators" of the prevailing values in their community.

The functionalist theory is unable to show any reason why this symbolic integration function of religion could not be taken over by some other institution of society such as the political institution. Presumably, patriotism and the cult of national heroes such as Abraham Lincoln could serve this purpose as well as religion. We have national feast days such as Memorial Day or the Fourth of July, each with a heavy overlay of religious-like ritual and symbol. Yet, they do not displace religious feasts such as Christmas, The

Passover, Yom Kippur, or Easter. In countries such as the Soviet Union, attempts to substitute nationalistic festivals and symbolic rites for religious ones have not been successful.

These facts should suggest to functionalists that there is some other role of religion in society besides that of lending its symbolic sanctity to society's values. Sociologists are indebted to functional theory for pointing out clearly *one* of the functions of religion in society. They need to go beyond this theory to discover *other* social functions of religion, e.g., religion as an innovative force, disruptive of social equilibrium.

University of California sociologist Charles Glock reviewed the status of theory in sociology of religion in *Sociology Today*. He concluded that every theory is essentially the functionalist approach to society as applied to the special area of religion. As noted above, we believe there is more to the subject than that. Glock also suggests that at the present stage of the development of sociology, we will achieve more fruitful results by concentrating on typology. In the following section of this chapter, we will review what this approach tells us about religion in society.

TYPOLOGY IN SOCIOLOGY OF RELIGION

The main usefulness of typology in sociology of religion is that it allows us to generalize about social processes in many different religions. In this section of the chapter we will explore three areas of typology: forms of religious expression, forms of religious organization, and forms of religious leadership.

Forms of Religious Expression

In *Sociology of Religion,* Joachim Wach states that religion is essentially an experience of the holy. The experience of the holy expresses itself in many different ways. It takes the form of doctrine, practices, attitudes, and collective worship.

Doctrine

Not every religion stresses doctrinal purity. In some faiths, such as Christianity, it is relatively easy to delimit what is heresy and what is orthodox doctrine — the true belief. Even though Protestant, Roman Catholic, and Eastern Orthodox Christians differ among themselves concerning certain doctrines, they combine to condemn other doctrines as heresy. Each branch of Christianity tends to define itself over against other branches in terms of special doctrines such as the Protestant emphasis on justification by faith not works and the Catholic belief in the infallibility of the Roman Catholic Church. Buddhism or Hinduism, on the other hand, finds room for such a conflicting and varied set of beliefs that it is impossible for an outside observer to say what is heresy and what is orthodox truth. One can believe almost anything and still be a good Buddhist. Religions which stress doctrinal purity usually draw up creeds or confessions of faith which serve as touchstones of true belief. Are there any sociological differences between Christianity and Buddhism which help to explain why doctrine is important in one and not the other? The Christian faith is embodied in highly organized churches, each of which has some authority structure which can define true doctrine. This authority may be the pope or a bishop or a presbyterian synod or a board of elders of the church. Buddhism is not formally organized in the same way as the Christian churches are. It lacks the sociological prerequisite of formal organization which would allow it either to define or enforce a "true belief."

Primitive religions among African or American Indian tribes express doctrine in myth stories, legends, and symbolic language. Water, fire, light, and darkness are used to symbolize man's relation to the gods. The bonds of custom tend to prevent individuals from changing or distorting traditional religious lore. Myth stories are passed on from generation to generation with a minimum of innovation. Organized religions such as Christianity, Judaism, or Islam also use myth and symbol to express their faith. Myth and symbol have their own kind of logic — much like the logic found in poetry.

Advanced religions go beyond myth and symbol when expressing religious doctrine. Most of them have some central book such as the Koran or the Bible or the Hindu Veda which contains the core doctrines of the faith. Continued reflection on these books leads to theology. Theology is an attempt to systematize and logically order the faith expressed in the central book. It uses abstract and technical language instead of symbol. The sociological prerequisites for theology are the invention of writing and contact with logical forms of thought. Theology only flourishes in those cultures where philosophy and science are found.

Theological education involves the seeming paradox that it tends to beget heresy. When men are taught to consider reflectively "the true faith," some men will always think the unthinkable. Pure indoctrination is sociologically incompatible with advanced education. We see an example of this in the conflict between intellectuals and

Wide World Photo

Buddhist religious rites.

the government in the Soviet Union. The intellectuals have an un-
canny habit of introducing revision — heresy — in the orthodox
Marxist faith.

Practices

The practice of prayer is universally found in religions of the
world. Prayer may be defined as talking to God — asking for favors,
thanking for benefits, and listening to find God's will. Prayer may
be either private and individual or collective. In some preliterate

tribes where the individual is believed to be simply an extension of the group there is little scope for purely private prayer.

Another universal practice is the setting aside of special times and places as sacred. The Moslem looks on Friday as a special religious day. Jews set aside Saturday, while Christians commemorate the Sabbath on Sunday. These religions also celebrate other special holy days such as Christmas or the Jewish feast of Purim. On special religious days profane activity comes to a halt. Stores close and commerce ceases. Ask a store-owner in your home town, "How's business from 12 to 3 on Good Friday?" and he will remind you of the fact that the economic system of any country is profoundly affected by religious holy days. Sacred places may be buildings (the synogogue, church, mosque, or temple) or cities (Moslem Mecca, Hindu Benares, Christian and Jewish Jerusalem, Roman Catholic Lourdes). Religious norms forbid certain activities in sacred places. One does not smoke, dance a jig, or eat a snack lunch in church!

Religion even effects food consumption habits. During the Moslem month of the great fast and the Christian Lent, believers abstain from certain kinds of food. Hindus do not eat steak because cattle are sacred. Orthodox Jews eat only kosher foodstuffs, served on kosher dishes. Religious practices, in short, are part of the cultural system of any society in which religion plays a leading part.

Attitudes

While attitudes are hard to measure, they exert real effect on social action. Consider varying religious attitudes toward war. The Quakers are pacifists who believe all war is evil. Even patriotic Quakers must refuse to serve in the armed services. They claim that their pacifism makes them more patriotic since they are serving the best interests of their country. Quakers are often unpopular people during wartime. In Aztec Mexico the god of war was the most popular deity. Every year the Aztecs offered human sacrifice to this god. The Aztecs saw war as a religious crusade. The Hindu attitude toward life is respect for all living creatures. Hindus should not kill other humans even in wartime. This fact explains why the Indian army has disproportionate numbers of Sikhs — a small Indian sect which rejects the major tenets of Hinduism.

The most important religious attitude from the viewpoint of its sociological effects is the attitude taken by a religion toward the material world or cosmos. There are three possible attitudes or stances which religion can adopt in relation to the world. Table 2 presents these alternative stances in schematic form.

TABLE 2

(A) Basically Good World	(B) Ambivalent World	(C) Basically Evil World
Belief: man can overcome all evil	man can conquer much evil — never elimi- nate it	the world is evil — man should flee it
Attitude: optimism	cautious optimism	Pessimism
Religious Groups: Homeric religion classic Confucianism modern Humanism Marxism	Christianity Judaism Islam	Hinduism most branches of Buddhism

The first possible attitude toward the material world is characterized by intense optimism. With time and rational control, man can overcome all evil. He can achieve utopia here on earth. Classic Chinese Confucianism, modern humanistic movements, and Marxism fall within this category. The second attitude is mixed or ambivalent. It is an attitude of cautious optimism based on the belief that good is more powerful than evil. So long as men exist, however, there will be evil. Christianity, Islam, and Judaism belong to this category since they all hold that men can sin. In all three there is a belief that, besides God, there is a principle of evil in the world which is not God and under God's control, the devil. The third attitude is pessimistic. Hinduism and most branches of Buddhism are sure that the world is evil, or at least a mere delusion. The happy man is the one who flees the world of material objects and sense knowledge and achieves communion with the All. Such a man reaches a state of Hindu *nirvana,* oblivion to care, pain, and external reality. The importance of these attitudes from a sociological point of view is their effect on the way a society accepts science and technology. The attitudes listed under *A* and *B* in Table II are both compatible with modern science and technology. The attitude under *C* is inimical to science. One can safely predict that to the extent that a society views the material world as basically delusion and evil, so modern industrialism and scientific exploration will be impeded. One of the most basic conflicts confronting India as it tries to become part of the modern world is the clash between classic Hindu attitudes and the values of modern science.

Worship

We have seen that the experience of the holy expresses itself in doctrine, practices, and attitudes. It is found most intensely in worship services. Many primitive religions worship God through sacrifice — the immolation of humans, animals, food, or the libation of special liquids which express the individual's or the group's dependence on God. Modern Jews do not practice sacrifice, although the Torah reminds us that their ancient ancestors did. Christians look on Jesus' death on the cross as the supreme sacrifice offered once and for all mankind. They commemorate and renew this sacrifice in the Christian liturgy of the Eucharist. Buddhism, Hinduism, and Islam do not practice sacrifice.

Most Christians know what they mean by a sacrament — a special religious rite or action which joins the Christian in faith especially to Christ, such as baptism or the Eucharist. There are parallels to the Christian sacraments in most world religions. In Japan there are sacred washings; in India sacred meals have a sacramental nature. These rites are external symbols which signify a special presence of the deity to the believer.

A third form of worship besides sacrament and sacrifice is ritual prayer meetings. Often incense and candles are used, as in Buddhist temples, to stress the special solemnity of such meetings. Collective forms of worship fall into three patterns. Some collective worship services follow a pattern of corporate silence. The group comes together, as in a Quaker meeting, and sits silently in prayer. Buddhism and Hinduism typically employ collective silence in prayer in their temples of worship. A second form of collective service involves prayer performed by one man or a select group of religious elite in the name of all. The Eastern Orthodox liturgy follows this pattern. Finally, there is a group liturgy in which all present participate by vocal prayer and singing. Christian and Jewish groups in our country combine all three patterns in their church or synogogue services. There are moments of silent prayer. The minister, priest, or rabbi reads scripture and offers prayer in the name of all. The congregation joins in singing and collective prayer. An interesting sociological study would be to try to determine whether identification with other members of the congregation is lessened when corporate silence or prayer by a leader in the name of the congregation is the predominant pattern of collective worship.

We have seen, then, that the forms of religious expression are doctrine, practices, attitudes, and worship. We must now investigate forms of religious organization.

Forms of Religious Organization

In a real sense all collective expressions of religion are organized. Some, however, are informally organized. Their principle of organization is cultural. As cultures they have their own norms, attitudes, ideas, and practices, but they are not, strictly speaking, societies. Hinduism and Buddhism are examples of such religious cultures. You cannot speak of the Hindu or Buddhist church. Other religious groups — the Greek Orthodox church, for example — are formally organized associations with visible authority structures and defined creeds. The first typological distinction, therefore, in discussing forms of religious organization is between religions which are natural groups and religions which are formally organized associations.

Religion as Natural Group

The most important natural groups are the family, extended kin groups or clans, and the nation. To the extent that these groups include religious expressions, they are religious natural groups. There is abundant evidence of religious natural groups.

Family cults as we find them in ancient Roman and Chinese society are often centered around ancestor worship. Prayers and familial rites for dead ancestors are prescribed parts of daily family life. Anthropologist Margaret Mead has documented one such family cult among the Manus people of New Guinea, who worshiped a creature called, "Sir Ghost." The head of the family wore the skull of the most recently deceased male in the family around his neck. This dead ancestor — the Sir Ghost — had to be placated before any important decision was made in the family. When another male in the family died, the skull of the former Sir Ghost was destroyed and replaced by the skull of this new Sir Ghost.

Besides ancestor worship, family cults often include special family patron saints or household gods such as the *lar familiaris* of ancient Roman family cults. Chinese families who follow the Taoist religion worship Tsao-Wang, the Taoist deity of the hearth. Family cults include religious rituals to commemorate the most important events in the family life cycle: pregnancy, birth of a child, name-giving to children, puberty, marriage, and death.

The clan, composed of many families who are actually related through a common ancestor or believe themselves related through some fictional ancestor, also has religious expressions which symbolize the unity of the clan. In Australian aborigine tribes the totem animal (kangaroo, bear, lizard, etc.) is considered to be the sacred

Wide World

Is this St. Patrick's Day parade in New York City a religious celebration or a national cult?

symbol of clan unity much as a school mascot takes on special symbolic significance at important athletic events. Clan religion was very important in pre-Mosaic Judaism. The book of *Genesis* in the bible draws out several features of the religion of ancient Israelite clans. Historically, the Christian practice of special patron saints is connected with the vast missionary effort to convert the barbarian clans of Northern Europe. When the Teutons abandoned Thor, Woden, and their other gods in order to embrace Christianity, they replaced their pagan gods with patron saints. These patron saints — not gods — were believed to take a special interest in each clan.

The best examples of national religious cults are supplied by ancient Rome and Japan. The Romans worshiped the *genius populi Romani* — the national (tribal) spirit of the Roman people. Later

they worshiped the emperor as a symbol of national unity. The early
Christian martyrs in Rome were looked on as unpatriotic citizens
who undermined national unity by refusing to participate in emperor worship. In Japan the national religion of Shinto was as much
an expression of national unity as a form of religion. In our present
day, Saint Patrick is both a religious saint of the Roman Catholic
Church and a folk-hero who symbolizes the national identity of
Irishmen all over the world. It is difficult sometimes to tell whether
Saint Patrick's day celebrations in Boston or New York are religious
festivals or national cults.

Even formally organized associations such as a church retain
elements of family, clan, or national cults. Besides Jewish synogogue services, Jews also have family worship services centered around
blessings at meals. The striking differences between Catholicism in
Latin America and in Germany point to the fact that national cults
do not entirely die out in organized religions. As sociologist Gerhard
Lenski reminds us in *The Religious Factor,* it is important to remember that religious beliefs and practices are not limited to what
goes on in a building on Sunday mornings. Our families and friendship groups also influence religious norms.

Religion as Formally Organized Associations

Formally organized associations have officers and a prescribed
set of rules and regulations for admission to and continuance in the
association. In the early part of this century a German sociologist
of religion, Ernst Troeltsch, distinguished between the formal organization characteristic of a *church* and the organization typical of a
sect. Since the word, church, has many different meanings — a
building, a set of beliefs — it is important to remember that Troeltsch
used it as a technical term to refer to a type of religious formal
organization. Troeltsch's division is an important typology for understanding religion as a formally organized association.

The church is a natural social group somewhat similar to the
family or the nation. It differs from these natural social groups in
that it is formally organized. One becomes a member of a church
by being born into it. Membership is ascribed not achieved. The
mere fact that a person belongs to a given family or nation makes
membership in the church socially obligatory. The church is an
inclusive institution which attempts to "baptize" the economic, cultural, and national interests of its members. The church stresses the
ethics of universalism, seeing its religious message as applicable to
all men, even the weak. Hence, as one work on the sociology of

religion puts it, the church "must represent the morality of the respectable majority, not that of the heroic minority."

As an educational institution, the church must train those born into it to conform to the beliefs and ethical norms of the religious groups. A church is formal, official, and doctrinal. Most of the best known denominations in America such as the Lutherans, the Roman Catholics, and the Methodists are organized as churches rather than sects. The ideal-type of the church is modeled on an established church in one of the European countries. Judaism is much like a church in organization, but is exclusive in its membership.

The sect does not approximate to the type of a natural social group. Like political parties or lodges, sects are voluntary associations in which membership is not an automatic birthright. One joins a sect as a responsible adult. Characteristically, sectarian religious groups are exclusive minority groups with a stringent ascetical and ethical code. Often, as in the early history of the Quakers, a special religious experience of sensibly felt conversion is a necessary prerequisite for membership. Members of religious sects tenaciously adhere to their own rigid interpretation of morality even at the cost of persecution or isolation. "Better persecution than compromise the true faith," these members reason. Because sects believe in a democratic priesthood of all believers, they reject the idea of an official clergy. Their worship services, rather than being organized around an official liturgy, are spontaneous prayer meetings.

On the American western frontier revivalist sects rallied around the slogan of "deeds not creeds" as they held their campfire prayer meetings. The important thing was sensible devotion, not dry ritual. A good contrast between sectarian services and church services can be gained by comparing a prayer meeting in a store-front revival congregation with the solemn high mass of the Roman Catholic church. Sectarian preachers dramatize the democratic nature of their organization by wearing lay attire. In the church ministers wear a ritual dress.

The history of Protestantism in Western Europe and America has been a continuous cycle in which sects have splintered off from official churches. In turn, these sects, solidifying into official churches as their membership began to include the children and grandchildren of the original converts, gave birth to new sectarian splinter groups. Contemporary Baptists and Methodists, who are more and more organized as a church, originally began their history as sectarians.

Table 3 gives a summary view of the organizational characteristics of the church and the sect.

TABLE 3

Church	Sect
1. natural social group	1. voluntary association
2. members are born into the group	2. Members join the sect after undergoing a special religious experience
3. an inclusive institution adapted to the morality of the respectable majority	3. exclusive group stressing rigid ascetical or ethical norms
4. stress on doctrine	4. stress on devotion
5. official liturgical worship	5. spontaneous prayer meeting
6. official clerical leadership	6. lay leadership—no official clergy

The ideal-type distinction between church and sect originated from a study of various Protestant-Christian groups in Europe and America. It is not limited in its applicability to Protestantism. The essential elements of sectarian organization are exclusive membership and rigid ethical demands. Monasticism in Buddhism, Eastern Orthodoxy, and Catholicism is sect-like in organization. Among the Jews, the Hassidim are a pious sect of orthodox Jews from Eastern Europe who refuse to cut their hair. The Hassidim are ethically strict. They try to avoid contact with modern society. It is like meeting someone from another world when a Hassidim migrant sits next to you on a New York subway train!

The Moslem brotherhoods — secret revolutionary societies throughout the Middle East — are sects. Certain movements within the organized church are much like sects. The religious orders in Roman Catholicism historically began as small bands of like-minded individuals who banded together into exclusive associations dedicated to living a "pure" form of Christianity. John Wesley's Methodism and General William Booth's Salvation Army began as exclusive pious groups within the Church of England.

With the passage of time, sects face a crisis of organization. F ased entirely on the principle of adult voluntary association, they have to face the problem of how to incorporate the children of sect members, In time, many sects simply die out. Others become institutionalized into churches.

Because of their rigid code of ethics, sects have to decide what attitude to adopt toward the rest of society. Some sects become purely passive, withdrawing from contact from society to their own special farm land. The Amish of Pennsylvania and the Dukobors of British Columbia in Canada illustrate this approach to the problem of how to relate to society. Other groups, such as the Jehovah's Witnesses, engage in intense missionary activity, hoping to convert society to their rigid regimen. Still other sects take on a militant revolutionary character. Some observers think the Black Muslim movement among the Negro poor is an example of a militantly revolutionary sect.

We must not think of the lines between the polar opposites in a typology as hard and fast. Formally organized religions include features of family or national cults. As the example of monasticism makes clear, sects may be either included or excluded by the church. Sociologist Peter Berger reminded us in an article in *The American Journal of Sociology* that "sectarianism appears more as a process than as a structure, a process that may also occur within the social structure of a church."

We have seen typologies dealing with forms of religious expression (doctrine, practices, attitudes, worship) and forms of religious organization (natural religious groups vs. formally organized associations; church vs. sect). We must now examine forms of religious leadership.

Forms of Religious Leadership

There are many different types of religious leadership. In speaking about leaders, sociologist Max Weber distinguished between two types of leadership. A leader is a man who possesses *charism* — a specific power for exercising authority over other men and influencing their life. The charism of leadership may be either personal or derive from an office or position of authority. Leaders who have personal charism generate an emotional, personal loyalty in their followers. A charism of office leads to a more rational, tempered obedience. An example can best illustrate this distinction. Any president of the United States, even an unpopular one, possesses charism of office. He can count on general support and obedience from all citizens including those who did not vote for him. These citizens respect the office of the president, if not the man. Some presidents arc more successful than others because, besides the charism of office, they have a special personal magnetism. They have personal charism. Applied to religion, we can state that some religious leaders have authority because of their office (pope, bishop, rabbi, or elder of the Mormon church). Others derive their leadership from personal holiness or magnetism (Christian saints, Gandhi). Let us consider some types of religious leadership found in world religions.

The Founder of Religion

The similarities among the founders of the great religions are very striking. Jesus, Buddha, and Mohammed — all began their careers without a charism of office. They were not part of the organized religious structures into which they were born. Each, by personal magnetism based on a special religious experience of God and a highly developed awareness of a mission to serve the religious needs of their fellowmen, drew to himself a small band of loyal disciples. Each had a balanced personality. At death, each became the object of a special cult. The religions which grew out of their experiences and became stamped with their names were spread by the loyal disciples who interpreted the message of their masters for succeeding generations.

The Priest/Minister/Rabbi

After the death of the founder of religion, certain men in each faith occupied the office of supervising the ritual worship service and safeguarding the traditional faith. Their successors today have the task of regulating worship and interpreting the message of the religious founder. This task is performed by the priest, minister, or rabbi. The authority of the priest, minister, or rabbi derives more from the office than from personal charism. Individuals may also have personal charism. But, even if they lack it, they retain authority because of their appointed office. Usually, candidates who perform the task of regulating worship and teaching are carefully screened beforehand. They must pass through an institutionalized course of training before being commissioned as priest, minister, or rabbi.

The Prophet

The authority of the prophet is highly personal. His magnetic leadership comes from an intense communion with God and a special insight into what God wishes for his religious community here and now. While the sociological model for the prophet-type derives from the portraits of the biblical prophets such as Isaiah and Jeremiah, the history of religion evidences that there are parallels to this type in other religions besides Judaism. Joan of Arc and Francis of Assisi had prophetic leadership, although both lacked official positions in the medieval church. Brigham Young is considered as a prophetic follower of Joseph Smith, the founding father of Mormonism. The Ghost Dance Movement which spread in rapid fashion from one American Indian tribe to another in the late nineteenth century began with Indian prophets who tried to communicate their intense religious experience to their fellow Indians. Their authority was personal. These religious movements never became institutionalized into official churches with defined offices.

The Reformer

Reformers only arise out of organized religious faiths which they attempt to reform. They may wish to change the form of religious expression or the forms of religious organization. Often, reformers appeal to an earlier historical existence of the religion. Guru Nanak in Hinduism and Martin Luther in Christianity exemplify the reformer-type. Reformers may attempt to remold religious expression either by remaining within their own religious group or by seceding from the parent religion. Since reformers often meet with intense opposition to their scheme of reform from the officials of the organized religion, they are more likely to break off relations or be excommunicated by the parent religion. Yet, as the history of the Counter-Reformation within Roman Catholicism makes clear in men like Ignatius Loyola and Francis de Sales, reformers often remain within the religion which they attempt to change. Reformers enjoy personal charism.

The Saint

In many religions, the holy man has special religious authority. Brahmin gurus, Christian hermits, Buddhist sages — all are religious leaders whose authority stems from a life of personal dedication and holiness.

Magician/Diviner

In primitive religions, magicians exercise leadership because they are believed to possess secret words or ceremonies which will force the gods to grant what is desired. The Diviner uses objects such as entrails of birds or cosmic signs (lightning, cloud formation, the flight of birds) to predict or interpret God's will.

This brief and over-sketchy review of types of religious leadership is very far from including all types of leadership in religion. You are advised to study religious leadership in your own local church or synagogue. You can begin by drawing up a list of all leaders whose authority flows from their position in the institution (priest, minister, rabbi, trustee, Sunday School teacher, member of the board of elders) and comparing these men with religious leaders whose authority derives from the power of their personality.

THE INTERACTION OF RELIGION AND
OTHER SOCIAL SYSTEMS

In this final section of the chapter, we will briefly treat of the interaction of religion and other social systems. In particular, we will consider the relation of religion to family system, political system, social stratification system, and economic system in society. None of these systems of society exists in isolation. They interact with one another because one and the same person belongs to several social groups. The religious believer is, also, a family man, a breadwinner in his work role, and a citizen of the political state. We should expect, therefore, that religion will leave its impact on other secular institutions of society.

Religion and Family System

Some of the differences which we observe in family systems from society to society are due to the religious factor. The historic Mormon family was based on polygamy in an attempt by Mormons to carry out the biblical command in the *Book of Genesis* to "increase and multiply." Even though the deacons of the Mormon church officially condemned polygamy in compliance with conditions set down by the United States Congress before granting statehood to Utah, newspapers occasionally report isolated instances of individual Mormon families which still practice polygamy in remote areas of Utah, Arizona, and Idaho. The low status of married women in many Moslem lands is bound up with the religious belief of Mohammedans that polygamy is the will of God.

The official condemnations by Roman Catholic churchmen of divorce with remarriage is well known. Almost all Christian, Jewish, and Moslem groups have distinctive family ethics. The Christian disapproval of premarital sexual intercourse has been echoed by most churches.

Religion and Political System

Religious man is also political man. When he enters the voting booth he brings with him his religious background. In Italy, Austria, Japan, and Holland political parties are closely alligned with varying religious groups. Much of the political unrest in South Viet Nam is due to tension between Buddhists and Christians in that country.

Anyone who has noticed the computer analysis connected with national election coverage is aware that the religious groups of America divide on political issues. American Jews vote heavily as a bloc, hand-ing to the Democratic candidate his most solid majority. Catholics, also, give the majority of their votes to the Democrats. Protestant groups in America have mainly voted Republican. Every Republican candidate for president since 1944, with the exception of Senator Barry Goldwater in 1964, has polled a majority of America's Protestant voters.

Jewish espousal of liberal causes is not limited to American politics. In Great Britain also, Jews tend to back the Labour party rather than its conservative opponent, the Tory party. Every one of the nearly two dozen Jewish members of the House of Commons stood election as representatives of the Labour party.

It is not only in the United States, then, that the religious factor has influenced voting trends. In France, for example, among practicing Catholics, 68 per cent of the voters in the Fourth Republic supported the M.R.P. or the independent party, both of which are politically conservative. On the other hand, nonpracticing Catholics gave 56 percent of their vote to the Communists or Socialists. Of those identified as "indifferent" Catholics, 63 percent supported the Socialist or Communist parties.

Faced with this kind of evidence and similar evidence for voting records in many countries, Seymour M. Lipset in *Political Man,* concludes that the religious factor can override social class differences in determining voting preferences of members of the religious communities. As Lipset states it, "Religious beliefs or loyalties and the political values associated with them . . . seem to have some independent effect on voting behavior."

Religion and Social Stratification

In countries where there is only one religion there is no special relation between religion and social class. Both rich and poor in Ireland are Catholic. Both the wealthy and the outcastes of Egypt are Moslem. Yet, in countries such as England, Canada, The United States, where there is a plurality of religions, there is often a close relationship between religious affiliation and social class position. Consider the example of the United States.

It has long been a truism among American students of social class that the religious denominations draw their membership from differing strata of society. Table IV presents a listing of the major churches in America in order of the social status of their membership. Those churches at the top of the list draw their faithful predominantly from the upper classes, those in the middle from the middle classes, those at the bottom from the lower class. The list was compiled from data derived from the American Institute of Public Opinion Polls and from a survey conducted in the San Francisco Metropolitan area.

TABLE 4:   The Rank Order of Denominations in America According to the Economic Status of their Membership

---

1. Episcopalian
2. Congregational Christian Church
3. Presbyterian
4. Church of Christ Scientist
5. Jewish Groups (especially, Reformed and Conservative Synogogues)
6. Methodist
7. Lutheran
8. Roman Catholic
9. Baptist
10. Nazarene
11. Assembly of God
12. Seventh Day Adventists
13. Jehovah's Witnesses

The Jewish group in America also has its denominations: orthodox, conservative, and reform. These denominations, like the Protestant ones, draw their members from different social classess. While lower class Jews tend to remain orthodox, the upper class Jew often attends his services in conservative or reform synogogues.

By and large, individual churches in America, in the words of Liston Pope, dean of Yale Divinity School, "tend to be class churches with members drawn principally from one class group." One exception is the Roman Catholic church which does not have denominations, drawing its members from every social class. Upper-class Protestant denominations usually organize according to the church principle; lower class denominations follow the sectarian principle.

Those who have closely analyzed the statistics concerning conversion from one denomination to another are often amazed to find that an individual American as he ascends the ladder of economic success will shed his lower-status church for a higher-status denomination. The workingman's son who begins life as a Baptist is likely to be a Presbyterian or Episcopalian by the time he becomes a corporation president.

Religion and Economics

Spokesmen for the major faiths have not been loath to commit their respective churches to definite stands on those economic issues which they believed to involve questions of morality. The medieval Catholic church condemned usury, the lending of money at interest, as a mortal sin for Christians. Recently, the World Council of Churches in Geneva and the popes in Rome have made important statements about religion and economics. In 1961 the late Pope John XXIII wrote his encylical letter, *Mater et Magistra,* in which he commented on world economic problems involving over population, trade unionism, aid to underdeveloped countries, and the reclamation of farm land.

In a book referred to earlier in this chapter, *The Protestant Ethic and the Spirit of Capitalism,* sociologist Max Weber argued that the reason Protestant Northern Europe was economically more successful than Catholic Southern Europe was due to the theology of John Calvin. While medieval Catholic theologians, following the lead of Saint Augustine, saw work as a burdensome task laid on man's shoulders as punishment for original sin, Calvin argued in his book, *The Institutes of Christian Religion,* that work was a divine vocation for each man. Those who achieved worldly monetary success could view their wealth as a sign of God's pleasure. The rich or hard working man was saved. The shiftless man was a sinner and damned. Since the Calvinist burghers of the seventeenth century were not allowed to waste their hard earned wealth on pleasure-goods for consumption purposes, they reinvested their money in their businesses. Saving and investment are the core requirements of a rational economy of capitalism. Hence, this Protestant ethic of Calvin, according to Weber's thesis, was a major cause for the success of capitalism in Northern Europe.

Weber's argument has been applied to religion and economics in India. Students of Indian society noted that a disproportionate number of Parsis, a Persian sect which migrated to India several centuries ago, are millionaires and industrialists. The Parsis do not share the Hindu belief that the world is evil. They view the world as basically good. This religious attitude put the Parsis in a unique position to occupy leading roles in finance and business — occupations which the upper-class Hindu Brahmins considered to be beneath their dignity. In effect, when talking about India, we can speak of "the Parsi ethic and the spirit of capitalism."

In the past few years there has been an ongoing debate among students of the sociology of religion as to the extent to which the "Protestant ethic" has relevance for contemporary society. Some sociologists, like William H. Whyte in *The Organization Man,* argue that the Protestant ethic has yielded to a social ethic in which conformity, good fellowship, and the cult of personality adjustment have replaced hard work and thriftiness as the prized virtues in work life. Few Protestant churches in modern industrial societies still hold the doctrines of predestination and work as a vocation in the way Calvin taught them.

In 1961 a sociologist from the University of Michigan, Gerhard Lenski, wrote a book entitled *The Religious Factor* in which he maintained that American Protestants are better equipped than Catholics to achieve economic and social success. Lenski contends that the Protestant ethic is still very much alive in America. He suggests that it may be operative in European nations as well. His findings substantiated that Catholics in America have more negative attitudes toward work than do the Protestants. The fact is obvious that greater proportions of the upper class in America are Protestant than Catholic. Catholics contribute disproportionate numbers to the working classes. The way Protestant Americans raise their children instills in them, reasons Lenski, a spirit of independence, as well as positive attitudes toward work and higher education. Catholics, on the other hand, have less interest in education and worldly success. Hence, fewer of them rise in the social ladder of success.

Lenski's findings have been seriously challenged by other sociologists such as University of California professors Seymour M. Lipset and Reinhard Bendix in *Social Mobility in Industrial Society,* in which they conclude, after reviewing comprehensive data on religion and economic success in four industrial nations including Germany and the United States, that no significant differences appear between Protestant and Catholic groups in degree of economic success. Whether Weber's hypothesis about the Protestant ethic and the spirit of capitalism was a correct reading of seventeenth-century history or not, as well as the question whether his hypothesis has any relevance in modern, post-Calvinist society, is a debate that will continue to rage between sociologists of religion. The outcome and final settling of this debate is a future task for students of religious system. Whatever the outcome, the conclusion remains good that religion does have an important bearing on the economic system in society.

CONCLUSION

We concluded the last section by pointing to a future task in sociology of religion. It must be admitted that the study of the religious system is still largely an uncharted area in sociology. There are a good many unanswered questions. We began this chapter with a descriptive definition of the sociology of religion. We can conclude it by stating that a deeper understanding of the religious system in society is one of the major tasks which still await completion by sociologists.

Major Concepts in Chapter 7

1. *Religion:* Man's attempt to relate himself to what is beyond him and of ultimate concern for him.

2. *Magic:* A source, either special words or ceremonies, believed to have power or control over God.

3. *Sociology of religion:* The scientific study of the ways in which society and culture influence religion — its origins, practices, and doctrine; the study of the types of groups and kinds of leadership which express religious experience; the analysis of social change or social conservatism caused by religion; and the study of the way religion influences other social systems.

4. *Functional theory of religion:* The theory which states that religion contributes to the preservation of society by acting as a symbolic integrator of the cultural values of society.

5. *Established religion:* The official, tax-supported, faith of a nation; a religion which enjoys official government recognition and support.

6. *Secularization:* The process by which religion and religious motives become isolated from influence on important decisions of national and everyday life.

7. *The "Church" principle of organization:* Natural social group into which members are born: an official, doctrinal, ritual, inclusive institution.

8. *The "Sect" principle of organization:* A voluntary association which members join after undergoing a special religious experience; an exclusive group stressing devotion and rigid ethical norms.

9. *Charism:* Specific power for exercising authority over other men and influencing their lives.

10. *Personal charism:* The power for exercising authority derives from the personal qualities of the leader.

11. *Charism of office:* The power for exercising authority derives from the position of the leader in an official authority structure.

12. *The Protestant ethic:* An ethic of work based on the theology of John Calvin, stressing industriousness, frugality, and saving. Worldly success is a sign of divine predestination.

Review Questions

1. How does sociology of religion differ from theology?
2. In what ways can Marxist Communism be spoken of as a religious faith?
3. How does magic differ from religion?
4. Describe the three different methods of approach to a scientific study of religion.
5. State and criticize Marx's and Comte's theories of religion.
6. What is an "ideal type" in sociology? Give some examples. How are ideal types used in the sociology of religion?
7. Why can't we discover the historical social origins of religion in society?
8. What does it mean to say that religion serves the function of symbolic integration of cultural values?
9. What is the sociological prerequisite for an emphasis on doctrine in religion?
10. How does a religious attitude toward the material world have sociological consequences?
11. What is the difference between religion as a natural group and religion as a formally organized association?
12. Compare the "church" and the "sect" forms of organization.
13. List types of religious leadership based on charism of office and types based on personal charism.
14. What effect does religion have on voting behavior?
15. What does the "Protestant Ethic" hypothesis of Max Weber say about the relation of religion and economics?

Discussion Questions

1. Discuss: "Religion is always a conservative force in society."
2. Was Durkheim correct in saying that the attitude which men have toward sacred objects or people in religion is the same as the attitude of respect which men have toward moral authority in law and society?
3. List facts supporting or denying the statement: "Religion is established by the government in the United States."
4. Do you think the United States has become secularized?
5. Discuss: "Pure indoctrination is sociologically incompatible with advanced education."

Bibliography

Demarath, Nicholas J., *Social Class in American Protestantism* (Chicago: Rand McNally & Company, 1965).

*Durkheim, Émile, *The Elementary Forms of the Religious Life,* trans. by Joseph Ward Swain (Glencoe, Ill.: The Free Press, 1954).

Feuer, Lewis S. (ed.), *Karl Marx and Friedrich Engels: Basic Writings* (Garden City, N. Y.: Doubleday & Company, 1959).

Glock, Charles, "On the Study of Religious Commitment," *Religious Education,* 57 (July-August, 1962).

Greeley, Andrew M., "A Moratorium on the Protestant Ethic," *Sociological Analysis,* 1.

——— *Religion and Career* (New York: Sheed & Ward, 1963).

Herberg, Will, *Protestant, Catholic, Jew* (Garden City, N. Y.: Doubleday & Company, 1955).

*Lenski, Gerhard, *The Religious Factor: A Sociological Study of Religion's Impact on Politics, Economics, and Family Life* (Garden City, N. Y.: Doubleday & Company, 1961).

*Malinowski, Bronislaw, *Magic, Science and Religion* (Garden City, N. Y.: Doubleday & Company, 1954).

Niebuhr, H. Richard, *The Social Sources of Denominationalism* (New York: Henry Holt & Company, 1929).

Nottingham, Elizabeth, *Religion and Society* (Garden City, N. Y.: Doubleday & Company, 1954).

O'Dea, Thomas F., *The Sociology of Religion* (Englewood Cliffs, N. J.: Prentice-Hall, Inc., 1966).

*Wach, Joachim, *Sociology of Religion* (Chicago: University of Chicago Press, 1944).

*Weber, Max, *The Protestant Ethic and the Spirit of Capitalism,* trans. by Talcott Parsons (New York: Charles Scribner's Sons, 1958).

*——— *The Theory of Social and Economic Organization,* trans. by A. M. Henderson and Talcott Parsons (New York: Oxford University Press, 1947).

Yinger, J. Milton, *Religion, Society, and the Individual* (New York: The Macmillan Company, 1957).

——— *Sociology Looks at Religion* (New York: The Macmillan Company, 1961).

* Also published in paperback edition.

Chapter 8

The Political System

WHY GOVERNMENT IS NECESSARY

GOVERNMENT, as we have come to know it in the United States as a large scale organization of impressive scope of activity, is relatively new on the world scene and is by no means universal. There exist many preliterate peoples (so-called primitives) today, just as in previous centuries of our own civilization, who are able to maintain order and to advance their own way of life with what appears to be an absence of red tape and little or no concern with *politics* as we understand the word. We might begin looking at political systems by asking ourselves why it is necessary to have government, especially on such a large scale in our own society, if many societies apparently are able to get along with a minimum of formality. Briefly, why do we need so many rules and regulations, while preliterate societies seem to be relatively free from such restraint?

In order to answer this question, let us examine the actual situation in simpler societies. At one time it had been supposed that preliterate peoples or simple agricultural folk behaved almost instinctively or automatically in an orderly fashion. To some extent this image of how less complex societies are governed still persists. The treatment of the American Indian in the movies illustrates this point. Sometimes he is seen as following his leaders on the basis of blind impulse. At other times he is viewed through rose-colored glasses as the noble savage, thoroughly romantic, whose pure, simple way of life has been destroyed. In either event he is depicted as obedient or law-abiding as a result of habits or sentiments which are somehow *natural* to him. Belief that this is the case, whether among American Indians, African

Even among the American Indians the complexity of their political systems varied widely.

tribesmen, or others whom we call less *civilized* than ourselves, is a convenient fiction which has served in many cases as an excuse for enslaving or exploiting these peoples on the part of nations which consider themselves superior.

Aside from not wanting to provide an apology for the greed of some nations, it is important that we correct this mistaken notion if we wish to understand why there are political systems and formal governments. There are really *three* basic fallacies implicit in this stereotype about preliterate peoples:

1. That preliterate and civilized peoples, or different nations, or different races, or various groups of human beings are motivated to act on the basis of inherent differences. This is saying, in effect, that people in simple societies have simple natures, that they are different in kind from people in complex societies who have complex natures. We have seen previously that there is no evidence to bear out such an assertion. Indeed, preliterate peoples show, as has been indicated, an enormous amount of variation in the political systems they have worked out. American Indians, for example, may be lumped together

in the mind of the European descendant but they ranged from the relative simplicity of political arrangements among the Digger Indians of California to the sophistication of the Iroquois League.

2. That preliterate peoples do not distinguish between those things they do out of custom or habit, on the one hand, and those acts they perform in the interest of attaining some personal or social goal on the other. This implies that members of such groups would be no more concerned at failure of an individual to respect the rules surrounding marriage or property than if he failed to eat or speak in a mannerly fashion. It has been shown in countless studies by those, usually anthropologists, who have lived among preliterate peoples that they, too, have a sliding scale of rewards and punishments depending on the importance of a form of behavior to the welfare of the whole society. Thus, as in our own society, sloppy eating habits may be considered as vulgar, and disrespect for customs of courtesy may be termed rudeness. These do not evoke the same sanctions as stealing another's property or spouse, however, since vulgarity and rudeness are not as serious threats to social stability as theft or irregularity of kinship relationships.

3. That human societies are possible without some system of leadership, however informal, whose function or task it is to coordinate the activities of individuals and groups; that is to say, that a kind of primitive state of anarchy is imaginable in human society. When we say that this is a fallacious assertion, we do not intend to suggest that all human societies have a group of leaders which could be identified as a government. We do mean that in all human societies, however simple or complex, the decision of some individuals or groups are considered more binding or imperative in matters of import to the whole society. Thus, when defending its territory or attempting any other cooperative task the members of a human society are aware that some few individuals will issue the commands. It is clear that, if the members of a society have some common goals they wish to achieve, there must be some coordination or centralization of command or the job simply will not get done. It is this *need,* which is recognized to a greater or lesser degree in all human societies, to which political systems are addressed.

As a result of exposing these fallacies about preliterate peoples we should now be in a position to understand that some kind of political system is necessary to all human societies if they are to continue functioning. However, we have still left unanswered the question about the reasons for different political systems. If we turn now to a direct answer, we find actually that we have asked two questions:

1. In the most general sense we are asking why political systems become complicated at all. To go back to our original example, we might ask why the United States needs such a complex system while American Indians seem to have met their needs with much less elaborate systems.

2. In a very concrete way we are looking for the reasons the United States, for example, although matched in complexity by other societies such as England or the Soviet Union, has developed political structures which do not find an exact parallel in these other societies.

In answer to the first way of putting the question, preliterate societies are limited in size and density of population and there is considerable homogeneity among individuals and groups with relation to their interests and goals. This does not mean that these interests and goals are lacking in depth or scope, it simply points to the fact that in societies which are small in numbers it is possible for each member to have fairly comprehensive knowledge of all the activities taking place within the society's boundaries. Furthermore, this knowledge is transmitted through the spoken rather than the written word and it tends to be given first-hand rather than through a series of remote observers who report to him via TV, newspapers, or radio. Since the members of the society can have this intimate, face-to-face contact and communication, obviously the amount of formal organization necessary to maintain order or to achieve common ends is much less extensive than in complex societies.

In the latter, the complex societies, it is not possible for each and every member to be in complete possession of all the information necessary to make decisions on behalf of the whole society. For example, if we return to the matter of territorial defense, it can readily be seen that only a small number of individuals could devote sufficient time to learning all the very intricate items which constitute the defense system of a modern nation. Note that even if all of us felt inclined to defend ourselves against the same enemy, that is we could agree on the same defense goals, the task of making the right decision would require a vast amount of specialized knowledge.

It is this point about specialized knowledge which should provide the key to understanding why political systems become complicated. When a society reaches the point that it finds continuous need for specialists who are empowered to make decisions on behalf of the whole society, we say that it has a government in the formal sense of the word. We cannot pinpoint precisely the stage in the development of human society at which this occurs. Nor can we assert that it is mandatory for human societies to reach this stage, as the present day

existence of a few societies which have not developed formal governments indicates. It is likely, however, that some form of governmental
control, in this formal sense, has been known for about 10,000 years.
This would coincide roughly with the time when some human societies
ceased their nomadic wanderings and settled down to an agricultural
way of life in the Tigris-Euphrates area. In this situation some men
would be laboring full-time as farmers and others in trades, perhaps
pottery or weapon or tool making. The role of coordinating all these
activities, choosing how the fruits of all these labors will be distributed,
and defending the entire settlement against marauding bands of no-
mads or against acquisitive neighbors who might prefer war to pastoral
life, most likely was reserved for a relatively small group of individuals.

We have not discussed how such a small group acquired this role
or who chooses the goals for the society. This is really the kind of
consideration implied in the second way of putting our question. It
should be clear, however, that increase in the total scale of a society,
in its many different dimensions, is accompanied by an increase in
the complexity of what we have called the political system. We can
get some basic idea of the increased scale of a society if we add to the
need for territorial defense even a few items which require coordination and specialized knowledge. For example: commercial or trade
activities beyond the level of simple barter; road building to connect
settlements within the society's territory; irrigation systems which
make optimum use of available water resources. All of these demand
that decisions be made on some regular or organized basis if the job
is to get done.

The second way of asking our question opens up, in turn, some
interesting considerations. When a society has reached that stage of
complexity which necessitates formal organization to direct and coordinate it toward the goals it deems desirable, there is a wide range
of possibilities open to it. That such a variety of forms of organization
is available can be seen, as we have already suggested, by contrasting
societies such as the United States, the Soviet Union, and England.
If one looks at the roster of the United Nations the differences in organization of political systems become even more striking. Some countries, for example, exhibit what appears to be a peculiar combination
of traditional rights and privileges side by side with newly adopted
features. Actually if we look closely enough at every society, we will
see that each one has a political system made up of a mixture of elements which may not appear to be logically consistent one with another. Thus, England retains its hereditary monarchy and at the

same time has a highly developed legal system in a democratic frame-work. Similarly we will consider some of the seeming contradictions in our own system. In this sense no political system can be said to be perfectly integrated. Nevertheless, we shall make some attempt further on to classify political systems according to the predominant type of elements they contain. We shall be in a better position to do this if we turn our attention first to some of the ways in which political systems develop and to the sources of variation in their governmental struc-tures.

HOW POLITICAL SYSTEMS DEVELOP

It should be noted initially that, when a society reaches that point where some formal government is felt to be necessary, all political functions do not pass automatically to that government. We should remember that the functions of the political system refer to the goals, the things worth striving for, upon which the members of the society agree to a greater or lesser extent. In our own society, for example, some of these goals are economic in character, such as a living wage, a decent standard of living. Until fairly recently in our society it was not considered legitimate for the government to exercise any coordination or regulation in the attainment of this goal. Even where there was agreement that this was a desirable goal, it was generally felt that the unregulated working of the market, the law of supply and demand, would automatically provide an adequate income for all. There is still disagreement, of course, as to how much governmental regulation is necessary in this area, just as there is in the many other areas in which agencies of the government operate. Thus, only *some* public action is deemed necessary with relation to specific goals, as contrasted with the action of private individuals or groups. It is this *public* action performed by a specific, fairly small part of the whole population which signals the appearance of government.

Now, which actions are defined as *public,* of concern to the society as a whole, and thus subject to governmental organization, will depend on the definitions which have developed in the history of a particular society. These definitions become part and parcel of the cultural values and they are, in turn, reflected in the rules or norms which constitute governmental institutions. It will be recalled from the earlier discussion of culture that its elements accumulate in a more or less systematic fashion, that is, in a *pattern*. This pattern tends to permeate all the systems, such as the political system, of the society.

The patterning of the political system would lead us to expect that, as a society develops, the way its government is organized will display a consistency in structure. In fact the existence of formal constitutions, written as in the United States or unwritten as in England, is evidence that human societies have attempted to guarantee this consistency. In a sense, from what we have been saying, we could conclude that all stable governments operate under something 'that may be called a "constitution." Constitutions are, in effect, the basic definitions of what are legitimate public actions. It is within the framework of these constitutions that the definitions of governmental functions in different societies are found.

These definitions of governmental functions may remain static over time, but when we look at complex, modern societies we notice that there is a continued development or change taking place. This process roughly parallels the development of the scale of the whole society. It will be remembered that it is this process of increasing scale which, in the first place, marks the onset of organized decision making, that is, government.

Not only is there variation in the areas in which public action is deemed necessary, there is also noticeable variation as societies develop in the composition of the group that rules. The earliest governmental organizations were probably the outgrowth of power which was vested in the hands of a very few individuals who had achieved their positions as a result of personal exploits. We can suggest a number of possible situations in which some personalities would emerge as dominant in relatively uncomplicated societies. They may have been conquerors or defending heroes in the struggle between tribes; they may have successfully led the group on a profitable hunting expedition and demonstrated their ability to do this season after season; they may have, with equal success, divined sources of water or said the right words which coincided with much needed rainfall. We can picture this only by imaginative reconstructions which probably are unconscious distortions of the long, slow process actually involved. Nevertheless, the myths of which we have record from different societies, such as those written by the Greeks or preserved orally by contemporary preliterate peoples, stress the *personal* prowess of leaders.

Just as there was a transition from informal to highly organized public actions, as we have been discussing, there has been a shift in the development of complex societies from rulers who have power in virtue of their personal abilities. As the need for public action became more continuous and extensive, there developed the corresponding need for a *class* of individuals trained to perform the various governmental functions. The existence of a class of civil servants and of leaders is a large step in the organization of political systems beyond that of the simplest preliterate societies. Still, membership in the class may be on the basis of heredity or some personal criterion which may or may not fit the individual for the role he is expected to play.

A final stage in development takes place when governmental roles are defined on an impersonal basis. Clearly, this is at a stage of societal development where the number of governmental functions is extensive and the relationships between the subgroups within the total governmental organization are complicated. In this case, each position in the government has a "job description" in terms of getting one or more tasks accomplished. The person who fills the position, occupies this role, is expected to do so on the basis of his capacity to perform according to universal rather than personal standards. It is not because he or she was born in a particular caste or class or in a particular lineage, but because of demonstrated ability to carry out the duties of the *office* — hence, an *official*. And the *official* operates within a large, formal *bureau* — hence, a *bureaucrat!*

Bureaus and bureaucrats, of course, also exist in other large, formal organizations such as economic and religious organizations. We should not think of them as devices invented for exclusive use in government. It is interesting to observe, however, that the term bureaucrat is used, especially with a negative value attached, when speaking of government bureaus. This, as we shall see, has a particular cultural significance in the United States but, in general, we can say that the impersonal aspect of large governmental operations would necessarily produce a negative reaction. Government, particularly at the federal level, is much more pervasive in its relations with the individual citizen than any other bureaucratic organization and, for that reason, would be the object of considerably more criticism.

TYPES OF POLITICAL SYSTEM

The developmental picture we have been trying to paint now gives us a basis on which we can classify political systems according to the type of elements that dominate within them. The purpose of such a *typology* will be to aid us in our understanding of concrete political systems. No single political system will correspond exactly to any one type in the pure sense of the word. As we had indicated earlier, all political systems contain a mixture of elements which appear to be nonlogical if we think of them in terms of a "pure" or "ideal" type definition. This kind of definition was employed by the German sociologist Max Weber (1864–1920). It is, in fact, his penetrating essays on bureaucracy and on political systems which form the basis of most present-day sociological analysis of these subjects. We shall employ his typology and attempt to use it as a method of looking very specifically at our own political system. There are other approaches to the subject, but it appears that this is the most fruitful in terms of relating to the concepts which have been employed throughout this text.

The basis on which we erect our typology is the kinds of authority which are characteristic of governments. There are three of these: *traditionalistic, rational-legal,* and *charismatic*.

Traditionalistic Systems

Traditionalistic systems rest their authority, as can be inferred from the label, on the fact of tradition itself. It is the past, the way things always have been done, which has acquired an aura of being sacred and thus gives the government its legitimacy. This applies both to the areas in which the government functions and to the composition of the group that rules. What we are describing is a system which is essentially adapted to an unchanging or inflexible way of life. One of the most detailed descriptions of such a society is that of the Zuñi pueblos given by Ruth Benedict in *Patterns of Culture*. Here we find an almost obsessive preoccupation with keeping every ritual word perfect from one generation to the next. The priest class dominated, making of the Zuñi a *theocracy*.

A great many preliterate societies have had traditionalistic political systems but by no means all of them. For example, Benedict also describes the Kwakiutl Indians of the Northwest, whose cultural values put equally obsessive emphasis, like many other American Indian peoples, on the vision, which is a characteristic of charismatic authority. Other preliterate societies choose entirely different groups to make decisions, for example, the Tiwi of North Australia, who have developed a *gerontocracy*, a system ruled by elders.

More complex societies have also developed traditionalistic governments. The feudal system of Europe and the Ottoman Empire as well as many dynasties in China and Japan were basically of this character. This should illustrate a very important feature of traditionalistic systems. We have said that traditionalistic systems are devoted to precedent, that they are best adapted to unchanging situations. However, except in the most isolated societies, it is impossible to anticipate the many new needs which the society might experience,

A sun priest of
the Zuñi Indians in
New Mexico.

Smithsonian Institution

such as we would expect to be the case in the societies we have just cited. Europe during the feudal period, if we look at the pages of history, was in a continuous state of flux. In circumstances like this, if there is no precedent for coping with new situations and the leaders wish to remain in power, they will have to exercise considerable personal discretion in making decisions. Their decisions, although possibly based on simple whim, go unchallenged because they have *traditionally* made decisions.

It can be seen that this emphasis upon the personal capacity of the leaders or ruling groups leads to many possible strains in the traditionalistic system. The result of the leaders making arbitrary decisions may produce dissatisfaction for the members of the society. This means that leaders have to maintain rigid control, in totalitarian fashion, to quell uprisings. The history of empires attests to the fact that such systems have had more than their share of discontent. There are not only popular revolts with which to contend; but, perhaps even more frequently, others who are seeking power will attempt to over-throw the leaders. The rebels, whether popular or rival factions, may also try to make their authority legitimate in terms of being more faithful to tradition than those they are trying to oust.

Rational-Legal Systems

Rational-legal systems, again as the label implies, derive their authority from: (*a*) the demonstrated ability of the office holders to perform the tasks called for by the office, and (*b*) norms which define quite clearly the scope of governmental operations and serve, there-fore, as the *principles* which guide governmental development. The emphasis is on the impersonal, on the rationality of action. When a goal is desired, the stress is on the means to that end. In a "pure" type of such a society the choice of means will, hypothetically, be that which is known to achieve that end most effectively. *Means,* in this sense, is intended to indicate both the specific course of action which will lead to the goal and the officials who perform the actions. Also hypo-thetically, the principles on which these means rest are broad enough to provide for new situations with which the society might be con-fronted.

These are characteristics which should be recognized, from our previous discussion, as descriptive of large, formal organizations, that is, of bureaucracy in general. We should recognize, also, that in a large, heterogeneous society this kind of organization is the most effective in the long run. This is not because a traditionalistic system cannot provide effective action in some situations. It is, rather, that the importance of rules, as opposed to persons, makes the working of a rational-legal system considerably more predictable. To this extent, we say that it is *functional* for the wider society.

It would be a gross exaggeration to say that rational-legal sys-tems always work as planned. Devising of rules is still a human ac-tivity and, despite the impressive knowledge of the professional or expert, they are subject to a great deal of error of judgment. The margin of error may appear to be somewhat less in a bureaucracy which has a very specific function, say the output of a single product such as an automobile. This is because we can measure the effect of different productive practices on output. In this kind of organization, however, the cost of other factors may be overlooked. For example, the introduction of a new practice, although increasing the number of automobiles coming off the assembly line, might also increase the tension between workers and supervisors. One might have to reckon this as a social cost. This may not seem to be of major concern in an economic organization. Yet, aside from the social awareness of the owners or managers, it has been demonstrated over and over again that employee dissatisfaction or low morale can lower production in the long run. Unless those responsible for planning formal organization, for setting up the rules, could anticipate the many possible consequences of these rules, we can hardly imagine a perfectly functioning system.

These remarks point to the fact that there are *dysfunctional* aspects of bureaucracies. Since responsibility is limited to one's official role, there can be a lack of initiative to institute needed changes. Furthermore, as we have been saying, any change in the rules may have a number of unexpected consequences for the whole organization. Knowledge that this is the case may lead to rigidity, since officials may be unwilling to stick their necks out unless they are sure of the results.

Government has the reputation of being much more plagued by these dysfunctional features. There are probably several reasons for such an impression. One of these is that the product of government is not as tangible as that of economic organizations. Thus, it is difficult to measure the results of governmental action, such as those in the field of foreign policy, or the administration of the Securities and Exchange Commission, or in the broad area of education. The number of governmental operations in a complex society is enormous, at a number of different levels, and most of them are of this less tangible character.

Similarly, the number of persons directly in contact with government at some level is far greater than any other organization. Given the diverse interest of a large population, not everyone will be satisfied with the rules which are made for all. Their very impersonality, which is intended to guarantee their impartiality and flexibility, can strike the individual citizen as a sign of inefficiency due to red tape. Add to this a cultural tradition which has stressed individualism and suspicion of big government, as in our society, and we see some of the reasons government is seen negatively.

Our own society has, of course, a rational-legal government. Before we turn our attention to its features, which will comprise the final part of this chapter, let us consider the one remaining pure type of government.

Charismatic Leadership

Charismatic leadership is the more proper term to use rather than charismatic system. System implies something which has relative stability, as in the traditionalistic or rational-legal governmental systems. The essence of the charismatic is a revolutionary spirit centered around one leader who is presumed (from the Greek derivation of the word *charisma,* meaning "gift of grace") to have such special qualities that he borders on the superhuman. Indeed, the charismatic leader may very well be believed to be almost divine, or at least able to interpret divine messages in a way that others find impossible. Since the disciples of the charismatic leader do not, by definition, have his powers and they are confronted with complicated decisions, the original revolutionary movement becomes something more routine. Weber uses the phrase "routinization of charisma" to describe this process. We shall return to it in a moment.

It is difficult to predict the moment at which political systems of the traditionalistic or rational-legal types will become ripe for revolution. We like to think that this happens more frequently to traditionalistic systems since they are, as we have pointed out, less flexible, that is more susceptible to rigidity in the way in which they can respond to new needs. This is not just wishful thinking, however, since rational-legal systems can, as we have intimated, become encrusted with tradition. As a matter of fact, all systems have to rely on tradition. What distinguishes them is their belief in the sacredness of tradition. When a rational-legal system begins to operate as though past bureaucratic decisions are correct because they have always been correct, then it is hardly distinct from a system which is committed to being traditionalistic.

Germany in the period between the two world wars (1918–1939) presents a case study revealing all these elements. The German monarchy, under the Hohenzollern kaisers, had maintained traditionalistic control up to the end of World War I. Like all traditionalistic systems in complex societies it was necessary that administration of the German empire be vested in a bureaucracy. The effectiveness of the German bureaucracy was almost without peer at the end of the nineteenth century and the beginning of this century. Since it was oriented to the service of a traditionalistic government, it, in turn, tended to take on a traditionalistic character itself. It is this tendency which we have discussed as a potentiality in all bureaucracies.

Following World War I the Weimar Republic, the democratic government of Germany, attempted to transform the society so that it could take its place in the ranks of modern rational-legal political systems. Interestingly enough, Max Weber was one of the most highly respected figures in the immediate post-World War I intellectual circles in Germany. He tried to inspire the younger generation with confidence and faith in a system which put law and reason above personal appeal of the demagogue. He died in 1920, well before Adolf Hitler made his initial bid for power and more than a decade before Germany gave itself over to the National Socialism (Nazi) movement in 1933.

It is hard to say whether or not the well-developed German bureaucracy could have been transformed. In the earlier discussion of the social system as a whole it was pointed out that the various subsystems must support each other. Certainly in Germany in the late 1920's there were very few mutually reinforcing elements in the whole society which would have made it possible for a rational-legal political system to have survived. This is not intended as an apology for the events that followed, but the sense of defeatism which set in made it almost inevitable that a Hitler would have emerged. Too much of the traditional order had ended with World War I and the ensuing years saw too little political and economic stability. Most nations in western civilization were going through major social revolutions. The changes in our own society, culminating in the depression of the 1930's, fortunately were met by major adaptations in the framework of the rational-legal system. In the case of Germany the odds against such a solution just seemed too great and the price of patience too great for the German people to pay.

Hitler arrived on the scene with what, at first, was considered by almost all, within and outside Germany, as a crackpot message. The sense of mission which he projected through a magnetic personality landed on sympathetic ears. He gave the German people a sense of personal identification, a trait absent for the most part in bureaucratic systems. He promised forthright solutions to problems which seemed insuperable. At one point he referred to himself as " . . . the German people, past, present, and future." We can only say his appeal was all but irresistible. The situation of uncertainty and the presumed personal qualities of the leader combined to produce what we are calling charisma.

Once having committed itself to a charismatic leader, as Germany did, a nation finds that overthrowing him is far from easy. The leader and his chosen disciples may spend much of their time proving that the leader's vision of authority is authentic. The attempts to prove their authenticity may involve the nation in courses of violent action which foredoom it to an even worse fate.

There are alternatives. The routinization of charisma, to which we referred above, is probably a more likely process than the violent end that came to Hitler and the Nazis. Perhaps we are too close to events, but it does appear that the revolution which brought about the Soviet Union has departed significantly from reliance on the charismatic qualities of its early leaders. Lenin, and later Stalin, were revered for their personal qualities. Their tomb in Red Square, from which Stalin's body has subsequently been removed, has about it the character of a religious shrine. Still, the complexity of life in the Soviet Union has demanded that the government accommodate itself by developing a more rational system of administration. There are remnants of charisma in the claims to authority by the present rulers. Actually they are appealing to tradition since the personally dynamic leaders have dissappeared. The situations they face, however, call for much more impersonality. This is clearly to be expected in a society on the *scale* of the Soviet Union at the present time.

This has been an extensive discussion of charismatic authority, but it has been for the purpose of leading into a discussion of our own political system. As indicated earlier, no system is without mixed elements. This means that all modern political systems contain features which, if developed, could move them more consistently towards the unchanging past or the flexible future. Without the proper balance between the values of the past and of the new demands of the future, it is extremely tempting to listen to the voice of the dictator who promises an easy solution to present difficulties. The appeals which pave the way for the dictator can be very subtle. Once men begin to believe that problems cannot be solved, it is relatively easy for them to hand over the solutions to those who have the simplest, most appealing answers. All modern political systems probably are beset with problems which seem overwhelming. All of them, also, probably fall heir to the temptation to seek the quickest and least demanding solution. This may be an understandable situation, but, for those of us committed to rational solutions, scarcely acceptable.

THE AMERICAN POLITICAL SYSTEM

For the remainder of this chapter we will examine our own political system. We do this, not only because it throws light on a subject which is of particular interest to us as Americans, but also because it affords us an excellent opportunity to see the usefulness of our typology. We have been stressing the point that we can label a political system according to the dominant elements in its governmental structure, recognizing that the actual reality will represent a mixture. This is fully illustrated in the case of the United States.

Our government emerged, as we should know, in revolt against

British attempts to execute the colonial policies of George III. Although Britain had restrictive laws for many years before the accession of George III, she had practiced the policy of salutary neglect, permitting the colonies a great deal of freedom. The colonies consequently developed into complex units with a systematic interrelationship all their own. George III, however, decided to enforce the mercantilist philosophy behind Britain's laws. His transgressions of colonial liberties led to the Declaration of Independence.

It was significant that this statement of purpose did not emerge until after the revolution had begun. This teaches us a great deal about revolutionary movements. The uprisings at Lexington and Concord in April, 1775, were more or less spontaneous reactions to the injustices of the colonial administration under the monarchy of George III, who misread the feelings of the British as well as those of the Americans. A simultaneous sense of rebellion brought the colonies into a united movement which soon acquired a common ideology.

During the years of the Revolutionary War the common purpose of the upheaval undoubtedly found a leader who expressed its sense of determination in the person of George Washington. As we look back upon him he has acquired a kind of charismic quality. Such legendary characteristics as his inability to tell a lie suggest that he was well on the way to being revered because of his personal gifts. It is difficult to say whether or not his contempories felt as reverential toward him as subsequent generations of Americans have learned to feel. In any event, during the struggle for independence, attempts were made almost immediately to develop a rational-legal system. The Articles of Confederation were proposed in 1777 and after 1781 represented the law of the land until the Constitution went into effect in 1789.

This was a remarkedly rapid development for what has proved to be a system of equally remarkable durability. The very traditionalistic system of George III against which the rebellion occurred, interestingly enough, contained within it the inspiration which apparently provided the necessary thrust to the colonies. In England, itself, there had been a long history of emphasis on the primacy of law, the *common law*. It is this tradition which we have inherited as the basis for our legal system and which is embodied in our whole approach to the enactment and administration of the laws affecting governmental operations. The ultimate purpose of this tradition is to serve the common good rather than the interests of a particular class.

Perhaps it seems peculiar that the word "tradition" should have been used in referring to the development of a rational-legal system. Actually all systems have to have traditions in order to operate in any

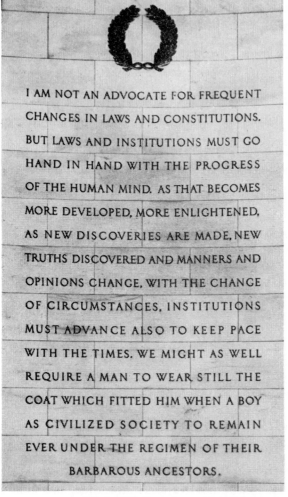

I AM NOT AN ADVOCATE FOR FREQUENT CHANGES IN LAWS AND CONSTITUTIONS. BUT LAWS AND INSTITUTIONS MUST GO HAND IN HAND WITH THE PROGRESS OF THE HUMAN MIND. AS THAT BECOMES MORE DEVELOPED, MORE ENLIGHTENED, AS NEW DISCOVERIES ARE MADE, NEW TRUTHS DISCOVERED AND MANNERS AND OPINIONS CHANGE, WITH THE CHANGE OF CIRCUMSTANCES, INSTITUTIONS MUST ADVANCE ALSO TO KEEP PACE WITH THE TIMES. WE MIGHT AS WELL REQUIRE A MAN TO WEAR STILL THE COAT WHICH FITTED HIM WHEN A BOY AS CIVILIZED SOCIETY TO REMAIN EVER UNDER THE REGIMEN OF THEIR BARBAROUS ANCESTORS.

Our founding fathers were aware of the need for developing a rational-legal system which respected tradition but allowed for change. This excerpt is from Jefferson's letter to Samuel Kercheval, July 12, 1816. It is inscribed on the Jefferson Memorial.

Photo by Abbie Rowe, Courtesy National Park Service

predictable fashion. What distinguishes a traditionalistic system, however is the insistence that traditional methods ought not to be changed. One of the traditions of a rational-legal system, on the other hand, is the insistence that a method, a law, can be changed if the occasion arises.

The Constitution provides an excellent example of a traditional framework which affords a predictable basis for rational action and, at the same time, has built-in provisions for amendment. This means that governmental authority is defined in the basic document which removes the definition from the realm of personal whim. Even the process of amendment is not an arbitrary one. It, too, is intended to be as rational as possible.

To some extent the intention of the founding fathers, the framers of the Constitution, has become the object of veneration. This seems to be a mixture of a belief in the almost charismatic qualities of the framers and a traditionalistic attitude toward the specific items set forth in the Constitution. Generally, this viewpoint, in its extreme, supports those who would like to see the role of government considerably reduced. The ability of the framers, however, is not in question when we say that they could not possibly have foreseen all of the situations which would arise in a complex society. As we have said, they were aware of this in making provision for amendment and in structuring the government in the broadest, most flexible terms. It should be remembered that in 1790, when the first census was taken, there were only about four million inhabitants in the United States and, of these, roughly five percent lived in the cities. The needs of the present 190 million, seventy percent of whom live in urbanized areas, could hardly have been foretold. (The first census was printed on 56 pages; the census of 1960 took about 100,000.) Add to this the impact of industrialization in the succeeding century and a half and the waves of immigrants with a diversity of cultural backgrounds and we see the enormous increase in the *scale* of the United States as a nation. The change in size, density, and heterogeneity in the intervening years has been spectacular. Again, it is remarkable that the original form of government, expressed in the Constitution, should have been flexible enough to adapt itself to all the turmoil of a rapidly expanding society.

THE POLITICAL SYSTEM AS A FUNCTIONAL SYSTEM

So far we have been treating the United States as though government only exists at the federal level. Naturally this doesn't even begin to describe the complexities of our political system. Still in a brief treatment of this kind it is important to begin at the most central point for understanding. The sociologist is interested, it should be stressed constantly, in the workings of social systems. We have been approaching the whole of the United States as a total social system. Having chosen this as the unit of analysis, then it is more fruitful for our purposes to look at the political system as a functional subsystem of the whole. The historian or the political scientist may object that we have overlooked the very important role of the States, particularly since so much of the Constitution is concerned with this. From our frame of reference, however, the States should be analyzed in terms of how they fit into the functioning of the whole system. Except for die-hard members of States' rights groups, the consensus would seem to coincide with what we have been saying. It is not a matter of the federal government taking over, but there are recognized national goals in which the federal government has a key role and in which States and other political subdivisions have *complementary* roles.

The federal government and the states are both described in the Constitution but other political subdivisions such as cities, counties, etc., are not. This should in no way imply that such units are without influence in the operation of national affairs. What we have described so far would be an extremely colorless and inaccurate picture if we did not try to fit in somewhere a consideration of the pressures that are brought to bear on Washington from lesser levels. This is intended to include not only lesser governmental subdivisions but also political parties, organized pressure groups, powerful influences, and the potential influence of citizens who may or may not have organized themselves. This is a most important point to bring in here since it brings to life the bare outline we have given of our political system.

The rational-legal framework for administration of the federal government still depends on a method for determining what problems are to be tackled and what kinds of solutions are available at any given time. This is a function of the diverse groups we have mentioned. They represent the many different interests contained within our whole society. It is evident that there is not a simple solution to the question of how this representation can best be achieved. If we look back at the history of our society we can see that there has been a continuous shifting of power back and forth from one subgroup to another.

The political parties, themselves, have had a peculiar history with regard to changes in the fortunes of power and influence. Even today the two major parties embrace within themselves philosophies of government which, at first glance, would appear to be irreconcilable. Elements of extreme conservatism and extreme liberalism will be found in the same party. Party traditions carry some weight in determining the party platform, but, to a great extent, the strategic demands of a particular campaign have even more influence. Choosing the party's candidate in a presidential campaign is another example of the kind of mixture we are talking about. Here, again, the party's traditions are important but the immediate interests of pressure groups are felt

Political gatherings often have a carnival atmosphere which seems unrelated to the seriousness of the system of government.

and the conventions play on the charismatic qualities of the man selected.

The temptation is to take none of this seriously since the carnival atmosphere of the conventions seems unrelated to the seriousness of a rational-legal system. Similarly, political byplay at the local level of the ward or election district is difficult to connect with the extensive aims of the national government. This is an unfortunate perspective to develop, both from the viewpoint of engaging more and more persons in political processes and in developing an understanding of the workings of our political system.

With regard to the latter, we have sketched only the most basic elements of our system. We should keep trying to fit in all the pieces, in jigsaw puzzle fashion, so that we are able to see our system as a system. That is to say, the long history of durability of our system should convince us that the many stray parts probably have some positive function. Much can be dysfunctional, of course, but one of the features of the system is to seek out unworkable elements and to attempt to remedy them. Thus, the local level is important because it shows up whatever discrepancies may exist. Those who represent us at the municipal, state, or federal level are constantly mindful that they are ultimately responsible to the electorate. Regardless of how "far out" the demands of the electorate might be, it is the continued consensus of the electorate which makes the whole political system work. Individuals express their wishes in a variety of ways about the purposes or goals which are desirable for the whole society to attain. It is a continuing sociological task to assess the various processes at work and to pick up the multitude of strands which contribute to the functioning of the system. No detail should be overlooked in further study, and every attempt should be made to fit each item into a systematic framework.

The necessity to engage more and more persons in the political process is basic to the preservation of democracy. It is also essential to interest succeeding generations in careers in government at one or another level. Fortunately, the trend is in that direction. The percentage of college graduates, for example, ready to devote themselves to public service has been steadily on the increase. This has been the result of a fundamental change in recent decades in attitudes towards government. Part of this change has been brought about by the prestige of those who have occupied high office and the integrity with which they have discharged their roles. At the same time the tasks with which society has been faced have been recognized as a moral challenge. There is an exciting sense of commitment on the part of those who have involved themselves in making our heritage of freedom to determine our own goals a reality.

Major Concepts in Chapter 8

1. *Formal organization:* That aspect of group interaction which is specifically aimed at attaining a goal or goals is called "organization"; it is said to be "formal" when the norms which define the organized behavior are given and supervised by specific persons. Armies, schools, and government agencies are obvious examples.

2. *Bureaucracy:* Sometimes used interchangeably with the term "formal organization." When the formal organization has developed to such a degree that there are very explicit rules or norms which define a whole hierarchy of roles or official behavior, we use the term "bureaucracy." "Bureaucracy" is often interpreted to mean an over-organized formal organization.

3. *Government:* In the formal sense of the word, refers to that group or those roles within a society which have a monopoly of control within a definite territory, whether by consensus or by imposition.

4. *Constitutions:* The basic definitions of the legitimate areas in which the government may exert its control.

5. *Traditionalistic systems:* Those which rest their authority or legitimacy (on the fact of tradition itself).

6. *Rational-legal systems:* Those which derive their authority from the ability of the office holder *and* from the lawful norms which define the role of the official.

7. *Charismatic leader:* One whose authority is derived from some presumed special qualities and who usually embodies a revolutionary spirit (Charisma literally means "gift of grace.")

8. *Theocracy:* A form of government in which the ruling *class* is made up of priests, ministers, or others with a religious orientation who claim to rule by divine authority.

9. *Gerontocracy:* A form of government in which control is in the hands of the elders of the society.

10. *Routinization of charisma:* The apparently inevitable process by which the original revolutionary spirit embodied in a charismatic leader becomes transformed into a stable form of government.

Review Questions

1. On what basis are societies classified into simple (pre-literate) and complex (civilized)?
2. Do all human societies have a government?
3. What *need* is met by political systems?
4. Why do political systems become complicated?
5. How is the decision made as to what is "public"?
6. How is the decision made as to who rules?
7. Why has there been a shift from personal power to civil service?
8. Why is a rational-legal system generally the most effective for a complex society?
9. Distinguish between traditionalistic, rational-legal, and charismatic authority.
10. Why is it difficult to compare governmental and business efficiency?
11. Do rational-legal systems operate without traditions?
12. What specific factors are indicators of the increased scale of a society?
13. What is the functions of political parties and pressure groups, etc.?

Discussion Questions

1. Who takes what side in the question of government action vs. private action in the "public" sector?
2. What kinds of career opportunities are there in business and government? From your point of view, what are the relative merits of each?
3. How does the constitutional system provide for flexibility?
4. In contrast to the federal government, how much autonomy should local or State governments have?
5. How much flexibility does the political party system provide?

Bibliography

*Benedict, Ruth, *Patterns of Culture* (Boston: Houghton Mifflin Company, 1934).

*Blau, Peter M., *Bureaucracy in Modern Society* (New York: Random House, 1956).

Childe, V. G., *Man Makes Himself*, 3rd ed. (London: Watts, 1956).

*————*What Happened in History*, rev. ed. (Baltimore: Penguin Books, Inc., 1964).

*Gerth, Hans H., and C. Wright Mills, *Essays from Max Weber* (New York: Oxford University Press).

*Harrington, Michael, *The Other America: Poverty in the United States* (New York: The Macmillan Company, 1962).

*Hart, C. W. M., and Arnold R. Pilling, *The Tiwi of North Australia* (New York: Henry Holt and Company, 1960).

Hertzler, J. O., *American Social Institutions* (Boston: Allyn and Bacon, Inc., 1961).

*Hunter, Floyd, *Community Power Structure: A Study of Decision Makers* (Chapel Hill, N. C.: University of North Carolina Press, 1953).

Hyman, Herbert, *Political Socialization: A Study in the Psychology of Political Behavior* (Glencoe, Ill.: The Free Press, 1959).

Johnson, Harry M., *Sociology: A Systematic Introduction* (New York: Harcourt, Brace & World, Inc., 1960).

Katz, Daniel, *et al.* (ed.), *Public Opinion and Propaganda* (New York: The Dryden Press, 1954).

Keller, Suzanne, *Beyond the Ruling Class: Strategic Elites in Modern Society* (New York: Random House, 1963).

*Lazarsfeld, Paul F., *et al.* (eds.), *The People's Choice,* 2nd ed. (New York: Columbia University Press, 1948).

*Malinowski, Bronislaw, *Argonauts of the Western Pacific* (New York: E. P. Dutton & Company, Inc., 1922).

———— *Crime and Custom in Savage Society* (New York: Harcourt & Brace & World, Inc., 1926).

* Also published in paperback edition.

Marx, Karl, and Friedrich Engels, *Community Manifesto,* trans. by Eden and Cedar Paul (New York: Russell & Russell, 1963).

Merton, Robert K., *Social Theory and Social Structure: Toward the Codification of Theory and Research,* rev. & enl. ed. (Glencoe, Ill.: The Free Press, 1957).

*Miller, S. M. (ed.), *Max Weber: Selections from His Work* (New York: Thomas Y. Crowell Company, 1963).

*Monsen, R. Joseph, Jr., and Mark W. Cannon, *The Makers of Public Policy* (New York: McGraw-Hill Book Company, 1965).

*Padover, Saul K. (ed.), *Thomas Jefferson on Democracy* (New York: New American Library, 1939).

Parsons, Talcott, *et al.* (eds.), *Theories of Society: Foundations of Modern Sociological Theory,* 2 vols. (New York: The Free Press of Glencoe, Inc., 1961).

Tawney, Richard, *Religion and the Rise of Capitalism,* Holland Memorial Lectures, 1922 (London: J. Murray, 1936).

*Williams, Oliver P., and Charles Press (eds.), *Democracy in Urban America: Readings on Government and Politics* (Chicago: Rand McNally & Company, 1961).

Chapter 9

The Economic System

IN THE previous chapter on the political system we saw that much of the activity of a modern, complex government, such as our own, concerns itself with economic matters. This is not accidental or arbitrary since, as was pointed out, so many of the important goals in our society are economic in character. A better way to put it, perhaps, would be to say that some of the fundamental things we feel are worth striving for are satisfied in economic organization. As examples of such basic goals, we have cited a living wage and a decent standard of living. We pointed to the fact that there is considerable debate on the role of government in assuring that our economic organization or enterprises will achieve these goals. Regardless of how we feel on this issue, however, we should be clear that economic enterprises are not the concern of the economist exclusively. The sociologist recognizes that involvement in economic organization has far-reaching effects in the life of the individual and of the family. This is not only true with relation to less complex societies where the family very often is the basic unit of production of goods and services, but, as we will discuss, is equally true of societies such as our own in which family life and occupational life seem to be fairly well separated.

This latter point, that is, the way in which the economy and the remainder of the social system are mutually influential, can serve as the general theme of this chapter. Just as in the discussion of the political system we saw that there were some fallacies with regard to our thinking in the matter, there is considerable myth-making with relation to economics. Examination of the most commonly accepted fallacy will launch us on our way toward understanding the functioning of economic systems.

It is frequently asserted that economic activity is the most basic aspect of human society and, as a consequence, all other aspects of the social system (e.g. political, religious, educational, familial) accommodate themselves to its demands. It would appear at first view, that this assertion would be relatively easy to refute. We all put great stock in such aphorisms as "men do not live by bread alone" and "money doesn't buy happiness." Furthermore, we may detect right away that subscribing to the view that economic activity is basic or fundamental in determining the structure of social systems is essentially Marxian. The materialism of Marxism is rejected by us as being an inadequate philosophy of human nature and an inaccurate explanation of social systems.

ECONOMICS IN THE SOCIAL SYSTEM

The difficulty with this out-of-hand rejection, however, is that it fails to specify either the importance of economic activity in human society, or the way in which other aspects of the social system in turn affect the economic system. So let us consider these items in order that we may keep a proper perspective on and begin to understand the workings of the economic system.

Now if human societies must adapt themselves to the available natural resources, that is to their environment, it would seem abundantly clear that societies are limited by their environment. Actually this is true in the extreme cases, so that we would not expect the Eskimos to have invented agriculture. What this actually says, however, is that the environment offers a *range* of possibilities but it does not help us to predict how they will be employed by man. Thus, we may be able to specify the environmental conditions or natural resources which are, as a minimum, necessary for the development of certain kinds of economic activity. We would not, for example, as in the Eskimo case, or the many island societies which inhabit coral reefs unsuitable to intensive tillage, imagine that these societies would develop an economy other than fishing or limited derivative industries. But given these ranges, we still would not be able to account for the tremendous variety which is observed to exist between societies with the same kinds of basic economies. There are enormous differences between the fishing economy of the Eskimos and any of the island peoples of the Southwestern Pacific

Certain environmental conditions are necessary for certain types of economic activity. Here Eskimos, with their fishing boats in the background, prepare to convert walrus tusks into ivory carvings.

or, even closer to home, the societies which developed along the whole Northwest coast of America.

Ultimately what we are saying is that, given the ranges of possibilities presented by the environment, the difference in economic systems is dependent on the uses which societies make of their resources. Since, however, these uses which societies make of their resources really constitute a definition of economic systems, we still have failed to specify how much weight should be given to economic systems in the determination of whole social systems. We only know that a crude statement about the natural resources and the kind of economy developed around them is not sufficient to explain economies or total social systems. Such statements have appeared in the history of sociological theory in various forms, all of which may be labeled as varieties of *environmental determinism*.

Even if it is not clear what role economic systems play in structuring the remainder of society, one might still argue that adaptation to the resources available is still the most fundamental problem with which societies are faced. Thus, regardless of what kind of system develops, the rest of the social system could be expected to accommodate itself to it. This is the essence of the Marxian propositions. It avoids the crudeness of environmental determinism but it sees economic activity as so universally pervasive and so indispensable to survival that it appears to be the most important social variable. Let us examine some reasons why this viewpoint is plausible, even if we have not committed ourselves ideologically to such a position.

First, economic activities are so highly *visible* since they do result in observable goods and services being produced and distributed. This is true, of course, only to the extent that we interpret these goods and services solely as having economic value. There are innumerable examples from preliterate societies of items which serve obvious, tangible economic purposes but which fulfill other functions as well. In these cases, although the activity itself is highly visible, it is difficult to determine its meaning to the participants. Arensberg and Kimball in *Family and Community in Ireland* have shown the dual function of the market days in rural towns: on the one hand they serve to effect the necessary sale of calves which is important to the whole fabric of the Irish economy; on the other hand, and no less importantly, the participants in these market days are acting out or reasserting their statuses in a wider system of social relations which are only partially economic in character. Here, as in so many other such cases, it is impossible to decide whether the activity fulfills exclusively an economic or other system function. Actually it is unnecessary to do so as long as we see the point that social activities, especially in simple, undifferentiated societies, are not essentially distinguishable into one or another category. Rather, sometimes such activity can be viewed as economic and sometimes as fulfilling other important functions in human society.

The Kula Ring

Perhaps the classic example of this is afforded in the case of the Kula ring, described by Malinowski in *Argonauts of the Western Pacific*, and in less detail, by Ruth Benedict in *Patterns of Culture*. Among the islands off the shores of New Guinea there has developed a system in which each individual finds a trading partner from another island with whom he exchanges shell bracelets, armbands, and necklaces which have great ceremonial value. Any one individual has such a trading partner on each of the islands with which his own island trades. When, as a young man, he first engages in such an exchange, his partners similarly will be young men from other islands whose statuses roughly correspond to his own. Since these are life-long partnerships, all of his trading partners are moving up in status within their own tribes as he is within his. At the outset the ceremonial shell objects which they exchange will have little significance to them. As they move up in status, probably largely on the basis of age, the objects which their peer group is exchanging also take on greater ceremonial value. The value of the objects derives from their history in the Kula ring, both in terms of how long they have been passed around the ring and the status of previous possessors. The objects are so well known to all the participants in the ring that they have acquired names which indicate their importance. They are exchanged with appropriately elaborate ritual in much the same way that we might exchange Christmas gifts with friends or relatives.

At the same time that this ceremonial exchange is going on, the partners are trading items which we would classify as economic, that is, having utility. The essential point, however, is that from the viewpoint of the participants the ceremonial exchange and the functions it serves are much more important than the economic exchange. The latter is more or less an afterthought.

Again we see that this one activity can be analyzed in terms of the different functions it serves for the system, and there is no necessity to begin with the assumption that it is essentially one or the other. It should be clear, however, that in the case of the Kula ring we are dealing with a situation in which the economic system has had to accommodate itself to other aspects of the social system. We shall similarly be able to document this mutual accommodation of the economic system with other aspects of the social system when we turn to a consideration of our own economic system.

Technology

A second argument which contributes to the plausibility of the independent role of the economic system is the apparent cumulative quality of technology. Thus, it can easily be shown that there are various stages in the harnessing of energy for use in the production of goods and services. No one would dispute that the history of mankind has shown a logical progression from (1) reliance chiefly on human energy, as in hunting and gathering economics, to (2) the use of the horse-, or other animal-power in agricultural economies, and then to (3) the harnessing of fuel, such as coal, to drive the machinery of an industrial society, with the promise in store of

Automated machining operations on a V-8 engine block. Only when factories are seen as a system of production are they said to be a part of culture.

Ford Motor Company

(4) large-scale use of atomic energy. This oversimplifies the actual history of such developments, but it represents the main outlines which can be filled in with reference to any standard history of technological development. Other technological devices could be similarly arranged on a progressive scale of historical development, in which each successive invention presupposes the previous one. This is illustrated if we look at means of water transportation, for example, which have developed from rough, dugout, canoe-like vessels relying on human energy, to enormous, elaborate cargo and passenger craft driven by atomic power.

Now, the appearances of these items, or inventions, which are sometimes labeled *material* culture, can be chronicled for all of mankind independently of the societies in which they occur. It is then often alleged that the remainder of culture, referred to as *nonmaterial,* lags behind in its adjustment to the appearance of these inventions. As one sociologist, William F. Ogburn, in his hypothesis of such "cultural lag," has suggested, it might be more proper to say that "Invention is the Mother of Necessity."

Very frequently we ask ourselves questions which would seem to support such assertions. For example, we might ask: "What effect has industrialization had on the family?" or "How has the automobile influenced the development of the suburbs and intensified the problems of the central city?" Presumably we could phrase many more such questions, all of the same character. They imply that the invention, or complex of inventions, acts as an *independent variable* to which the rest of the system must adjust.

There are several ways of replying to this which will amplify the general theme of this chapter, that is, the way in which the economy and the remainder of the social system are mutually influential. First, factories and automobiles, despite the fact that they can be touched, are no more *real* than other items of culture. That they are material does not mean that they enter into culture patterns and, hence, into social systems automatically. It is only when factories are seen as *systems* of production and automobiles as *means* of transportation that they are said to be part of culture. In this sense, they are as abstract or nonmaterial as every other aspect of culture or social systems. This may be seen most clearly, perhaps, by considering a stone as something which is quite obviously material, tangible. In one culture it can become a weapon and in another an object of veneration. It is still material, but it is different in the two cultures because of some meaning, abstract, nonmaterial, which has been attached to it.

Second, technology and the economic system are not the same thing. Or to put it another way, technology is only one factor in the whole structure of activity which we label as economic. Whether or not a society possesses the necessary knowledge of techniques, that is technology, for producing certain kinds of goods is much the same in its impact on the whole economic system as climatic environment. It only sets the range of possibilities of what the economic system can do. Thus, knowledge of the way in which automobiles can be mass produced is obviously a necessary precondition for the development of the automobile industry. Clearly, however, such knowledge does not provide a blueprint for the complex system of social relationships which characterizes such an industry. The design of the assembly line may indicate the necessity for a wide variety of skilled personnel but it does not explain the intricate social structure into which these skilled roles will be woven.

Finally, the decision to develop and accumulate a technology which will serve in the productive activities of a society is the result of the stress on the value of these activities. Once the society has made this choice, then we would expect that, within the range of its knowledge of productive skills, it will develop them to the fullest. It is important to see that all societies make these choices in terms of their cultural values, stressing those aspects of life which are most meaningful to them.

We can see this element of choice if we go back to the case of the Kula ring. The tribes participating chose to ignore, for the most part, the material aspects of what they were doing in the exchange. Instead, they decided to elaborate the ceremonial aspect, even further ignoring the possible profit to be gained in the trade of scarce, valuable items such as the necklaces and armbands. In our culture such items might have enormous economic value as heirlooms or antiques.

The Kula participants chose not to concern themselves with increased productivity or with more efficient means of transportation and focused their attention on elaborating patterns of social interaction involving the shell bracelets. If they had decided to elaborate their economic system, paying attention to production and transportation, then their ceremonial exchanges might well have fallen into disuse. We would not then ask what effect the production system or the means of transportation had on the ceremonial life. We would realize that the time spent on the former would be at the expense of the latter.

Thus, social systems in which there has been an accumulation of technology and an elaboration of the economic system and in which these have become important aspects of life are the only ones in which the hypothesis of "cultural lag" takes on significance. In the Kula ring we might properly say that the technological and economic aspect of it lag behind the ceremonial patterns which serve the function of renewing the ties between trading partners and of reaffirming the status of the participant. Many examples of the so-called "lag" working in this opposite direction can be shown in the case of preliterate societies, because in most of these societies emphasis has been put on other than economic values.

This leads us, then, to a consideration of societies in which the economic system does play a relatively major role. In looking at them we can ask two questions: (1) How did they get that way? (2) How do they function or, more precisely, how does the economic system relate to other subsystems in such societies?

With relation to the first of these questions, we have already seen that economic systems will not develop, that is, become complex or differentiated, where the culture pattern of the society places greater emphasis on other kinds of activities, as in the case of the Trobriand Islanders or the Irish farmers. Consequently, we can see immediately that a change in value orientation is necessary to effect the shift in emphasis to the economic system.

Now, it is not at all clear at what point in the history of any

Arabian American Oil Company

The revenues from oil-rich sheikdoms of the Middle East may not produce large-scale economic development unless there are changes in the values and social systems of these countries as well.

society this shift will take place. When we look at the societies which are currently called underdeveloped, we see that they are most likely undergoing such shifts in emphasis right now. It is apparent, however, that they are not all doing so at the same rate, even though some or all of them have had equal exposure to the highly developed economic systems of western societies. It is difficult both to weigh the amount of emphasis these societies each give to those values which are resistant to economic development and to spell out the exact conditions which represent the turning point, so to speak, in the direction of more concern with economic activities.

It is probable that most of us assume that these societies inevitably will "westernize" their economies. This seems to be a perfectly safe prediction because it is hard for us to imagine that many such societies could remain isolated from the mainstream of world-wide economic development and still maintain their integrity as societies. We have seen, especially since World War II, that the remotest nations have taken their places in the United Nations and that they are addressing themselves to internal development of their resources. This would seem to support the view, which we have previously discussed, that economic development is inevitable, that is, that it is really the independent variable in explaining social systems. In our arguments against this view we have pointed to those societies which are preliterate or underdeveloped and now we find that they too are taking advantage of the accumulated technology of the western nations. At first view this appears to be a significant rebuttal to all that we have been saying.

On closer inspection, however, we can see that in large measure the pressures to develop differentiated economic systems does not come from inside these societies. The extreme case, perhaps, is offered by the oil-rich sheikdoms of the Middle East. These societies, which consisted for the most part of nomadic tribes, would hardly have been expected on their own initiative to have exploited their oil resources. Obviously, the value of these reservoirs to societies, already dependent on large quantities of fuel, meant that if necessary, force would be used to establish pipelines and refineries. Even as it is, without other profound changes in values and changes in other aspects of the social systems of these countries, the oil revenues which accrue to them may not produce large-scale economic development.

Sadly, this is the case in so many of the societies which are economically underdeveloped, particularly those which have previously been under colonial administration. The colonial powers were often not interested in tampering with the going social system since their basic interests may have been only to obtain one or a few abundant natural resources or to occupy the territory as part of a wider system of defense. In this situation a limited number of skilled technicians and lower level civil servants would be trained from among the indigenous population but their impact on the rest of their societies was generally minimal.

Where colonial powers had to come to terms with local rulers of a feudal type, this may have had the effect only of entrenching the latter in their positions and preserving the social system pretty much intact. This has been, for example, one of the major criticisms of the various aid programs undertaken by the United States in the post-World War II period. It is alleged that, as well meaning as our effort has been, it has the unintended consequence of preserving the status quo. At the same time those who have been exposed through education or travel to the abundance of goods and services available to those in western societies become dissatisfied with the conditions of disease and famine which accompany the low standard of living in their own countries. For many, as we know, resentment towards the United States sets in. Since we could not, even if we so desired, *force* these societies to make major changes in social structure to accommodate economic development, we find ourselves on the horns of a dilemma. Further action on our part may simply aggravate an already tense situation; failure to act may be seen as indifference to the consequences of the programs we have already undertaken for political, economic, or humanitarian reasons.

This should not be construed as an argument for an isolationist or ostrich-like policy on our part. It only underscores the difficulty in changing entire social systems by the manipulation of one segment of it and makes it more imperative that we attempt to understand how economic systems do come to play a relatively major role.

Economics in Western Culture

In a sense, the only major model we have of such a turn of events is provided by the highly industrialized nations of the West. This is not to suggest that the processes which lead to economic development can only take this form. Japan is one notable exception since it managed in the 19th century to incorporate the technology of the west into a total social system which bore little resemblance to events in the rational-legal political systems of the west. Similarly, as we look at such major oriental societies as China, India, and Indonesia, it is not at all certain that they want to or must imitate the model of western economic development. The Soviet Union may very well serve as an alternate model. Still, there may be enough elements common to economic development in these diverse societies as well as in the history of western societies to suggest that some equivalent changes must occur.

The dominant mode of productive activity in Europe was agricultural, at least until the sixteenth century. At the same time, trade across the continent and into the east was considerable and probably had been so since the time of the Crusades in the eleventh and twelfth centuries. The trade had produced urban population concentrations such as the Italian city-states and the cities in the Hanseatic League. Other urban concentrations became centers of learning or church authority. Within these urban centers a variety of craft and merchant guilds flourished. The legacy of art and architecture which has been handed down to us intact attests both to the skill and to the high degree of differentiation of productive functions. Here, the parallels to China can be clearly seen.

Significantly, however, the political systems were *traditionalistic* in the various societies which now form the nations of Europe. Feudal obligations were pervasive and these were based on the overlord's authority, however it had been established. The particular hierarchical patterns which occurred were far from uniform. In fact, if anything, they represented a political crazy-quilt. Nevertheless, the mutual feudal obligations had developed because the population of a specific territory, or dominion, had need of protection which only the lord could provide. In return for his guarantee of protection and stability, the population gave their loyalty to him. In situations which were primarily agricultural the system worked to everyone's benefit, even if we would look upon it as one of inequality today. Essentially, there were no elements of conflict within such situations since the concern of the worker of the land was to obtain enough produce to sustain his family. The loyalty which he owed to family, or even to a wider friendship group, was not at odds with the loyalty he had pledged to the lord of the manor. The demands of the latter for payment, chiefly in kind or in labor, even if excessive, were part and parcel of the tenant's daily round of activities in any event.

The worker of a small holding of land was constantly reminded of the lord's power since the manor house or castle was frequently adjacent to or within view of his place of work. This would be true even if the lord was an absentee landlord or if a land agent was as close as the worker ever got to the person of the lord.

In all of this a commitment to a common set of religious values served as a kind of cement which held the social relationships together. In this case, the religious orientation helped to maintain the going patterns and provide an ultimate justification which integrated the whole structure of the feudal society.

The towns and cities were another matter, however. They, too, were dependent for protection on the lord, whatever his formal title, whether prince, duke, or count. The loyalty of their inhabitants, on the other hand, was not so easily assured. This was not, initially, because they did not share a common commitment to ultimate values. Rather, the differentiated occupations in which they were involved, whether as artisans, merchants, or academicians, made demands upon them which cut across the undivided loyalty demanded by the lord who had dominion over the territory they inhabited. Thus, the master of the craft guild can be seen as a figure whose authority was much more imminent for the apprentice or journeyman than that of the ruler of the municipality.

The political turbulence of these centuries which we call the Middle Ages and on into the Renaissance suggests that there was considerable strain generated by the attempts of the feudal lords to maintain dominion over their territories where they were divided in this fashion. The feudal system was essentially suited to a relatively undifferentiated agricultural society. As a result the cities were able to wrest a considerable amount of autonomy away from the ruler in the form of *charters*. The city as a whole, under the terms of these charters, agreed to make payment to the lord in return for his protection. The structure of relationships within the city was not under his control, however, but subject to the regulations imposed by the craft or guild.

It is important that we see that this is quite a different orientation than we have previously described as characteristic of the preliterate society or of the rural portions of the feudal society itself. It is also important to see that by itself it does not produce a change in the subservience of the economic system to the political and/or religious systems, for example. Despite the obvious strains in the feudal system, to a great extent these represented a jockeying for power among political units. The system did endure as the dominant one for several centuries in Europe. China and India both have managed, until fairly recent times, to retain a pervasive feudal structure despite the fact that their cities and towns similarly posed a threat to the autonomy of territorial rulers.

The Protestant Ethic

Again it is Max Weber, to whom we referred in the previous chapter, who has supplied us with a clue to understanding the unique developments in Europe. In perhaps his best known study, *The Protestant Ethic and the Spirit of Capitalism,* Weber advances the view that, until those engaged in the productive or commercial enterprises of the city had acquired a religious justification for their work, the particular economic system which we label *capitalism* would not have emerged. The religious justification was, as implied in the title of his work, supplied in the sixteenth century by the Protestant Reformation.

To understand this, let us refer back to the distinction made in the previous chapter between traditionalistic and rational-legal political systems, since the same kind of distinction applies to economic systems. In fact, as implied in our discussion then, there is an intimate connection between the political and economic systems. Thus, the agrarian feudal economy, itself, was characterized by traditionalistic modes of production, both as to techniques and as to the relationships between tenant and lord. These modes of interaction reinforced, and were reinforced by, a traditionalistic political system and a religious system which was traditionalistic in structure and other-worldly in orientation. In general, Christians were proscribed from the taking of interest on loans, as the prolonged arguments among theologians in these centuries attest, and the notion of profit making was frowned upon.

On the other hand, the modes of production in the urban centers were characterized by considerable technical rationality, as one would suppose from the nature of the craft guilds with their emphasis on ability to perform. They were, however, still very much enbedded in traditionalistic relationships, for example those which obtained between master and apprentice. However, these relationships, both within and between guilds, became increasingly characterized by formal rules so that they took on the aspect of rationality. Membership in the guilds, by way of illustration, though essentially hereditary, more and more became a matter of free choice dictated by aspiration or demonstrated performance.

Similarly, the relationship between the whole city and the feudal lord took on the formality of a charter, an instrument which spelled out in rational detail the terms of the relationship. Significantly, it was the city as a whole, not the individual townsmen, which was specified in the charter. This kind of instrument minimized the hereditary relationships which were at the base of the traditional feudal system and made of the city a corporate unit with defined rights and limitations.

The pressures toward increased rationality in these aspects of urban life still lacked the legitimacy which we accord them in our system. As Weber argues, it was not until the Protestant Reformation, especially in the Calvinist orientation, that this legitimacy was forthcoming. Calvin's message appealed very particularly to the wealthy merchants and craftsmen of the city. It is this *middle class,* between the lords, that is the landed aristocracy, and their vassals, whom we have labeled the *bourgeoisie* and who became the innovators of a capitalist economy.

Calvin's views struck at the heart of the traditional, hierarchical system which was central to Catholicism. The reforms which he,

Calvin's message made
occupational performance and saving
a virtue.

Bettmann Archives

and others, encouraged were intended to strip Christianity of the
feudal trappings it had acquired through the centuries. In accom-
plishing this, it gave the powerful members of the bourgeoisie a
weapon and motivation to resist the traditional order. The Calvinist view which put a premium on performance in this world
as a sign of being one of God's elect in the next world made occupational performance a virtue.

The emphasis was puritanical, however, so that asceticism
surrounded the performance of one's duties. Thus, whatever profits
accrued from engaging in commercial enterprises were not to be
used in the pursuit of pleasure. Too frequently the feudal lords,
after the fashion of the Medicis in Italy, had used their accumulated
wealth to erect lavish monuments to themselves, thereby perpetuating,
at least symbolically, the traditional reverence which they expected
of their subjects. Calvinism, on the other hand, encouraged the
ploughing back "into the business" of excess wealth by stressing
the importance of thrift. In other words, saving became a virtue also.

Saving as a value, or what is referred to by sociologists as
"deferred gratification," served as a major element in the transition to the dominance of the economic system. It is this willingness
not to spend all one's income which made it possible for capital
to accumulate which, in turn, could be invested in further enterprises. Of course, having something to save would be a necessary

precondition for saving, but under feudalism even those with a comfortable surplus of wealth did not think along those lines. In the post-Reformation period even those for whom saving entailed some sacrifice were willing to do so. The result was that larger and larger sums of money became available to the powerful merchants of the middle class with which they could further trade and commerce.

The potential power which was placed in the hands of the bourgeoisie by concentration of capital was not immediately realized since the rights of the traditional lords still limited the expansion of trade and commerce. Where, as in England, the most powerful of the rival feudal lords enlisted the financial help of the merchant princes and were willing, in return, to make many concessions to them, the business of finance flourished. Thus, the political aspirations of some feudal lords in combination with the wealth of the middle class made the emergence of unified nations possible. It should be noted that such developments were not uniform throughout Europe but, in fact, were confined to those societies where the political rulers were most willing to abandon traditional prerogatives in the interest of the expansion of trade, commerce, and ultimately production.

In this respect, England stole the march on continental powers such as France both in terms of a much earlier limitation on the absolute powers of the monarch and the rationalization of finance. For example, it was not until the time of Napoleon, in the nineteenth century, after the French Revolution, that the Bank of France was established and the bourgeoisie came into power. In England, on the other hand, the Bank of England was first chartered in 1694, six years after the "Glorious" Revolution which deposed the "divine-right" Stuart monarchy and firmly established a rational-legal political system. Under this system, the Parliament actively encouraged the further development of economic enterprise in the seventeenth and eighteenth centuries.

Meanwhile, the corresponding political body in France, the Estates-General was totally without power and did not meet. Despite the efforts of Louis XIV's controller-general, Colbert, to rationalize production and finance, the whimsical autocracy of the monarch discouraged the growth of the middle class. After the death of Colbert, Louis XIV revoked in 1685 the Edict of Nantes, which had guaranteed religious freedom to Protestants, and forced the 300,000 or more Huguenots to emigrate to England, Holland, and Germany. The Huguenots were Calvinists, mostly merchants and skilled craftsmen, who in the countries to which they fled were representative of the middle class which was rising to more and more power.

Science and Economics

Among other measures enacted by the English Parliament in the seventeenth and eighteenth centuries which paved the way for the dominance of the economic system under industrial capitalism were the various acts which encouraged the enclosure of agricultural lands in the name of more "scientific" farming. This had the consequence of forcing the small tenants out of the rural areas and into the cities where ultimately they would provide the pool of industrial labor. Where an agrarian peasant class had existed which was tied to the land in much the same fashion as it was under feudalism, or as it is in underdeveloped societies today, an urban proletariat was created. Where the peasant had been assured status by inheritance of a land holding, now when he found himself adrift in the city he was impelled to rely on performance in an occupation, chiefly a technically rational one, to assure him of similar status.

Indeed, this transformation was not accomplished overnight, so that eighteenth-century England was beset with the problems of a status-less or role-less urban mass population. However, when the accumulated capital of the mercantile system was put into industrial development in the nineteenth century, the transformation was complete. What had been an amorphous urban proletariat now found a meaningful status in the industrial system, that is to say, in the factory.

The inventions or innovations in productive techniques which made the factory a possibility were themselves the products of the this-worldly orientation that the Reformation had ushered in. The seventeenth- and eighteenth-century acceleration in science, with its implication for later technology, came about only when the pursuit of knowledge was no longer subject to traditionalistic orientation. This is illustrative of the point we made earlier in the chapter, that the development of technology is dependent on the values of the society to encourage it. Thus, the trial of Galileo early in the seventeenth century would, perhaps, have gone unnoticed if it had not signalized both the demise of traditionalistic control over knowledge and the rise of the rationalistic spirit of inquiry in a new social order.

Since the machines, such as the spinning jenny in the fabric

The spinning jenny accomplished eight times the work of one person and was an important factor in the subsequent development of the textile industry.

Bettmann Archives

industry, were too large for the individual craftsman to contain in his home and too expensive for him in any event, they could only be located in the factories which were financed by the wealthy upper bourgeoisie. To compete for their investments with trade and commerce required the maximum rationalization of industrial production. What remained of the more traditional cottage industries and small shops of craftsmen gave way to the technical efficiency of the large-scale plant. In this way, the individual worker became accustomed to deriving status from an economic system which was divorced from his kinship system or, for that matter, from any of the more parochial loyalties to which he had previously owed allegiance.

This historical case-study of one major model of economic development should actually have provided clues not only to answer the first question we posed much earlier, that is, how did economic systems come to play a relatively major role in some societies. We should see, at the same time, that we have been answering the second question, how does the economic system relate to other subsystems in such societies. Thus, the emergence of the economic system as dominant in the societies of the West was not, as we have seen, because it was independent of other subsystems, but precisely because it changed hand-in-glove with them.

Let us look a little more closely at this notion, by way of summary of all we have said and of making clear our understanding of how societies function as total social systems: (1) When the goal-attainment systems of the societies in Western Europe, that is the political systems, were no longer traditionalistic and had become rational-legal, the urban trade and commercial centers, which had legal charters and rational techniques and modes of production, rose to prominence; (2) when the pattern maintenance and tension management system, chiefly the family, was freed from its traditional relationship with the feudal lord by moving into the urban setting, a whole class of workers was available to contribute its labor to the economic system in return for wages; (3) when the integrative system of the societies, that is the system which addresses itself to the solidarity of the units in the system by making explicit or reinforcing the common values of the society, legitimized such things as profit, saving, and the free entrepreneur, there was a middle class of urban entrepreneurs which benefited. Thus the Protestant Reformation signaled the introduction of a whole new set of relationships in the society since it minimized the hierarchical order of feudal society and replaced them with relationships based on role performance in a rationalized work setting.

Weber, as we saw, argued that this latter shift is perhaps the most important in explaining the unique development in Western societies, but he did not mean to imply that the other elements we have discussed were unimportant. He was much more interested, by illustrating with this one case, that the Marxian model of economics change oversimplified the matter. The lesson to be drawn, then, when we look at currently underdeveloped societies is that change in their economic system will require profound changes in the rest of the social system. Europe had centuries in which to change from a feudal, agrarian society to an industrial one and even at that slow rate the transformation was accomplished only with considerable violence and upheaval. The rapidity with which newly emerging societies are attempting to reach the same end would lead us to predict that they, too, will require similar social revolutions but on a scale and at a pace for which we have no precedent. These revolutions need not be violent or cause enormous social dislocation, but this may be easier said than done unless there is very careful consideration on the part of those whose job it is to assure the attainment of the goals of the society.

AMERICAN ECONOMIC PROBLEMS

It would be misleading, on the basis of the discussion we have had so far, to suggest that the economic system in the United States has reached a point of such rationality in techniques and in modes of production that it works like a well-oiled machine. Even if this were the case, there would still remain the problem of the relationship of the economic subsystem and the other functional subsystems of our society. We say "problems of the relationship" because it should be clear that our society is not in some kind of static equilibrium. In the previous chapter, for example, we noted that there has been considerable disagreement over how much government regulation over economic activity is necessary or desirable.

The remainder of this chapter, then, is devoted to a consideration of some of the problematic aspects of the American economy. There are probably many more than those we will deal with here, but those singled out are the ones with which sociologists have been concerned. To some extent sociologists choose only those problems which correspond to the general area of concern of the society as a whole. For example, since social status is so closely linked with occupational status, sociologists have directed much of their attention to the way in which the economy ensures that heads of household will have a position in the occupational structure and the opportunities for mobility within it. This is a concern, however, which is not unique to the sociologist. Certainly since the Great Depression of the 1930's, and especially in the atmosphere of the War on Poverty in the 1960's, this is a problem from the viewpoint of the entire society.

It is well to remember, from Chapter 5 on "The Social System," that each one of the functional subsystems, such as the economy, may be treated as a system itself. Thus, the economy is that subsystem which meets the *adaptive* needs of the total society. Seen as a *system* itself, it has needs for goal attainment, integration, pattern maintenance, and tension management, as well as adaptation to its environment, that is to the other subsystems of the society. These needs are not automatically or easily met precisely because (*a*) the economy is not a single or simple organization of automatons, and (*b*) it does interact with the other subsystems. Like any complex system which functions in the context of an even more complex system, then, we can expect that there will be problems of operation.

Even though the economy cannot be identified with any single group, the business firm has dominated the American economic system. It has been estimated that there are about 1,270,000 corporations in the United States. All but about 71,000 have assets of less than a million dollars. In 1962, only 638 corporations had assets over two and a half billion dollars. The same corporations tend to be the largest employers, so that a small fraction of firms producing goods and services in our economy employ a significant part of the labor force. A large number of other employed persons depend for their livelihood on activities which are allied to the major industries. As one example, surrounding most large industrial plants there will be a host of service enterprises such as gasoline stations, lunch counters, etc., which probably would cease operating if the major industry in the area went out of business.

In order to keep the wheels of such large industries in constant operation it has been necessary to make their operation as rational as possible. This has meant that bureaucratic organization has been called for, that is to say, formal organization. As we saw in our discussion of bureaucracy in the political sphere, this is both functional and dysfunctional. It is functional in the *economy* to the extent that the productive goals are presumably best achieved by having the occupant of any role chosen on the basis of his ability to perform. It is dysfunctional insofar as the individual workers lose sight of the overall organizational goals.

The existence of a formal organization presupposes that there is some blueprint of operation, some patterns or norms of operation, which must be maintained. Hopefully this would permit some flexibility, but frequently the person assigned a role in the bureaucracy is pressured not to stick his neck out. As a consequenc he may insist on perpetuating outmoded techniques. The formal blueprint, in this situation, is adhered to ritualistically, in much the same way that traditionalistic societies operate.

This ritual adherence to the norms can occur at any level in the productive enterprise. It is no more observable at lower status levels of the organization than it is in top level management. It is not some *habit* which the employee brings to the role with him. Rather the anxieties are generated within the organization, where no one individual has the "big picture," so to speak. The uncertainty about how long one's position will be necessary may produce feelings of insecurity, the response to which is rigidity, a kind of compulsive conformity. As there arises the desire for a shift in organizational goals such a response of resistance to change may make it difficult to produce the required flexibility to meet new needs.

This rigidity or resistance to change may be observed most clearly where informal organizations develop. As we saw in Chapter 5, on "The Social System," the bank-wiring group was just such an informal group. It had developed, as we should remember, norms which prevented members from "rate busting." The effect of this was ritualistic adherence to a formula of productivity. It can be seen that this was generated in the bureaucratic structure of the work situation since the members of the group were fearful of the intrusion of supervisory personnel. At the same time, it illustrates the earlier point we made that the economy interacts with other subsystems. The individual worker is dependent on his occupational role in our social system for wages or salary with which to maintain his family. Thus, any anxieties or tensions which develop in the work situation are also a threat to the integrity of the family.

In essence, we have been saying that emphasis on the efficient, predictable performance of the worker does not guarantee that the outcome of his actions in the work role he is playing will always be predictable from his viewpoint. If the communication process within the formal organization does nothing to dispel this uncertainty, the worker will attempt to create predictability by such means as relating informally to members of a group at his level. He *knows* he can count on them.

At higher levels of the organization, for example within management, the same phenomenon has been observed repeatedly. Recruitment into the ranks of management is very often controlled on the basis of ethnic and/or racial origin and by social class considerations. In these cases, the universal criteria which are expected to operate are replaced by particular or personal ones. For example, where a college degree may be the basic qualification for a position as a management trainee, sometimes *which* college the degree is from is of greater importance. From the viewpoint of those in management, selection on the basis of a particular college may increase the predictability they have about the kind of person they are recruiting. It is not because they know that he is more technically competent but, as the members of the bank-wiring group felt, they *know* they can count on him.

When we say that this is a dysfunctional aspect of the bureaucratic organization of the large industry, we should not overstate the case. These may be inevitable outcomes of any large, formal organization which simultaneously is producing goods and coping with a complicated network of social relationships among personnel. Actually, on balance, these informal groupings may contribute to productivity by improving employee morale. If the informal cliques in which the worker is involved do, in fact, reduce anxieties which he would otherwise have, then it would be hard to argue that they are always dysfunctional for the goals of the economy.

However functional such practices are for getting the economic job done, to the extent that they erect discriminatory barriers to hiring and promoting they must be seen as dysfunctional from the viewpoint of the system goals of the wider society. The transformation from feudal society which we described above highlights the importance of work role as the source of status for the head of household in our society. The whole fabric of our system hinges on the individual being motivated to find a place in a highly differentiated economy. Unless this had happened, as we indicated, the economy would never become such an important subsystem. If large segments of the population are barred from performing a work role on the basis of *ascribed* characteristics, much as race or social class, and *achieved* abilities are ignored, the goals of the society, itself, are threatened.

There is considerable evidence that poverty and unemployment are becoming increasingly hereditary. Those who are born into such conditions, especially the minority groups in our society, find it more and more difficult to escape. We can see that there is a vicious circle in operation here: certain groups are barred from participation in the training which will lead to jobs or promotion; therefore, they are unable to demonstrate their capacities; therefore, they are defined as not having demonstrated their capacities; therefore, they are barred from participation in the training which will lead to jobs or promotion; and so on and on.

This problem admits of no easy solution because the component organizations of the economy see their role as the production of goods and services and not providing for full employment. This is not to say that producers are without a social conscience in this matter. In economic terms alone it can be demonstrated that full employment means greater profit for the business firm and, perhaps, less taxes diverted to the support of those receiving relief or unemployment compensation. Nevertheless, the structure of the industrial organization makes it difficult for it to take on the additional function of guaranteeing a role for everyone.

This latter point explains the rise to prominence of unions as part and parcel of the economy in industrialized societies. The unions are not, in actuality, part of the productive structure. That is to say, they do not enter into the formal or blueprint organization. They arose precisely because the formal organization was unable to develop mechanisms which would provide predictable employment and working conditions for the wage earner. To some extent, as bureaucracies, they have become inflexible and admit members on the basis of ascribed characteristics rather than demonstrated abilities. Certain unions systematically pass on membership within families or ethnic groups. Basically this is the same kind of mechanism which we have just seen at work in the industrial firm. It should be understood as resulting from a similar dual role. The union is both meeting the problem of adapting to the needs of the economy *and* coping with a complicated network of social relationships among its members.

This discussion of the problem areas which have concerned sociologists is intended to emphasize for us what we stated as the theme of this chapter: the way in which the economy and the remainder of the social system are mutually influential. Since this is the case, we frequently find that collective action is taken through the political system and we find that the government has played an increasing role in the ordering of the economy. Our system has generally been inclined against the government operating even a substantial share of the economy. We have felt that this would run counter both to our values and to meeting the adaptive needs of the system effectively. Still, how much government regulation is necessary, and at what points, will continue to be arguable subjects. It is, indeed, a measure of the pivotal importance of the economy in the functioning of our system that we debate the matter of the best means to keep it operating smoothly.

Major Concepts in Chapter 9

1. *Environmental determinism:* The view that one or more factors, such as climate, natural resources or geography, actually specify the form which societies will take.

2. *Technology:* The science of practical or industrial arts; the *knowledge* of how to do things, the range from the simple stone age arts to the complicated techniques of an automated industry.

3. *Cultural lag:* The hypothesis that the so-called non-material items of culture do not change as rapidly as the material items.

4. *Traditionalistic modes of production:* Those which, as in traditionalistic political systems, are employed because they have always been used.

5. *Technical rationality:* The use of the most efficient available means of production rather than those which always have been used.

6. *Capitalism:* An economic system which puts great emphasis on having available flexible funds, not concentrated in a single organization, which can be used to the best advantage of the economy.

7. *Bourgeoisie:* Literally the burghers or two dwellers who emerged as a middle class in the waning days of feudalism.

8. *The Protestant Ethic:* The phrase used by Max Weber to describe

the cluster of values stemming from the Protestant Reformation which were most conducive to the rise of Capitalism; hard work and savings become, in this Ethic, the paramount virtues.

9. *Marxism:* In sociology, the view that the organization of the means of production is the fundamental or determining features of all human societies.

10. *Deferred gratification:* The notion, which prevails in the Protestant Ethic, that it is important to deny now oneself in order to enjoy the fruits of one's labors in the future.

Review Questions

1. To what extent does environment determine the type of economic activity?
2. Why does the economic determinist's position seem plausible?
3. What does determine if a society will develop and accumulate a technology?
4. What is the "cultural lag" hypothesis?
5. What is the major function of the Kula ring?
6. What was the role of religious values under feudalism?
7. Do cities always change the economic-political balance of the society?
8. Why did England, in contrast to France, undergo the kinds of economic and political change it did?
9. How do events in England during the 17th and 18th centuries illustrate the importance of values in the development of science and technology?
10. How did the reformation aid the rise of Capitalism?
11. Why are there "problems of operation" in a modern economy?
12. Why is occupational status so important to the individual in our society?
13. Is selective hiring always dysfunctional?
14. Why do unions exist?

Discussion Questions

1. Compare change in the political, education or religious institutions in our society with that in technology.
2. Look at the currently underdeveloped countries and discuss the general problems of their development: population growth; capitalization of industry; educational and skills levels.
3. To what extent does the "Protestant Ethic" still operate in our society? Is it confined to Protestants? Are all Protestants imbued with it?
4. Whose responsibility should "poverty" and "low skills" be?
5. Discuss some of the Marxian ideas of society.

Bibliography

Arensberg, Conrad M., and Solon T. Kimball, *Family and Community in Ireland* (Cambridge, Mass.: Harvard University Press, 1940).

*Benedict, Ruth, *Patterns of Culture* (Boston: Houghton-Mifflin Company, 1934).

Blau, Peter M., and W Richard Scott, *Formal Organizations: A Comparative Approach* (San Francisco: Chandler Publishing Company, 1963).

Caplow, Theodore, *Principles of Organization* (New York: Harcourt, Brace & World, Inc., 1964).

Chinoy, Ely, *Automobile Workers and the American Dream* (Garden City, N. Y.: Doubleday & Company, 1964).

*Etzioni, Amitai, *Modern Organizations,* Foundation of Modern Sociology Series (Englewood Cliffs, N. J.: Prentice-Hall, Inc., 1964).

Form, William H., and Delbert C. Miller, *Industry, Labor, and Community* (New York: Harper & Brothers, 1960).

Gouldner, Alvin W., and Richard A. Peterson, *Technology and the Moral Order* (Indianapolis: The Bobbs-Merrill Company, Inc., 1966).

*Harrington, Michael, *The Other America: Poverty in the United States* (New York: The Macmillan Company, 1962).

Hertzler, J. O., *American Social Institutions* (Boston: Allyn and Bacon, Inc., 1961).

Lenski, Gerhard E., *Power and Privilege: A Theory of Social Stratification* (New York: McGraw-Hill Book Company, 1966).

*Malinowski, Bronislaw, *Argonauts of the Western Pacific* (New York: E. P. Dutton & Company, Inc., 1922).

Marx, Karl, and Friedrich Engels, *Communist Manifesto,* trans. by Eden and Cedar Paul (New York: Russell & Russell, 1963).

Merton, Robert K., *Social Theory and Social Structure: Toward the Codification of Theory and Research,* rev. & enl. ed. (Glencoe, Ill.: The Free Press, 1957).

*Mills, C. Wright, *White Collar: The American Middle Classes* (New York: Oxford University Press, 1956).

Moore, Wilbert E., *Industrial Relations and the Social Order* (New York: The Macmillan Company, 1947).

*Nash, Manning, *Primitive and Peasant Economic Systems* (San Francisco: Chandler Publishing Company, 1956).

Smelser, Neil J., *The Sociology of Economic Life,* Foundations of Modern Sociology Series (Englewood Cliffs, N. J.: Prentice-Hall, Inc., 1963).

*Tawney, Richard J., *Religion and the Rise of Capitalism* (London: J. Murray, 1936).

*Veblen, Thorstein, *The Theory of the Leisure Class: An Economic Study of Institutions* (New York: The New American Library, 1912).

Weber, Max, *The Protestant Ethic and the Spirit of Capitalism,* trans, by Talcott Parsons (New York: Charles Scribner's Sons, 1958).

*Whyte, William H., Jr., *The Organization Man* (New York: Doubleday & Company, Inc., 1956).

* Also published in paperback edition.

PART THREE

AMERICAN SOCIAL PROBLEMS

Chapter 10

The Community in America

URBAN sociology has long been a core concern of sociologists. Its main concept has been the problem of community, as population increase produces a strain upon the way of life that is only possible under the conditions of small population. So while earlier philosophical conceptions of an ideal community may have contained a smattering of insight into the small community like the one envisioned by Plato in his *Republic,* how much can one man's observations, no matter how painstaking or brilliant, be extended to provide a picture of the major dimensions of a community of *millions* of families such as comprise many cities of today and most of the cities of tomorrow?

KINDS OF COMMUNITIES

The United States census, as we shall see in this chapter, provides sociologists with a great deal of data for scientific research. The census bureau has developed a concept of metropolitan community which should help us illustrate our point about the size of American communities. The Standard Metropolitan Statistical Area (SMSA) consists, according to the census bureau, of one central city of not less than 50,000 population, the entire county which contains the central city, and other adjacent counties which are places of employment or residence for workers in the central county. These surrounding places must have important economic and social relationships with the central county. Sometimes two cities of the required size will fall within twenty miles of each other, in which case they are considered the same SMSA, or, in our terms, the same metropolitan community.

The flow of people to suburbia is affecting a change in the pattern of the community in America.

One look at the metropolitan communities in Table 1 should suffice to convince the student that the United States is rapidly becoming a nation of such heavily populated communities. These 24 SMSA's, each with a population of more than a million, illustrate the great growth of population in the United States, and even more strikingly bring home the fact that we have become a nation of metropolitan dwellers. Metropolitan communities (SMSA's) contain about 60 percent of the total U. S. population. A total of 212 SMSA's were mentioned in the 1960 census! The problems of the metropolitan community have become the predominant internal problems of America.

Studying the modern city and understanding it in such comprehensiveness as to be able to relate one part of the modern community to other parts is just now beginning to be done. Urban sociology is gradually coming to be a basis for city planning and urban renewal. In this present chapter we shall see some of the consequences of not having developed a field of inquiry earlier in our history and the urgency of the need for understanding the metropolitan community.

Our method of introducing you to the problem of community will be through observation. Your attention will be drawn to the results of scientific observation of the community, the results of socio-logical investigation, which, as we have indicated, are not enough to understand all of the problems of the metropolis. Your observations are intended to fire your imagination and to make your training in sociology more interesting. Metropolitan problems are everyone's business. Perhaps many students will wish to make these problems their particular concerns, either as professional social scientists or as concerned citizens. In either case the conceptions of community phenomena discussed here provide a foundation for further study.

TABLE 1

1960

Rank	Standard metropolitan statistical area	Population
1	New York, N. Y.	10,694,633
2	Los Angeles-Long Beach, Calif.	6,742,696
3	Chicago, Ill.	6,220,913
4	Philadelphia, Pa.-N. J.	4,342,897
5	Detroit, Mich.	3,762,360
6	San Francisco-Oakland, Calif.	2,783,359
7	Boston, Mass.	2,589,301
8	Pittsburgh, Pa.	2,405,435
9	St. Louis, Mo.-Ill.	2,060,103
10	Washington, D. C.-Md.-Va.	2,001,897
11	Cleveland, Ohio	1,796,595
12	Baltimore, Md.	1,727,023
13	Newark, N. J.	1,689,420
14	Minneapolis-St. Paul, Minn.	1,482,030
15	Buffalo, N. Y.	1,306,957
16	Houston, Texas	1,243,158
17	Milwaukee, Wis.	1,194,290
18	Paterson-Clifton-Passaic, N. J.	1,186,873
19	Seattle, Wash.	1,107,213
20	Dallas, Texas	1,083,601
21	Cincinnati, Ohio-Ky.	1,071,624
22	Kansas City, Mo.-Kans.	1,039,493
23	San Diego, Calif.	1,033,011
24	Atlanta, Ga.	1,017,188

For our purposes we may distinguish three types of community, the *preliterate* and two types of literate human aggregates, the *preindustrial* and the *industrial* communities. The student (unless he is an anthropologist studying primitive or *folk* society, which is highly unlikely) lives in a literate community; he can read and write. Aside from the obvious difference in life style which reading and writing bring to a people, some not-so-obvious consequences for community life will be developed through sociological analysis later in the chapter. Nor is it likely that the student lives in a preindustrial community, since, for one thing, he would not likely be reading a book in English unless he lived in an English-speaking country, almost all of which have undergone the Industrial Revolution. So, by elimination, the student probably lives in an *industrial* community, one whose way of life is on the one hand complex and often difficult for the individual to understand and identify with, and, on the other hand, one which offers greater potential opportunity for individual development than the other types of community mentioned. The SMSA's, the metropolitan communities shown in Table 1, are precisely such industrial communities.

Community Defined

We shall develop further these differences among the various kinds of communities. But before doing so, let us define *community* sociologically so that we may understand more precisely what the thing is that we are dealing with. When sociologists speak of a community we mean (1) *an aggregate of people,* (2) *a geographic locality which contains that aggregate,* (3) *a network of social system which relates everyone in the aggregate to everyone else in the aggregate,* and (4) *a set of values* which is, at least to the dominant people of the network of social systems, a compelling set of conceptions of the "good life," the way life ought to be lived.

The first reaction of the alert student may well be that no such thing as "community" exists. From his observations it may seem that no two segments of his town or city agree on anything. During elections, for example, almost everyone seems to feel that his combination of candidates have the key to the "good life" and failure to elect them will bring ruin. The remainder seem to feel that everything has already fallen into ruin so that there is no necessity to vote; "there is no good life anymore." We shall demonstrate later in the chapter that community does exist and that the example given here illustrates the problem of community in an industrialized, urbanized country such as America. First it is necessary to develop the ingredients of our definition of community more fully.

"An aggregate of people" taken alone does not seem to provide much of a basis for sociological analysis. Yet, the sheer *size* of the number of people who comprise an aggregate imposes upon its people certain limitations of style of life. The student must surely have seen or read about an isolated village of one or two hundred people which would, of course, be totally incapable of industrializing without importing (among many other elements of production) many more people. On the other hand, the people of the crowded cities would not (excepting in the daydreaming sense of "getting away from it all") accept the unchallenging simple life of a feed store proprietor or any of the small handful of occupations that would be available in the small town.

Since each of the ingredients of our definition depends upon the others, something more can be learned of the nature of the community aggregate as our definition progresses.

"A geographic locality" gives this particular aggregate a dimension which distinguishes it from others. Territoriality, another term for geographic locality, refers to people who share the same space in common. The locale may be small, as in the example of the small village, or if we wish to stretch the concept of territoriality to the limit we may apply it to the entire earth! At present (and apparently for a long time to come) it is unrealistic to consider world society as a community. The one-world view that some men have achieved is not ridiculed, at least by sociologists, some of whom may even share the vision. Rather, it is the function of sociologists to evaluate these visions in the light of social reality. In point of fact, the remaining elements of the definition of community rule out the notion of world community at least in the present. While the societies of the world are becoming increasingly more interdependent, through trade and other intercultural exchanges, (1) it can hardly be said that everyone in the world is presently related to everyone else in the world through a network of social systems, and (2) it would be even more absurd to assert that the world's people have a common set of values!

So in order to have a meaningful conception of community, scientific caution dictates that we limit our definition to aggregates which have territorial boundaries. This raises the question of national boundaries. For example is American society a community? Here again, the concept of community is attenuated (stretched out) too far. For sociological purposes, the largest territorial aggregate that we shall consider a community is *a metropolitan area,* a combination of artificially bounded cities that contain a naturally bounded aggregate. At first this seems a very complicated distinction but it helps to unravel a very complicated predicament in which the urban people of America have historically placed themselves.

Natural boundaries of an aggregate of people are crescive, they just grow. When someone who works in a city moves out farther than anyone else residentially, he extends the natural boundary of that city by as far as he has moved. If he happens to cross a city or village boundary which has been created by law (hence artificially), the natural boundary is now greater than the artificial one. We shall expand upon this problem when we consider the modern community. We introduce the idea of natural boundary here to illustrate that territoriality is not an administrative concept. Artificial boundaries may be passed by laws, but people and their social relationships determine the natural boundaries of a community.

SYSTEMS OF RELATIONSHIP

How then do sociologists discover boundaries of modern communities? The question we ask is simple. What common interests do people have which unite them as a community? The first approach to a solution of this problem is through a scientific description of the things that people *do* in common. Sociologists study *behavior,* and infer systems of relationships from people's activities. From the facts which are available we formulate conceptions of a higher order of abstraction like "interdependence" and "community." Some of the evidence for the existence of a community is obvious; some evidence is just as sound but not so obvious. This latter evidence calls for "analysis." It is more work mentally, but highly rewarding in revealing the existence of community.

We can illustrate this procedure for discovering community by analyzing three steps of sociological analysis. First we consider the major activities of all human beings, the things that people, as people, do no matter where they are. Second we examine the evidence that *these* people, the aggregate we are studying, regardless of the political boundaries that unite or separate them perform these major activities in concert. And thirdly we infer the existence of social systems and community among them. Let us start off by considering industrial activity since work can logically be considered the prime function of the modern (industrial) community:

Activity	Evidence (data)	Social Systems
Work	Tax reports	The existence of a
	Industrial distribution	common economic system
	Manufacturing patterns	
	Use of automobiles	
	Public transportation	

Now we can see how the inference about the existence of an economic system was made. We started with the notion that a given geographic locality contained a community. Recognizing that all human beings must work or be dependent upon other human beings who do work, we raised the question "Is there some connection, some interrelationship, in the work of the people in this locality?" Referring back to our diagram it can be seen that our data do throw light on our question.

In the first place, some tax reports give us valuable information about large payrolls and therefore alert us to concentrations of workers in the locality we are analyzing. Other tax reports and data about industrial distribution help us to understand the concentration and dispersion of plants, factories, warehouses, and other industrial facilities throughout the area. Manufacturing patterns tell us much about the kinds of work that are done in the locality and the kinds of trades and skills the work force has. Now we know something about the division of labor in the locality.

The concept of the division of labor is a crucial one for understanding the differences between the modern community and the simpler communities which preceded it historically. In the preliterate community, the division of labor was simple, just as economic life was simple. A family, or (more properly) a clan, performed most life sustaining activities within its own membership. Under the supervision of elders the fishing, hunting, gathering, or agriculture that was undertaken was broken down into child's work, adult's work, or elder's work. That is, there was a rudimentary division of labor by age category. Too, there was often a sex differentiation into men's work and women's work. But that about exhausts the social categories involved in the primitive community-clan, sex, and age.

In the preindustrial communities that followed the preliterate community the invention of writing, together with technical advances in transportation, made possible more commercial activity and marketing. Typically in such feudal communities a few wealthy families controlled the economic system of the community. This was the origin of social classes as we have them today. The main differences between preindustrial communities and the modern metropolitan community is that social classes are now reflections of the highly specialized division of labor in the modern economy. Modern work requires great skill and proficiency at many highly specialized tasks. Less technical work is also necessary (though increasingly less so) and carries less prestige. Again the United States census provided us with data to illustrate our sociological conceptions. The census has an elaborate system of classifying occupations from which we have selected four general classifications for our analysis.

1. *Professional, Technical, and Kindred*
   Sample occupations: lawyers, scientists, social workers, teachers.
2. *Clerical and Kindred Workers*
   Sample occupations: bank tellers, bill collectors, file clerks, insurance examiners.
3. *Craftsmen, Foremen, and Kindred Workers*
   Sample occupations: baker, book binder, stone carver, brick mason.
4. *Laborers, except Farm and Mine*
   Sample occupations: truck drivers' helpers, stevedores, gardeners.

The alert student will have noticed that the occupations are listed by the census bureau in such a way as to suggest that laborers are not as high on the scale of occupations as professional, technical, and kindred, not even as high as craftsmen nor clerical workers which share a middle position between the low status laborer and the high status professional workers. This ranking of occupations by the U. S. Census Bureau is a reflection of a basic fact of social life in the modern community.

Social Stratification

Sociologists call this ranking *social stratification,* since it refers to the process by which the modern community divides its families into strata or layers. The Industrial Revolution ushered in a phenomenon unknown in folk and feudal, preindustrial, societies. With some exceptions, the tendency in modern industrial communities is to stratify the families of the community into classes according to *the occupation of the family's breadwinner.* Both the competitive nature of American culture and the ways in which social stratification works are discussed in other chapters of this book. Our purposes in this chapter are served by showing the general relationship between work and the family in the modern community and, of course, by showing that this relationship is a prime distinctive feature of the modern industrial community — namely, social classes based upon functional specialization in the work force.

This method of operation enables us to undertake another analysis of the workings of the modern community, *family life,* using essentially the same method of inquiry.

Activity	Evidence (data)	Social Systems
Family life	occupation education income place of residence	the existence of a social stratification system

From common sense we know that the primary functions of the family are to regulate the sexual relations of adults and to procreate and educate new members of society. But we are considering the family here in a special aspect, as a link for the various systems of the modern community. Census procedures help us to do this. The basic unit which it provides us is the *Census tract.*

All metropolitan communities have, as we have said, at least one central city which is "tracted." This is to say that the census bureau has divided these cities into clusters of blocks which are roughly homogeneous, that is, areas where land is used in the same ways. See below for an example of a census tract map. The center of a city is the most expensive area of land, and, in the economically competitive society it is used for the highest economic return, *business.* The downtown area is bustling and exciting during the business hours of the day and later bustles with the nightlife of cafes, theaters, and night clubs. Obviously not desirable for family residence, the census enumerations (which are taken every ten years; years ending in zero are censal years, e.g., 1940, 1950, 1960) reveal that the occupations of the

A Census Tract Map

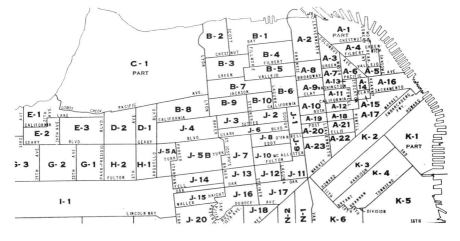

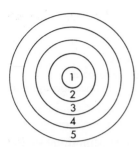

1. Business areas
2. Zone of transition ("slums")
3. Area of workingmen's homes
4. Area of better apartment houses
5. Suburbs

Relation between socio-economic class and neighborhood.

heads of households in these downtown areas are predominantly in the ranks of the craftsmen and laborers with few professional, technical, and kindred occupations being reported there.

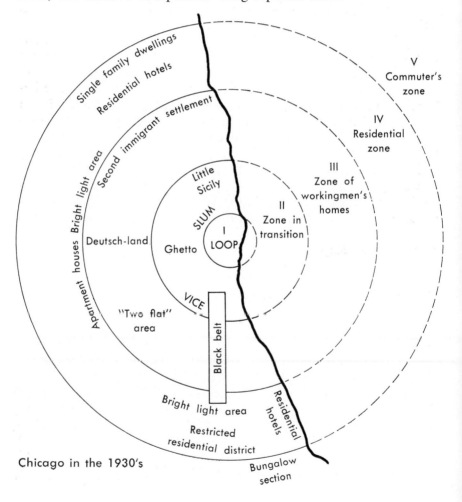

Chicago in the 1930's

In Chicago in the 1930's, sociologists led by Park and Burgess developed a scheme which illustrated the relationship between socio-economic class and geographic neighborhood in the modern city. The general principle which they developed was that the city had expanded (under the pressure of population increase) *outward from the center* in concentric circles. The more privileged families (professional, technical, and kindred) moving always outward to more desirable residential land when "less desirable" people invaded their former neighborhoods. The end result tended to resemble, with noteworthy exceptions, a pattern of family residence in the metropolitan community which looks like the following diagram. The scheme applied to large cities *at the time* the theory was developed and does not, of course, take into acount urban redevelopment since that time.

Several observations can be made about this patterning of family residence in the metropolitan community.

1. It should be noted that, in general, it can be proved very simply — by driving from the center of the city to its outskirts one can observe that housing improves and neighborhoods get better.

2. There are exceptions to this general pattern, some of which we can illustrate briefly. The presence of lakes and rivers may alter the pattern. For example, Lake Michigan forced Chicago to expand outward from its shores so that even in the city where Burgess developed his theory in the 1930's the pattern of urban settlement looked as shown on p. 236.

Urban redevelopment, high price apartments, and great traffic arteries further complicate the basic concentric pattern.

But unless we are to become lost in a morass of technicalities about urban residence patterns, let us sum up what we have discovered about the social systems of the metropolitan community. Firstly, the people making up the community have a division of labor in the local economy. They have many different kinds of jobs; some with higher and some with lower prestige. Secondly, they live in neighborhoods or social areas which form natural boundaries and reflect the economic division of labor (and the prestige ranking of jobs). Thirdly, most of the working people share a residence with their family.

The first generalization we can make about the interrelationship of social systems in the metropolis is that the economic system and the family system are connected through the social stratification system. Now we can turn to the family system and ask how it works (functions) within the network of other systems in the community. We can start with some simple sociological research findings. For the sake of convenience let us call professional, technical and kindred, white collar workers. Certain other census occupational categories could be similarly labeled, but for the sake of convenience let us contrast the white collar professional with the blue collar worker in the craftsmen, operatives, and laborers categories. Thus simplified, our terminology enables us to assert that:

1. Children of white collar families receive more education than others and are far more likely to end up in white collar occupations as adults.
2. Due to residential and social distance children of white collar families tend to grow up, associate, and recreate with children of other white collar families.
3. Young men and women from white collar families intermarry predominantly within their own ranks.
4. The white collar family tends to perpetuate itself through time and the blue collar family tends to maintain its less favored position through time.

In a word, the family serves to maintain the pattern of occupational difference in the economy and residential differences in the geographic area of the community from one generation to the next. In the next chapter on social stratification, channels of *social mobility,* ways of moving up or down on the social ladder, are discussed. It suffices here simply to note that there is such a ladder.

So far we have analyzed the economic, the familial, and the stratification systems sufficiently to provide grounds for considering them a network. These three systems are at the core, however, of an even more extended network. Religious systems, political systems, health and welfare systems, and other systems interrelate with them.

The Network of Social Systems in the Metropolitan Community

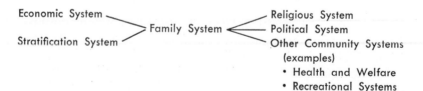

Values and Community

It may seem that the relative importance of one system or another is not recognized in our diagram. Some might argue for the economic as the dominant system in the industrial community. But the sociological facts argue that despite the fact that the family is caught up in economic and social competition all of the community social systems depend upon the family. If families did not subscribe to the beliefs and values which hold these systems together, if the young were not imbued with these values they could not survive, at least in their present forms. In fact, as values change, social systems change. As we said earlier, values are conceptions of the good life. When external events occur people reassess their values, often without full consciousness of their reasons for doing so. American values which have structured community life stem from the "American Creed" which is stated in the Preamble of the Constitution:

> We, the people of the United States, in order to form a more perfect union, establish justice, insure domestic tranquility, provide for the common defense, promote the general welfare, and secure the blessings of liberty to ourselves and our posterity, do ordain and establish this Constitution for the United States of America.

The values implicit in the Preamble pertaining to personal freedom are spelled out even more explicitly in certain Articles of Amendment to the Constitution, asserting the freedoms of religion, assembly, and free speech, and from political discrimination because of sex, race, or national origin.

In essence, these *values,* codified into law, constitute the groundrules for competitive life within the community. The problems of the metropolitan community reflect in large measure the conflicts in values and conflicts *between* American values and actual behavior (usually but not always in the economic sphere and in the area of struggle for social status).

Values in Conflict

The values embedded in the Constitution have often come into conflict with other traditional American values such as strong individualism and absolute rights to property. If, on the one hand, an elite of economically powerful families should be free to enjoy its economic success how can this be reconciled with the lessened freedom of families who are economically deprived? While we are reserving the fuller consideration of social problems to a special chapter, for our present purposes we can see that many problems of community have arisen from this one value conflict.

It is true, as it has often been said, the American communities have been made up of immigrants. However, the "Old Americans" (white Yankees) early dominated the community and were successful (not without struggles) in passing their individualistic values on to the people who migrated to America, especially to immigrants from Western Europe. These in turn (again, after many struggles) mediated between the "Old Yankees" and the newer immigrants from Southern and Eastern Europe.

It is quite true that the American community was a "melting pot," but the student should be careful to note the full meaning of the concept. While the older Americans dominated the downtown business area, they moved their residences and their way of life to outer regions of the city. This resulted in the proliferation, or multiplication, of small political units outside the central city. These small towns, villages, and satellite cities naturally took on a conservative tone. In the meanwhile the central city, artificially bounded by city limits, but still the natural heart of the metropolitan community received waves of immigrants from foreign countries and from rural America. No matter how foreign their origins, all succumbed to the American dream of material success and freedom to enjoy the good life. In sum, the melting pot has produced a wide variety of social classes, ethnic and racial groups, vying for success.

The Pluralistic Community

So because of its heterogeneity of groups and interests the American community is in ferment as far as values are concerned. This in turn leads to social discord which is always at least *potentially* present among the various individuals, social classes, ethnic and racial groups, and various elements jockeying for their rights. But the picture is not so glum as many writers depict it. There is a consensus that there can be no argument about the need for justice, law, and order. Voting is highly predictable in certain instances, for example, when a bond issue for raising money for more recreational facilities occurs those who live in the better districts tend to vote against it and those who live in congested neighborhoods tend to vote in favor of it. Not unpredictable! Reduced to its simplest terms those who feel that they have to pay for it oppose those who will make more use of the facilities in question. But not all voting is in self-interest. An emergent set of values gives equilibrium to the modern community. For lack of a better term we shall call this ethic, or complex of values, the *ethic of pluralism.*

The pluralistic ethic relinquishes none of the values of freedom for individuals and groups in the community. Pluralism recognizes the legitimacy of economic and political struggling for economic and social betterment of all individuals and groups. This ethic opposes a maintenance of the *status quo* when differences between segments of the community are "frozen" so that struggling individuals and groups are unduly hampered in self improvement. The pluralist fears too much concentration of power in any segment of the community. A democratic equilibrium of power is the political goal which is sought. Unlike the ideal society of Plato, which existed only in imagination, the far-from-ideal American community is the result of a successive series of experiments, a series of compromises in otherwise hopelessly irresolvable values in conflict.

Major Concepts in Chapter 10

1. *Urban sociology:* The special application of general sociology to the social adaptations and problems induced by the concentration of population within limited geographical areas (population density).

2. *United States Census:* Periodic enumeration of the population and certain characteristics of the population. Inaugurated in 1790 and continued regularly at ten-year intervals. The stated purpose of the U. S. Census was to provide a basis for reapportioning seats in the House of Representatives.

3. *Ecology:* The study of the spatial distribution of people and institutions in cities.

4. *Community:* A subgroup having many characteristics of a society but on a smaller scale. Characterized by common territory, contact, interdependence, and some special basis of coherence (common values).

5. *Metropolitan community:* Community which has as its geographic locale a natural boundary in which are contained a central city or cities of 50,000 or more.

6. *Preliterate community:* A small primitive or folk community whose technology and values limits its capacity for development.

7. *Preindustrial community:* Includes preliterate communities but especially designates large communities not yet industrialized. Employs animate energy (men and animals), unable to achieve density of modern community.

8. *Industrial community:* Variously called "modern," "urban," or "developed," this community is able to concentrate large numbers of

people in a relatively small space. Employs inanimate energy (steam; electricity).

9. *Industrial Revolution:* The complex of changes which ushered in modern industrialism. In America, growth of factory modes of production in place of the small workshop in the eighteenth and nineteenth centuries and the advanced developments in the mechanization of industry.

10. *Social distance:* Reserve or constraint in social interaction between individuals of different (inferior and superior) social status.

11. *Social mobility:* The movement of persons from social group to social group or from social class to social class.

12. *Channels of social mobility:* Means by which social mobility occurs. Examples are marriage, education, employment promotion.

13. *Values:* Standard of judgment accepted by persons or groups. Conceptions of the "good life."

14. *American Creed:* Values of Americans. Stated in the Preamble to the Constitution and in several constitutional amendments; chiefly in the "Bill of Rights" (the first ten amendments).

15. *Value conflict:* The situation where holders of different values interact and disruptions of the interaction occur because of the clashing elements in their values.

16. *Melting pot:* In social lore, the idea that all immigrant groups that have come to America have simmered their Old World heritages into one homogeneous American heritage.

17. *Consensus:* Group decisions in which all members consciously participate.

18. *Ethic:* The sum of the characteristic culture traits of a group which differentiates it from other groups.

19. *Pluralism:* A value shared by many diverse groups which stresses tolerance of differences and overrides the ethnocentric values of each group.

Review Questions

1. Why is the problem of community a central one for urban sociologists?
2. How do you distinguish between urban sociology and just plain sociology?
3. What is the significance of population size for the community?
4. What is the significance of population density for the community?

5. What is the United States Census? It was begun in 1790 before there was a science of sociology to make use of its data. Why?
6. On what basis did we distinguish three types of community?
7. Define community. Is your neighborhood a community?
8. Why did cities grow out from the center? Why are better neighborhoods found in the outer concentric circles?
9. Explain: "Sociologists observe behavior, examine evidence, and infer the presence of a social system."
10. Why does land use help us to know something about the division of labor in a given geographic area?
11. Are there any preliterate communities in the world today?
12. Have feudal societies disappeared from the earth?
13. Will all communities ultimately be industrialized? Could you call urbanization and industrialization "progress"?
14. Can you find U. S. census publications on "Characteristics of the population" for your city or one nearby? If so, can you pick out census tracts that have a high social (prestige) ranking? What evidence could you use?
15. Is there a census tract map of your city? Would the concentric zone scheme roughly correspond to residential patterning in your city? If you try this, make your concentric zones about one-half mile each.
16. What modifying features would have to be taken into account in doing a concentric zone analysis of your city?
17. Do you think social stratification is undemocratic?
18. What are the values of your neighborhood? Are they the same as values in other selected neighborhoods of your city?
19. What is the American Creed?
20. How can Americans live up to the American Creed in our modern industrial communities?

Discussion Questions

1. What are the arguments for a regional government over all of the municipalities that make up a metropolitan area?
2. What are the arguments against such a regional government?
3. Could it be argued that metropolitan community, as the concept was developed in the chapter, is not really a "community"?
4. Discuss: "Urban redevelopment always hurts the poor."
5. Discuss the Civil Rights Movement as an aspect of the "metropolitan problem" in America.

Bibliography

Anderson, Nels, *The Urban Community* (New York: Henry Holt and Company, 1959).

Bergel, Egon Ernest, *Urban Sociology* (New York: McGraw-Hill Book Company, 1955).

Bernard, Jessie, *American Community Behavior,* rev. ed. (New York: Holt, Rinehart and Winston, 1962).

Beshers, James N., *Urban Social Structure* (New York: The Free Press of Glencoe, 1962).

Bollens, John C. (ed.), *Exploring the Metropolitan Community* (Berkeley, California: University of California Press, 1961).

Chapin, F. Stuart, Jr., and Shirley F. Weiss (eds.), *Urban Growth Dynamics in a Regional Cluster of Cities* (New York: John Wiley & Sons, Inc., 1962).

Cities, A Scientific American Book (New York: Alfred A. Knopf, 1965).

Clinard, Marshall, *The Sociology of Deviant Behavior* (New York: Holt, Rinehart & Winston, 1957).

D'Antonio, William V., and William H. Form, *Influentials in Two Border Cities: A Study in Community Decision-Making* (Notre Dame, Ind.: University of Notre Dame Press, 1965).

Dreiser, Theodore, *The Genius* (New York: Boni and Liveright, 1923).

*Editors of *Fortune* magazine, *The Exploding Metropolis* (Garden City: N. Y.: Doubleday & Company, 1958).

Gibbs, Jack P. (ed.), *Urban Research Methods* (New York: D. Van Nostrand Company, Inc., 1961).

Gist, Noel P., and L. A. Halbert, *Urban Society,* 4th ed. (New York: Thomas Y Crowell, 1951).

*Greer, Scott, *Governing the Metropolis* (New York: John Wiley & Sons, Inc., 1961).

*Hunter, Floyd, *Community Power Structure: A Study of Decision Makers* (Chapel Hill, N. C.: University of North Carolina Press, 1953).

*Jacobs, Jane, *The Life and Death of Great American Cities* (New York: Random House, 1961).

Mumford, Lewis, *The City in History: Its Origins, Its Transformations, and Its Prospects* (New York: Harcourt, Brace & World, Inc., 1961).

Nelson, Lowry, *et al., Community Structure and Change* (New York: The Macmillan Company, 1960).

*Presthus, Robert, *Men at the Top: A Study in Community Power* (New York: Oxford University Press, 1964).

Queen, Stuart A., and David Carpenter, *The American City* (New York: McGraw-Hill Book Company, Inc., 1953).

*Redfield, Robert, *The Little Community* (Chicago: University of Chicago Press, 1955),

*Riesman, David, *The Lonely Crowd* (New Haven: Yale University Press, 1950).

Sirjamaki, John, *The Sociology of Cities* (New York: Random House, 1964).

*Williams, Oliver P., and Charles Press (eds.), *Democracy in Urban America: Readings in Government and Politics* (Chicago: Rand McNally & Company, 1961).

---

* Also published in paperback edition.

Chapter 11

Social Classes in America

THE FACT OF SOCIAL STRATIFICATION

IN EVERY American school there are groups of students who are "in." They belong to the elite of the school. Star athletes, class officers, honor students carry greater weight around school, receive more deference from teachers and fellow students, have higher status than do ordinary members of the student body. If you wanted to, you could analyze your own school by breaking the student body into groups which rank higher and lower on a prestige scale.

What holds true of the American school also holds for other organizations in the United States. Why, for example, do all sergeants in an army camp salute first when meeting a colonel? Why do executives working for General Motors enjoy special privileges like the use of a company limousine and access to executive washrooms which are denied to janitors working in the same office? Why are bishops more visibly honored than simple rural curates? The army, corporations, the church — each organization divides into groups of people occupying different levels of strata of respect, authority, status. Each is a stratified society. Careful reflection shows that the larger American society contains many groups (rich *vs* poor; educated *vs* non-educated; immigrant minority *vs* native born) which have higher or lower positions of power and prestige. The United States, also, is a stratified society.

Social stratification refers to the breakdown of society into higher and lower economic classes and prestige groups. Bernard Berelson, a sociologist, has defined social stratification as "the ranking of people in a society by other members of the society into higher and lower social positions so as to produce a hierachy of respect or prestige."

245

There is a close link between social stratification and unequal distribution of status or prestige in society. Let us take an example. If you were a waiter in a local restaurant, would you give prompter service to a rich, well-mannered, handsomely dressed society matron or to a ditch digger dressed in boots, khaki shirt, and overalls? Perhaps your greater care in ministering to the wants of the society woman would be motivated by a desire for a good tip. It is very probable, however, that the society lady would command special service by her very manner of bearing herself. Unconsciously, an awareness of her own prestige would manifest itself in her external actions, eliciting from you, her waiter, an acknowledgment of her status. Her very way of carrying herself says, "I am used to being well served and expect the same from you." In all likelihood the ditch digger would be more nonchalant and familiar in his dealings with you.

The Skid Row wino is not as important as the bank president. Messenger boys command less respect than astronauts. Student body officers have higher rank in school than lowly freshmen. Indeed, in every society there is an unequal distribution of prestige.

This ranking of people into higher and lower social positions is a highly informal process. There is no law which states that doctors deserve greater prestige than garbagemen. Members of any group spontaneously size up their fellows, ranking them in a hierarchy. Consider how naturally and informally you rate groups of students within your own school as "in" or not.

Although in your own high school, students rank high or low mainly because of their personal qualities, in the larger American society individuals are rated on impersonal traits such as income, place of residence, family connections. Social stratification studies bear not so much on individuals, as such, but on strata or classes in society. Certain groups (immigrants, millionaires, college graduates), certain occupations (clergymen, doctors, longshoremen), and certain organizations (universities, the army, corporations) are ranged in a hierarchy of prestige. Individual members of these groups share in our collective judgment of the entire group. By abstracting from personal qualities, we can rank all college graduates higher on the status scale than all non-college graduates. We can readily see, therefore, that judgments based on social stratification are superficial. The student should carefully note throughout this chapter that what is said about the prestige level of groups does not exhaustively define the personal qualities of the individual members of these groups. By standards other than social class position, the struggling poor may be nobler persons than high society rich people.

THE NECESSITY OF SOCIAL CLASSES

Most Americans, indoctrinated by the lofty principle that "all men are created equal," feel very uneasy about admitting that social classes exist in the United States since a class system is synonymous with inequality of opportunity. We know really that in the United States the wealthy have greater chances of success than the poor because it is easier for rich people to send their sons to elite colleges and use connections to gain them an entrance into high levels of the business world. Nevertheless, most of us think that a perfectly classless society is the democratic ideal. Actually, a little thought will reveal that a classless society is not even possible in America.

Mankind's closest approximation to a classless society is found in primitive tribes in which all adult males have the same round of work, hunting and farming in the same traditional ways. There is very little to distinguish one adult male from another in status. Yet, even in very simple tribes some distinction exists between the elite consisting of chiefs, witch doctors, skillful hunters and the non-elite ordinary tribesmen.

As the primitive tribe becomes larger in population, wealthier and more skilled, there occurs within it a process of *division of labor*. Sociologists define division of labor in a society as the process by which the various jobs to be done in a group are divided up, with certain people specializing in performing definite tasks. While most members of a simple agrarian society engage in traditional farming, a few must specialize in governing and making laws, caring for the religious or health needs of the group, trading goods, fighting the wars with neighboring states. As you saw in the chapter on the family (Chap. 5), early in man's history classes of specialists sprung up, resulting from a division of labor: kings, warriors, priests, merchants. Such specialization is essential in human groups if there is to be growth and progress in wealth and technical skill. Because specialists perform a singular service to society, they have always been peculiarly honored and rewarded for their labor. In time, they become the richest, most powerful members of any society. Human nature being what it is, specialists try to use the power and wealth they have personally gained by passing on advantages to their own children and families. Whenever wealth and power is perpetuated within families for generations, with fathers transmitting special opportunities to their children, we have classes in a society.

Our sense of justice demands that there be inequalities of prestige and material rewards in society. Some jobs demand unique skills and knowledge. Others carry with them decision-making authority. There has to be an incentive for members of a group to take the time and trouble to gain the necessary skills for these jobs. Would it be fair to offer the same rewards and honor to a doctor as to a beachboy? Doctors deserve high prestige as a recompense for their long years of training and the invaluable service they render to the health needs of the community.

It is obvious, therefore, that we cannot avoid class divisions unless we abolish either division of labor or the institution of the family. No industrial society has succeeded in exterminating either one. Technical efficiency demands specialization. Human nature perpetuates the family.

Writing in the early stages of the Industrial Revolution, Karl Marx, the nineteenth-century philosopher and economist, proposed to rid society of class divisions. He naïvely thought that modern man could avoid specialization. In his projected utopian society, all men would be universally educated. Jobs would be rotated in such a way that everyone, eventually, would have a chance to occupy a position of power and authority. Recently, the Chinese Communists have attempted to break down the institution of the family in an effort to destroy class privileges. Both the Marxist Utopia and the Chinese Communist experiment are doomed to failure since they run counter to history and to human nature.

Although the Soviet Union pays lip service to the ideal of a classless society, it is clear to all, except the brainwashed, that classes exist in the Communist state. One sociological analysis of Soviet society, conducted by Professor Alex Inkeles of Harvard University, estimated that there are no fewer than ten gradations of class in Russia. Certainly, the communist bureaucratic élite enjoy privileges which are denied to Siberian peasants. It does not seem to have been a mere accident that while Nikita Krushchev was premier, his son-in-law held the important party post of editor of *Izvestia,* the official Communist newspaper. The Soviets do not like to admit that classes exist in their state. One leading Communist, Milovan Djilas, formerly vice-president of Yugoslavia, was jailed for publishing a book entitled, *The New Class.* In this book Djilas mocked the Communist hypocrisy of maintaining that they have a classless society when the revolutionary party members have appropriated to themselves the same powerful class privileges which formerly belonged to the ruling classes overthrown by the Communist revolution. Perhaps, the most telling satire on the Communist brand of classless society is found in George Orwell's book, *Animal Farm.* In this modern parable, all the animals on the farm conspire to overthrow the tyrannous farmer. The revolution begins in absolute equality. Soon, however, the pigs on the farm get the upper hand, enjoying privileges once exclusively those of the tyrant farmer. The pigs end up by changing the official doctrinaire slogan, "All animals are equal," to the ridiculous parody, "All animals are equal but some animals are more equal than others!"

In our own day, in Israel, there has been an effort to establish free collective farms, the *kibbutzim*, in which class distinctions have been rooted out. All positions of power and leadership were to be rotated. Even here, however, efficiency demanded that some men specialize in certain key jobs. Today, sociologists claim that they can see a class of officials emerging in the *kibbutzim*. All of these examples illustrate most clearly that in a modern industrial society, a classless society is impossible.

CRITERIA FOR DETERMINING SOCIAL CLASS

On what basis are some groups more highly esteemed than others? No general answer which will be valid for all societies can be given. Our answer to this question will be determined by the values of the particular society we are studying. For example, our Western industrial society sets a premium on wealth as an index of power and prestige. In the Indian caste system, family background and religious status were all important. A low caste millionaire received very little honor. Even within one nation different geographical regions vary in the standards they use to evaluate groups. Thus, a hundred years ago, while in Boston the social scions of established Mayflower-lineage families ruled supreme, out west on the frontier rugged cattlemen and rich barons reigned. In a similar way, in times of military crises the status stock of military leaders soars higher than it does during peacetime.

Although many factors influence the prestige judgment Americans make about groups, the following seven items represent the most important values which determine class status:

I. *Income: How much is there and from what source is it derived?*
   Although, in general, the rich have greater prestige than the poor, source of income is an important factor. A medium income doctor has more status than a millionaire head of a crime syndicate.

II. *Education: Amount of schooling and type of school attended.*

For Americans, the distinction between college and non-college graduates looms large. It makes a difference whether the degree was granted by Harvard or Podunk University.

III. *Occupation and Skill: How much skill and learning is required by an occupation?*

In an occupational prestige rating Americans ranked lawyers above accountants because they believed that the law required more skill and learning than accounting.

IV. *Family Connections:*

This criterion is used to contrast recent migrants to a community (the minority groups) with older established residents. Kinship connections assume greater proportions of importance in the upper strata of society.

V. *Authority and Power: How much political influence does a group wield in the community?*

Political influence or power is best measured by the number of persons' lives which a group or occupation affects. Such power may be either direct (by actually occupying political office) or indirect (through pressure which can be applied to politicians).

VI. *Prestige: How well known and highly regarded are members of this group or occupation?*

The method used to determine prestige is the public opinion poll. Sociologists do not feel competent to say that a certain group *deserves* more prestige than other groups. If a sociological survey finds that doctors have higher status than schoolteachers, this should not be interpreted to mean that doctors are better people than schoolteachers or even that they perform a greater service to society. It simply means that, when polled, Americans said that they thought doctors have more prestige than schoolteachers.

VII. *Service to the Community: How much benefit to the community does the group or occupation contribute?*

It is difficult to ascertain how much service a group contributes to the community. But, that this value is used sometimes in determining status is reflected by the fact that police officers and clergymen rate higher in public opinion polls than do other occupations which pay more.

No one of these seven criteria alone is employed by Americans when they judge the hierarchy of rank which groups occupy within their society. Usually all of these factors, combined, form the basis of judgment.

If you met a man on the street for the first time, how would you go about deciding where to place him in the class structure of the United States? W. Lloyd Warner, a sociologist who has contributed more than anyone else to social stratification studies, has devised an *Index of Status Characteristics* (ISC) which could be used to find the relative social position of an individual. The index consists of six variables: occupation, amount of income, source of income, type of house owned or lived in, residential location, and education. Each item on the index is weighted differently. Greatest weight is given to occupation, amount of income, education.

Occupation, more than any other variable, determines an individual's status in urban society. You saw this in the chapter on *community* (Chap. 10). The occupational position a man holds is both affected by his educational background, and, in turn affects his annual income. In its turn, income decides what type of home and residential location a man can afford. Occupational prestige, therefore, is central in deciding class position. The best known survey of occupational prestige was conducted by the National Opinion Research Center, under the direction of Professors North and Hatt. This study, known as the North-Hatt scale, asked a representative statistical sample to rank ninety occupations using the criteria of prestige, authority and power, income, education, requisite skill. This opinion poll demonstrated, among other things, that whether those questioned placed greatest stress on income, education, or requisite skills, they tended to rank the ninety occupations similarly. We can conclude from this study that there is a high degree of relationship between the various criteria used to determine prestige. Common sense itself tells us that most jobs which pay well also demand special education and skill. Such jobs usually confer authority on their occupants. Of course, there is always some status discrepancy between items on a prestige scale. Those who most benefit society may not be adequately rewarded. Again, a near-illiterate popular singer who merely "groans" for a living, performing no great service to society, may have an exorbitantly high income.

Occupational rankings show remarkable agreement across national boundaries. Professor Alex Inkeles of Harvard, in collaboration with Professor Peter Rossi of Chicago University, conducted surveys in seven industrial nations, including the United States, Great Britain, Japan, West Germany. Their multi-national survey demonstrated that people in other industrial nations rate occupations in orders that are similar in many points with those made by North Americans. Class distinctions based on occupational placement in these industrial countries are also similar.

Occupation as an index of status is especially important in determining class in large urban centers because it is a visible, objective criterion. In the past thirty years American sociologists have extensively studied social stratification in small communities and larger urban cities of the United States. They have found that in smaller communities of 10,000 population or less, prestige ranking is based more on personal criteria such as family lineage, length of residence in the community, membership in exclusive local clubs. In larger communities objective standards like occupation are needed to place an individual in the status hierarchy.

An interesting project that the student might attempt in your own community would be to draw up a list of representative occupations and ask members of your community to rank them on a scale of prestige. Your teacher could help you devise the scale and give you some background on statistical techniques needed to employ a valid scale. Or you could do this with the United States census as suggested in the chapter on *community* (Chap. 10).

One final point needs to be emphasized concerning the criteria for determining class position. When different groups in America are polled concerning class divisions, they do not use the same criteria to evaluate classes. The upper classes seem to have the clearest ideas about the number of classes in the United States. The lowest class tend to bunch together several of the classes above them, viewing them as one "rich" class. Sociologist Bernard Berelson has summed up some of these different points of view toward class. In evaluating class division in America, he found that "the lower classes use money as the main criterion; the middle classes use money and morality; the upper classes, ancestry and style of life."

THE NUMBER OF SOCIAL CLASSES
IN AMERICAN SOCIETY

Class lines in America are not as hard and fast as they are

in other countries, like Ecuador, where it is very easy to define an individual's class position. Because it is possible in the United States to change status during an individual's lifetime, the distinctions between classes are not clear cut. W. Lloyd Warner in his extensive studies of social stratification in representative communities throughout the United States divided America into six classes. These classes represented subdivisions of the classic upper, middle, and lower classes. We will use Warner's class categories which were first presented in his important study of a New England town, the *Yankee City* series.

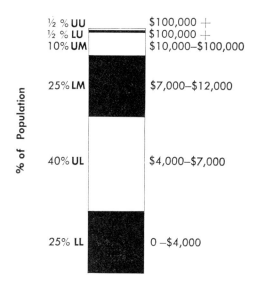

The Upper-Upper Class (UU)

This highest class in America is comprised of the very rich, most of whose members have material assets of well over $100,000. Many, of course, are millionaires. Money alone, however, does not provide the key of entrance into the upper-upper class. Wealth must be both legitimate and old. One's money is made legitimate by being derived from approved sources: inheritance of occupations which command respect, such as banking, property management, steel, the railroads. Although a multimillionaire boxer or popular entertainer may have more money than upper-upper society scions, his wealth is not considered dignified enough to gain him access to high society. Upper-upper class wealth also must be old, that is, well-established in the family for several generations. The "new rich" millionaire must bide his time before his family gains acceptance by the élite club of upper-uppers.

The upper-upper class is heavily concentrated along the Eastern seaboard of America and in older established cities like Baltimore, Chicago, Boston, New York, St. Louis, and San Francisco. At present the best index of whether a family is truly upper-upper is the fact that their name is listed in the *Social Register,* a roster of exclusive families. Social registers are compiled in fourteen of our largest cities. The upper-upper class is virtually nonexistent in smaller cities.

This class lays great store on tradition, family lineage, and kinship connections. Priding themselves on their gracious style of living, they eschew flashiness in clothes and home styles. Their children attend élite private secondary schools, going on to matriculate at the prestige Ivy League universities.

Less than one-half of one percent of America is upper-upper class. Because this class is so small statistically, not universally found in every city, some sociologists think that we should not consider this class separately from the lower-upper class. Nevertheless, the upper-upper class represents a unique strata of society, heavily inbred, treasuring tradition, given to a gracious way of life. For an interesting portrait of upper-upper society as contrasted to middle-class America, the student is invited to read John P. Marquand's novel *Point of No Return.*

In their occupational careers, upper-upper males have clustered in the world of investment and finance, especially as bankers and stock brokerage consultants. Many, of course, do not work at all, constituting an army of unemployed gentlemen of leisure. In recent years, politics and government service have attracted the young scions of upper class families. Names like Nelson Rockefeller, William Scranton, Henry Cabot Lodge, W. Averell Harriman, C. Douglas Dillon, Adlai Stevenson, Franklin Roosevelt, Jr., are as familiar to the readers of the daily newspaper as they are to devotees of *The Social Register.*

The Lower-Upper Class (LU)

The major difference between the lower-upper class and the upper-upper class is that the wealth of the former is neither old nor legitimate. They are the new rich, often much wealthier than some old established upper-upper class families.

In residence, style of living and ambition, lower-uppers are very similar to upper-uppers, although less hidebound by tradition.

The lower-upper class divides into two sharply distinguishable groups. On the one hand, there are the recent millionaires who ape the mannerisms of the upper-uppers, sending their children to the same private schools, waiting their allotted time until their wealth becomes old enough to gain them acceptance into upper-upper society. On the other hand, there are the celebrities, sports figures, entertainers, some businessmen who keep their roots in the middle class. Although they are very wealthy, their style of life remains much like the man next door. Altogether about one percent of America belongs to the top two classes.

The Upper-Middle Class (UM)

Whereas wealth is decisive for determining whether or not a man belongs to the upper classes, the identifying badge of the upper-middle class is the college diploma. This class constitutes what the journalist Vance Packard has termed "the diploma élite." The core members of this class are the professionals: doctors, dentists, lawyers, college professors, clergymen. They comprise the most educated class in America. Furthermore, they have come to view college education as a right for their children, often regardless of their children's intelligence quotient or proven ability to do university work.

While upper-middles are not independently wealthy, they enjoy substantial incomes, ranging from $10,000 to $100,000 a year. The upper-middles derive their income from their occupation. This distinguishes them from the wealthy upper-class which generally owns large sums of money, invested in stocks and property. Upper-middles use their income to purchase substantial homes in comfortable residential neighborhoods, usually identifiable as the area where doctors, wealthy lawyers, and business executives live.

The upper-middle class is less family-centered than upper class Americans. Partly, this is due to the fact that, for many of them, their occupation demands that they be highly mobile. Business executives, especially, must be prepared, on short notice, to transfer to a different plant or branch of their national corporation in another city. Not only is this class the most mobile group in America, it is also the class of joiners. More of its numbers, proportionately, are active members of lodges, civic organizations, churches in the United States than any other strata of society. You can test this fact, yourselves, by obtaining a roster of members of some service club or civic organization in your community such as the Rotary Club, Optimists, United Appeal. Wives and children of upper-middle males are also active members of women's auxiliaries and youth clubs. Because of the key positions they hold in civic organizations and vountary associations, upper middles wield greater political power and civic influence than their relative numbers warrant. Approximately 10 percent of America ranks in the upper-middle class.

Because a substantial portion of upper-middle society is recruited from professional classes of self-employed like doctors, lawyers, architects, this class has been the bastion of defense for the traditional American ideals of self-initiative and individualism over against government intervention. The most vocal political conservatives are drawn from the upper-middle class. Recent shifts in the number of professional men in the employ of giant corporations has somewhat mitigated this strong middle-class emphasis on the values of individualism, with greater weight being given to the virtues of the "company man."

The Lower-Middle Class (LM)

There are many similarities between the upper-middle and the lower-middle classes. Both represent strata whose numbers are expanding proportionately in our society. Both include employees who are white collar workers. The lower-middle class differs statistically from the upper-middle class in amount of education, income, and opportunities for career advancement. Vance Packard has called the lower-middle class, "the limited success class."

Almost all lower-middles have a high school diploma. Some have attended a few years of college. Those who have a college diploma are not employed in occupations whose prestige, income, and authority compare with upper-middle class jobs. A sample listing of some lower-middle occupations includes: high school and elementary school instructor, police officer, fireman in an urban fire department, clerks in business offices, routine salesman, accountant, minor officials in the civil service bureaucracy, small businessman.

Lower-middles are relative successes inasmuch as their comfortable salaries allow them to purchase their own homes, automobiles, home furnishings. Their jobs, while sometimes routine or dull, are respectable, clean, demand certain skills. Their salary ranges from $7,000 to $12,000 a year. Besides white collar occupations, the lower-middle class includes substantial numbers of skilled craftsmen like plumbers, carpenters, and electricians. The salary, residential location, and career aspiration for their children places such skilled craftsmen on the same level as white-collar workers. A very high proportion of the lower-middle class go on to college.

Career opportunities and, therefore, potential earning power of lower-middles is limited by the fact that they lack the essential ticket to a successful rise into the upper-middle class: the college diploma. The lower-middle class includes approximately 25 percent of American society.

The Upper-Lower Class (UL)

Below the white collar workers and skilled craftsmen is a strata of blue-collar, semi-skilled factory and manual laborers. Although this class represents almost 40 percent of the American population, its numbers are diminishing because of automation which displaces many semiskilled jobs. This class contains a disporportionate number of immigrants and first generation Americans. Almost half of its number have never completed high school.

Career advancement is almost impossible in upper-lower class occupations. An adult of fifty draws the same salary for unskilled labor as the lad of eighteen just starting out. Since their jobs tend to be routine, dull, mechanical, upper-lowers measure success by pay increases. Their life's ambition includes owning their own modest home and getting by financially. Few upper-lowers are taken in by the American Horatio Alger dream of success since they realize that their salaries leave little margin for investment. They are hardest hit by any economic recession.

The Lower-Lower Class (LL)

The lowest social class is an amorphous amalgam of many different types of people: the aged, retired, the unemployed or un-employable, migrant farm laborers, deserted families on relief. Because it contains so many disparate groups, it is best to define the lower-lower class as an economic category. A lower-lower class family is one with a combined annual income of less than $4,000. Michael Harrington, an economist, has described this class, which represents nearly 25 percent of the total population, as "the other America." It is in behalf of the lower-lower class that the majority of government sponsored welfare programs are directed. This social group has the lowest amount of education proportionate to the general population, the highest incidence of crime, disease, and family instability. It is very important statistically to divide this class into two groups — those who because of retirement or unemployment have descended the social ladder from a higher social class; those who have lived their entire lives in deprivation. The former group resembles the upper-lowers or the middle class in their values and way of life.

W. Lloyd Warner's categorical breakdown of American society into six social classes has been verified by social stratification studies undertaken in many urban centers in the United States. It reflects social reality. Nevertheless, it must be admitted that any division into a defined number of classes is arbitrary, depending on the criteria chosen to distinguish between social strata. Thus, not all sociologists are in agreement concerning the number of classes in America. Some argue for a five-part class structure, meshing together the top two classes; others postulate only the classic three strata: upper, middle, lower. One sociologist, Richard Centers, conducted a nationwide survey using the tripartite division into upper, middle, lower class. When he asked people to rank themselves into one of these three categories, over 80 percent of those responding claimed middle-class status for themselves. Large numbers of those whom we have labeled upper-middle class described themselves as upper-class, while a sizeable proportion of the upper-lower class considered themselves to be middle class. When, later, Centers added a fourth category, working class, to his number of choices, 45 percent of those who had previously claimed to be middle-class preferred to label themselves, "working class." Since most upper-lowers consider themselves to be middle-class, some sociologists prefer to lump together the lower-middle and upper-lower classes into one category, calling them the working middle class to distinguish them from the upper-middle class which they term the professional-middle class.

Two points concerning the number we assign to classes in our society seem obvious. First, the manner of determining the number of social strata is arbitrary. Hence, if we choose occupation as our criterion for selecting class labels, the United States divides into unemployed rich, professionals, nonprofessional bureaucratic officials, white collar clerical, skilled manual, unskilled laborers, the unemployed poor. On the other hand, if income alone decides social strata, our society includes those who make less than $5,000 annually, those in the $5,000–$10,000 bracket, those who make $10,000–$15,000 a year etc. A purely economic category, however, does not do justice to the cultural differences which exist between classes. The second point is that, although sociologists are in conflict on the number of classes they assign to American society, all agree that, for a meaningful analysis of social stratification, more than three categories are necessary. The student is advised to picture American class structure in terms of W. Lloyd Warner's six classes.

SOCIAL SPAN AND SOCIAL SHAPE

Every social class system has a span. *The social span* of a class structure refers to the range of difference between the upper-upper and lower-lower classes in terms of income, power, and prestige. The greater the inequalities which exist between the highest and lowest classes in a society, the greater the span between social classes. The concept of social span is a spatial metaphor about social distances which we usefully employ to measure social inequality. It is probable, for example, that the span or gap between the very rich and very poor is greater in India than in the United States. If the very rich receive smaller proportions of the national wealth than formerly because of high taxes, while the poor are allotted larger percentages of the national income than previously because of increased wages and government security programs, social span decreases. Do you think that the social span between the higher and lower classes in the United States has increased or decreased over the last one hundred years? When the gap between social classes is wide, there is little social contentment among the lower classes. In urban societies lower classes are intensely aware of the gap even though it is narrower than agricultural communities. Feudal agrarian societies have the widest span of all social structures.

A reduction in the amount of economic inequalities in society need not entail a lessening of social inequalities of status or prestige. The economic span between a modern-day Rockefeller and a shoe shine man may be less than the gap which existed between their respective grandfathers. It is debatable whether the prestige or power span has been reduced along with the economic gap. This example illustrates, once again, the folly of studying social class structure from a purely economic standpoint.

Spans of social class difference relate only to the distances between social extremes. They do not tell us how the population is distributed, i.e., what percentage of the nation belongs to each social class. Let us consider an example. Suppose that the span between the richest and poorest members of a given society is wide. The rich are fabulously rich and the poor are very poor indeed! Nevertheless, there may be only a few rich and poor persons in the society. Besides social span, therefore, we need to consider *the shape* of a class system in order to reckon the distribution of the population into classes.

Social structures come in two basic shapes. In feudal societies like prewar China in which the vast proportion of the population is peasant poor with only a small number of middle class and an even smaller number of upper class, a pyramid shape serves as a model. On the other hand, in countries like the United States in which the majority of the population clusters toward the middle class, with percentages tapering off as you ascend or descend the social scale, the model shape looks like a diamond.

Not only whole societies but also cities and local communities have varying spans and shapes. Some exclusive suburbs consisting solely of the two upper classes, have a span so slight that social distance is almost impossible to measure. There are rural small towns in America with only negligent numbers of upper or lower class. On the other hand, certain industrial suburbs with over fifty percent in the lower class have a shape modeled on the pyramid. In general, larger cities in the United States have different shapes and spans than smaller towns, mainly because the largest cities contain the greatest concentration of the upper and lower-lower classes. The student is advised to analyze comparative spans and shapes of various communities in his area. He should ask himself whether any differences can be observed between communities of slight span *vs* those of wide span, communities which include all social classes *vs* those of only one or several classes, communities which are pyramid shaped *vs* communities which are patterned on the diamond model.

OPEN AND CLOSED CLASS SYSTEMS

A major distinction between class systems in various societies is uncovered by asking the question: Is this class system open or closed? A closed-class system or *caste* assigns each individual the same status as his parents, with slight opportunity for advancement Most students are familiar with the example of caste system in pre-Ghandian India. In the caste system, family connections are more important than personal initiative and skill in deciding an individual's life opportunities. Can you think of some advantages and disadvantages of a closed-class system? Castes are only possible in static, unchanging, traditional societies. Until recently many Latin American nations had distinct castes. As a nation becomes more industrialized, technical changes constantly open up new areas of

There are still remnants of a closed class system in India.

job opportunities. It becomes impossible to assign all occupations by inheritance so that all carpenters' sons become carpenters, *etc.* Can you think of some new career opportunities which technical progress has created in this country since World War II? Television, space research, frozen food processing are only a few of the new technical areas which did not exist twenty-five years ago. The greatest criticism which can be leveled against a closed-class system is that it is socially wasteful. By an accident of birth, many men are unable to use their talents in the most socially useful way. They lack the family connections necessary to receive an education to fit them for the careers for which they have talent. Do you think that a social structure built on a closed-class system is just? Is it consonant with the democratic ideal?

In the ideal order a perfectly open-class system is the most efficient and the most democratic. Status and wealth are accorded to those men whose personal skill and initiative have earned them. In the open-class system innumerable opportunities exist for social advancement and success so that a butcher's son may grow up to be president. The son of a dockworker has no fewer chances of getting ahead than the son of a bank president. Do you think that there are any perfectly open-class systems in the world? Is the term a synonym for the impossible classless society? Certainly, in equalitarian America, while any man can advance in the social system through talent and hard work, still, one who begins in the lower class must work harder to succeed than the son of a millionaire. He does not have the same advantages as the rich boy. The United States is a relatively open-class system inasmuch as all enjoy real opportunities to advance. But, to the degree that these opportunities are not completely equal for all, to that degree the social structure of our society is not perfectly open. Actually, no social class system is perfectly open or closed. Even in rigid, feudal-caste societies there are always people, however few, who advance beyond their parents' status. Any given society only approximates to one or the other type of class system.

Several questions should be asked about the openness of our class structure. First, is the United States more open in its class structure than other industrial countries? Second, is our class system becoming more open or more closed as time goes on?

The answer to the first question is not the answer most Americans expect. Yet, the sociological evidence derived from comparative studies of social stratification in the United States and Europe, indicates that European countries are no less rigid than America in their class structures. Because of massive subsidies by European governments, doors of opportunity have been opened for sons of laborers in England, Germany, and France.

There is an interesting point that should be made concerning the way Americans view the social reality of their class structure when compared with the way Europeans see their class systems. Sociological studies have demonstrated that Americans generally think that their class structure is more democratic than it really is, overlooking obvious differences in the opportunities available to various classes. On the other hand, Europeans see their class systems as more rigid and closed than they are in reality. Can you explain why this is so?

One answer can be derived from the past histories of both types of countries. The United States was never a feudal society. It has always lacked hereditary titles, privileged nobility, a special estate established by law. It was founded as a nation on the principle that all men were created equal. Hence, Americans tend to see the reality of their social structure through rose-colored glasses, tinted by the official American dream of equality. On the other hand, Europeans, with national backgrounds of landed gentry and special classes, still view their social systems through the lenses of their own past histories of inequality.

The answer to our second question involves us in a comparison of our present-day class structure with the class system of earlier periods of our history. Since careful sociological analysis of social stratification in the United States only dates to the 1930's, it is not possible scientifically to determine whether social class structure is relatively more open or closed today than it was earlier. What evidence we have, however, points in the direction of the conclusion that social class structure is getting more open.

W. Lloyd Warner and James Abegglen conducted a study of successful businessmen in our country, *Big Business Leaders in America*. They attempted to compare these successful business leaders with their counterparts of fifty years ago. The fact that 71 percent of today's business successes are sons of fathers who occupied the same level of economic and social status, illustrates that the best way to become a success is to be the son of one. Nevertheless, Warner and Abegglen conclude that there is slightly greater opportunity to rise socially today than there was at the turn of the century.

Even fifty years ago, the Horatio Alger story of a rise from rags to riches was a myth. Sociologist William Miller analyzed the backgrounds of the richest 200 business leaders in America for the years 1901–1910. He found that 79 percent of them were sons of professional men, 75 percent were fourth generation Americans, 76 percent were college graduates. Only three percent had made the long climb upwards from the lower-lower class. So, even fifty years ago, the American class system was no more open than it is today.

One American sociologist, August Hollingshead, has extensively analyzed social class differences in the American high school. His work, *Elmtown's Youth,* based on studies in a central high school in a small midwestern town, is a sociological classic in the field of social stratification studies. His research in Elmtown and in New Haven, Connecticut, confirms that the higher classes have greater opportunities to attend college than the poor. Let us consider that on intelligence quotient tests a definite score is deemed the minimum requisite intelligence quotient for successful college-level studies. (On one such examination, *The California Test of Mental Maturity,* a score of 110 is considered the cut-off point for college aptitude.) Hollingshead discovered that students from upper-middle or higher classes had twice as many chances to attend college as children of the lower two classes, even when they ranked below the minimum mental aptitude for college work and the lower class children ranked considerably above college level.

Another fascinating finding in Hollingshead's studies was that a greater percentage of children from the upper three classes receive higher grades (*A's* and *B's*) than children from the lower classes. A teacher in an American high school was surprised to discover the number of students in his school in remedial classes who were sons of lower-class fathers. Sociological studies have shown that in comprehensive high schools in which there is a three track system (college preparatory course, commercial course, vocational course) a greater proportion of the children from the upper three classes are in the college preparatory course. These studies have also established that the lower two classes contribute most to the numbers of high school dropouts. These facts may reflect favoritism on the part of teachers. If such favoritism exists, it is probably due to the fact that middle-class students share the values which teachers, themselves middle class, consider important. A more likely explanation is that families of students from the upper three classes exert greater pressures on their children to obtain good grades so that they may attend college. Students from the upper classes, therefore, are better motivated to do school work. Whatever the explanation, it is obvious that, like the pigs on George Orwell's *Animal Farm,* when it comes to educational opportunities, although all Americans are equal, some Americans are more equal than others!

SOCIAL MOBILITY

Open-class structures allow relatively free movement across class lines. Sociologists term this movement of individuals into new class positions, social mobility. Social-mobility studies distinguish between career mobility and generational mobility. Career mobility refers to ascents or descents in class position achieved by one individual in his occupational lifetime. The man who starts his work life as a simple bank clerk and ends his career as president of the bank has achieved career mobility. Generational-mobility studies compare the relative class positions of fathers and sons. Although the myth of the rags-to-riches rise in the social scale has provided novelists and screenwriters with abundant material for fiction, social stratification studies demonstrate that mobility jumps from the lower to the upper class are rare. Most social mobility involves a movement into an adjacent social class, for example, from lower-upper to lower-middle.

When we are born, we are assigned the same social status as our families. These families impart to us our motivation for life success. They teach us, informally, a style of life and manner of behavior consonant with our social class. In extensive studies of social class behavior in New Haven, Connecticut, sociologist August Hollingshead found that 83 percent of the marriages in New Haven were contracted between parties on the same social class level. Of the 17 percent of inter-class marriages, most took place across adjacent class lines i.e. between upper-middle and lower-middle marriage mates. Women are more likely to marry men above their class level than vice versa.

Even friendship patterns are established between people of the same class. In his study of Elmtown's youth, Hollingshead carefully analyzed the friendship cliques of the adolescents. Three in every five students associated most closely only with friends of their own social class. Two in every five students had close friends from an adjacent class. The chances were only one in twenty-five that two close friends came from social classes which were two or more levels removed from one another e.g. upper-middle and lower-lower. The student can test this fact in his own school. Begin by identifying the series of informal friendship cliques within your school. This can be done by charting sociograms, asking a representative sample of students to name their five closest friends. Then, determine the social class background of each member of the clique, using the criteria of father's occupation, income, educational attainment, place and type of residence. The student might be surprised to find that, even in informal friendship patterns in his own school, the fact of social stratification is manifest.

There seems good evidence to link together social class mobility and neurosis. Neurosis is a mental sickness which distorts a person's view of social reality. Neurotic people are often compulsive, insecure, fearful. The social climber often has neurotic fears that people will discover his lower-class origin or that his behavior will be inappropriate to the new social class into which he has risen. He lacks a sense of ease with his achieved social status. There is, further, some indication that social-class mobility and prejudice, especially against Negroes, are interconnected. Perhaps, it is because many social climbers are not totally secure in their own social status that they take out their own fearfulness in hostility toward a group which is predominantly lower-class in the American social structure.

Class mobility can be either upwards or downwards. Although we have a term, social climbing, to refer to upward social mobility, no term exists to describe descent in social class status. The effects of downward mobility on the behavior of individuals has not been as closely analyzed by sociologists as social climbing.

Behavior Differences and Social Class

An earlier chapter on culture system outlined the manner in which groups to which we belong affect the way we think, act, see reality. Since social classes represent subcultures of the larger American society, they also determine our ideas, norms of action, attitudes. It is impossible in an introductory chapter on social stratification to do more than sketch a few of these cultural differences which exist between the classes.

Class and Political Behavior

Sociologists have undertaken extensive studies in order to ascertain the effect of class membership on political ideology and voting habits. It is a visible truism that the majority of the upper three classes (upper-upper, lower-upper, upper-middle) register and vote Republican, while, on the other hand, the major portion of the lower three classes identify themselves with the Democratic party. The lower-middle class acts as a bellwether in electoral contests inasmuch as this class contains a large percentage of switch voters who alternate between the two parties in casting their ballots. Sociologist Richard Centers designed a research scale to measure conservative *vs* radical political identification. There are conservatives and radicals in both political parties. Centers interviewed 1100 Americans who formed a cross-section of our social structure, asking them a graded series of political questions. He defined a conservative voter as one who was satisfied with things as they are, opposed federal intervention in sensitive welfare areas such as education, health, race relations, and defended isolationism in foreign policy. Radical political thinking was identified as a deep concern for social change and strong support for government welfare programs. Each respondent was classified according to occupation. Table 1 summarizes Centers' findings:

TABLE 1		
	Conservative or ultra-conservative	Radical or ultra-radical
Large business	87%	2%
Professional	70%	11%
Small business	74%	8%
White collar	56%	16%
Skilled manual	39%	27%
Semiskilled manual	21%	49%
Unskilled manual	23%	38%

The general conclusion to be drawn from Centers' study is that the chances of a respondent being a political conservative sharply decrease in proportion as his social position is lower on the class scale. Two slight exceptions to this rule are evident in Table 1. The professional class includes a higher percentage of radicals than the small business class. This fact is explained by considering that the professional group includes in its number college professors and intellectuals who traditionally are more radical politically than other groups in society. The second exception is that semiskilled manual workers are more radical in their political thinking than unskilled manual laborers. This finds its explanation in the fact that semiskilled laborers are more likely to belong to organized unions which engage in active political indoctrination through trade journals, political programs *etc.*

One general reason why upper-middle class career men are more conservative politically than any other segment of the population is that they suffer the largest tax bite when high taxes are necessary to finance government welfare programs. Unlike the very wealthy upper-class, they cannot afford clever corporate lawyers who will help them to find loopholes in the tax laws.

Class and Child-Raising Patterns

The sociology department of the University of Chicago has conducted studies on comparative child-raising practices across class lines. In one such study, all students in the fifth through seventh grades of a comprehensive public elementary school in Chicago, which included students from each social class, kept a daily diary of their activities.

The diaries were very revealing of social class differences. Children from the lower-class had the greatest amount of freedom from parental control. Fewer pressures from home were brought to bear on lower class children to succeed academically. The lower-class child attended more movies and spent more hours away from home without adult chaperones than children from higher classes. On the other hand, middle and upper-class children spent more time taking special lessons in music or dance, reading books from the public library, engaging in adult supervised activities like the boy scouts or little league baseball. In another study undertaken at the same university, it was discovered that middle-class mothers introduce their children to sphincter control toilet training an average of three months earlier than lower class mothers. Upper and lower-class parents are permissive in matters of discipline. Middle-class adults have the strictest child-rearing norms, demanding of their children greater independence and self-control. One result is that middle-class youngsters tend to be more inhibited, less free to express themselves than lower-class children. One sociological study brought this point home when it grouped together children from the lower class and those from the middle class. After each child was given paper and paint, he was asked to fingerpaint a picture. The lower-class children had fewer inhibitions about dipping their fingers into messy paint. Finally, the classes also differ in the manner in which they punish rebellious children. Whereas a lower-class father is likely to use a stick to apply corporal punishment to his disobedient son, middle and upper-class parents tend to threaten to withold their love and affection unless the child behaves.

Class and Language Patterns

Not only do social classes raise their children differently, they also speak different languages to them. Sociologist E. Digby Baltzell, in conjunction with the University of Pennsylvania, studied Philadelphia's élite high society. He noted many interesting contrasts in vocabulary usage when comparing the upper-class with middle-class speech patterns. Table 2 represents a list of some of the differences.

TABLE 2	
Upper Classes	Middle Classes
wash	launder
sofa	davenport
long dress	formal gown
dinner jacket	tuxedo
rich	wealthy
hello	pleased to meet you
what	pardon
I feel sick	I feel ill

The middle classes are more pretentious in their choice of words. Because they feel secure in their class position, the upper classes can afford to be blunter in language, calling the proverbial spade a spade. Hence, for example, it is more likely that an upper class speaker will speak of *sweat,* while the middle class person, anxious to present a good impression, talks about *perspiration.* The following quote from Baltzell summarizes other differences in language usage according to class: "The upper classes *live* in a *house* . . . use the *toilet,* the *porch, library,* or *playroom.* The middle classes *reside* in a *home* . . . use the *lavatory,* the *veranda, den,* or *rumpus room.*'"

Games and Social Class

The national woman's magazine, *Mademoiselle,* polled its readers concerning their athletic hobbies. It found that college-educated women from the top three classes are seven times as likely to play golf or tennis than non-college readers. This latter group preferred bowling, fishing, boating. Similarly, sociological surveys indicated that bridge is a card game almost exclusively limited to the upper three classes. Bingo, on the other hand, draws its enthusiastic devotees from the lower three classes.

CONCLUSIONS

There are many other significant variations in behavior patterns among social classes. The lower-lower class has the highest incidence of alcoholism, suicide, divorce or desertion, felony convictions, juvenile delinquency, and high school dropouts. The middle classes are the most faithful church attenders. The upper classes maintain the closest relations with kinship relatives. Lower-class families are mother-centered because of the high percent of divorce or male desertion in these families.

A German proverb relates that at the dinner table social class distinctions manifest themselves. Exotic dishes are enjoyed by the upper classes. In the well known novel, *To Kill a Mockingbird,* authoress Harper Lee has Scout, the little heroine of the book, invite Walter Cunningham, a shoeless, lower-class rural farmboy, to dinner at her house. While Atticus, her upper-middle class lawyer father, entertains Walter, Scout looks aghast as the farm boy takes molasses and smears it all over his meat, potatoes, and vegetable. Scout, later reproved for her rude remarks about Walter's table manners and food preferences, is reminded that "that is their way."

In recent years advertising agencies have conducted fullscale social stratification surveys on the behavior differences by class in an attempt to identify the predominant class values of those people most likely to purchase a certain product. They have discovered that the beer drinkers of America are recruited mainly from the upper-lower and lower-middle males. Motivation research studies uncovered that this group likes to think of themselves as rugged outdoorsmen. Many beer ads, therefore, appeal to this image, using outdoor sports motifs for backgrounds to their ads.

The author of this chapter designed a project to help open the eyes of his students to behavior differences among classes. Each student chose three different business establishments catering, respectively, to upper, middle, and lower-class clientele. The type of establishment chosen for study varied from undertaker parlors to department stores. The students spent several hours at each store observing the customers, merchandise, sales techniques, and business personnel, noting down the differences they observed. The subsequent class reports they wrote revealed many variations in social class behavior which they discovered in their on-the-spot observations.

A psychologist at Harvard University interviewed all incoming Harvard freshmen over a period of several years. He discovered that students from the upper classes, most recruited from private prep schools, oriented their lives toward *the past,* content to continue in family tradition. Their fathers had been so successful that there was little chance that the sons would surpass them. On the other hand, middle class students tended to project their lives toward *the future,* strongly intent on achieving higher social status than their parents. The evidence points to the fact that the lower classes focus their attention on *the present,* eager to obtain immediate sense gratification and pleasure. The feel that the future presents little towards which to look forward.

Table 3 concludes this chapter with a summary of the most important values or attitudes which shape the thinking and behavior of the major portion of each social class. Like any generalization, this summary view admits of many exceptions.

TABLE 3

Most Important Values or Attitudes of Each Social Class

Upper classes:	gracious living, leisure, refinement in culture, the extended family
Upper-middle:	career success, visible status symbols of career success (home, automobile, official occupational titles, expensive education for children)
Lower-middle:	respectability, economic security
Upper-lower:	"getting by" financially, home comforts
Lower-lower:	apathetic resignation to the fate of being poor, immediate sense gratification

We began this chapter by noting that many judgments based on social class differences are superficial. You can best test this truth yourself by becoming acquainted with members of all social classes. As you draw your friends from every social strata, you will recognize that beneath the superficial cultural differences based on class, there lies the unity of essential humanity. The student's own life will be enriched by cultivating close friendships with people from every level of the social structure. By doing this he will also contribute towards making the American class system more open and democratic.

Major Concepts in Chapter 11

1. *Social stratification:* The ranking of people in a society by other members of the society into higher and lower social positions so as to produce a hierarchy of respect or prestige.
2. *Division of labor:* The process by which the various jobs to be done in a group are divided up, with certain people specializing in performing definite tasks.
3. *Social class:* The perpetuation of wealth, power, and special opportunities within families for generations.

4. *Index of status characteristics:* An index devised by sociologist W. Lloyd Warner to measure the relative social position of an individual. The scale includes six weighted items: occupation, source of income, amount of income, type of residence, residential location.

5. *The six American social classes:* (*a*) *Upper-upper* (*UU*), rich, established families; (*b*) *Lower-upper* (*LU*), the new rich; (*c*) *Upper-middle* (*UM*), professional class; (*d*) *Lower-middle* (*LM*), white-collar workers and skilled craftsmen; (*e*) *Upper-lower* (*UL*), semi-skilled laborers; and (*f*) *Lower-lower* (*LL*), families which make less than $4,000 annually.

6. *Social span:* The range of difference, measuring social distance between upper and lower classes in society.

7. *The shape of social structure:* The distribution of population in a class structure. Shape is determined by the percentage of population in each class. There are two basic model shapes: the pyramid and the diamond.

8. *Closed class system:* A class system which allows little opportunity for social advancement, with each individual inheriting and remaining in the same status as his parents.

9. *Open class system:* A class system which permits open access to all members of society to advance in social position.

10. *Social mobility:* Movement of individuals from one class position to another.

Review Questions

1. List the most important values which determine class status.
2. How do sociologists measure prestige?
3. Which is the most important variable in W. Lloyd Warner's *Index of Status Characteristics?* Explain.
4. Do members of different groups in America use the same criteria to evaluate social class?
5. What is the major distinguishing difference between the upper-upper class and the lower-upper class?
6. Explain the terms "diploma elite."
7. Why is the lower-middle class aptly called "the limited-success class"? Explain the terms "limited" and "success."
8. Explain the difference between the social span and social shape of a society? What does the concept of social shape tell us about social class differences in society?
9. What is a caste? In what types of societies do we find a caste system?

10. Explain the differences between the way Americans perceive their class system and the way Europeans see their own class system.
11. What effect does educational opportunity for all have on class structure? What effect does class structure have on educational opportunity?
12. What is the difference between career mobility and generational mobility?
13. What effect does social class membership have on voting patterns?
14. What are some differences between the social classes in the methods of rearing children?
15. Of what use are sociological studies of social class to the advertising agencies of the United States?

Discussion Questions

1. Discuss: "A classless society is an impossible ideal."
2. Discuss: "Any division of American society into a defined number of classes is arbitrary."
3. Discuss: "The social span between the higher and lower classes in the United States has decreased over the last one hundred years."
4. List facts supporting and denying the statement, "The American social class system is an open class system."
5. Discuss: "The Horatio Alger story of a rise from rags to riches is a myth."

Bibliography

Amory, Cleveland, *The Proper Bostonians* (New York: E. P. Dutton & Company, Inc., 1957).

Barber, Bernard, *Social Stratification* (New York: Harcourt, Brace and Company, 1957).

Bendix, Reinhard, and Seymour M. Lipset (eds.), *Class, Status and Power: A Reader in Social Stratification* (Glencoe, Ill.: The Free Press, 1953).

Centers, Richard, *The Psychology of Social Classes* (Princeton, N. J.: Princeton University Press, 1949).

Clinard, Marshall, *The Sociology of Deviant Behavior* (New York: Holt, Rinehart and Winston, 1957).

*Dahrendorf, Rolf, *Class and Class Conflict in Industrial Society* (Stanford: Stanford University Press, 1959).

*Dollard, John, *Caste and Class in a Southern Town,* 3rd ed. (Garden City, N. Y.: Doubleday & Company, 1957).

Feuer, Lewis (ed.), *Marx and Engels* (Garden City, N. Y.: Doubleday and Company, 1959).

Gordon, Milton M., *Social Class in American Society* (Durham, N. C.: Duke University Press, 1958).

* Also published in paperback edition.

Hatt, Paul K., "Occupation and Social Stratification," *American Journal of Sociology*, 55:533–543 (May, 1950).

Hodges, Harold M., Jr., *Social Stratification: Class in America* (Cambridge, Mass.: Schenkman Publishing Co., Inc., 1964).

*Hollingshead, August B., *Elmtown's Youth: The Impact of Social Classes on Adolescents* (New York: John Wiley & Sons, Inc., 1949).

Lerner, Max, *America as a Civilization: Life and Thought in the United States Today* (New York: John Wiley & Sons, Inc., 1949).

Lipset, Seymour M., and Rinehard Bendix, *Social Mobility in Industrial Society* (Berkeley: University of California Press, 1959).

*Marquand, John P., *Point of No Return* (Boston: Little, Brown, 1949).

*Mills, C. Wright, *The Power Elite* (New York: Oxford University Press, 1956).

*———— *White Collar: American Middle Classes* (New York: Oxford University Press, 1956).

*Vidich, Arthur J., and Joseph Bensman, *Small Town in Mass Society: Class, Power and Religion in a Rural Community* (Princeton, N. J.: Princeton University Press, 1958).

*Whyte, William F., *The Organization Man* (New York: Simon & Schuster, Inc., 1956).

Chapter 12

American Social Problems

THE SOCIOLOGIST LOOKS AT SOCIAL PROBLEMS

IN THE course of our everyday lives we confront problems. Some problems — difficult questions on a physics test — are academic. Others are purely personal: blemishes on the face, crooked teeth, a fight with parents over the use of the family car. Still other problems are social. What are some of the social problems in your life? How do you decide which problems are purely personal and which are social?

Personal vs. Social Problems

Almost every social problem affects some part of our population in a personal way. Sociological statistics do not highlight the personal dimensions of social problems. In the sociology of the family, statisticians indicate that widespread divorce is a social problem in contemporary America. They do not lay bare all the personal suffering felt by a child from a broken home. In the last analysis, behind the statistics about social ills such as alcoholism, juvenile delinquency, and poverty, there lies a whole series of personal tragedies, sadness, and failures. Novelists and film writers try to give us a glimpse of the personal dimension of social problems.

While it is true that every social problem involves personal problems, the opposite statement is not necessarily true: not every personal problem causes social concern. For example, an adolescent feels keen anxiety at his lack of physical coordination and awkwardness caused by rapid physical maturity. In a sense, however, society does not even care about his personal problem.

What, then, makes a problem *social?* To earn the adjective *social,* a problem must touch the lives of a sufficient number of people in the group so as to cause group concern. There are two main reasons why some problems are called social problems. Society, itself, defines which problems are important enough to divert its energies to their solution. No matter how important a problem may be objectively, if there is not widespread social concern about it, it is not a social problem in our sense of the term. In sum, those problems are social problems which society defines as important. A second reason for calling certain problems social is that they are the direct results of social structure or organization. Whenever, for instance, there is a breakdown of organization in society because of rapid social change or changing value systems, the problems which result are social, i.e., caused by society.

Society Defines Social Problems

We learn a great deal about the values of any society by asking, "Which problems does it consider important?" Thus, for example, Hindu India finds the large minority of Moslems in its midst a severe social problem. The Soviet Union views with alarm any religious practice within its borders. Are foreign immigrants a social problem? For some countries, yes. Yet, the United States during its colonial period and up through the nineteenth century welcomed foreign migrants. Do racial differences always cause social tension? In Brazil, distinctions of color go unnoticed. In the Union of South Africa men are judged by the shades of color which distinguish them. Very primitive tribes do not have problems of traffic congestion or water pollution. Their problem is sheer survival.

The definition of social problems does not depend entirely on culture. Science can help us define them by pinpointing objective social changes. Sociology, especially, does this. Even in the realm of science, social problems change their shape over a period of time.

If we were to consult any book on *demography* (the sociology of population problems) which was written before 1940, we would be surprised to discover a concern about underpopulation in the world with predictions of a rapid decline in world population. This concern seems puzzling to us who have read accounts about a population explosion. How do we explain the change in the population problem? Population experts writing before World War II predicted trends from statistics based on the depression years when birth-rates were declining. After the war, however, population statistics had to take into account the post-war baby boom as well as drastically reduced infant death rates in the underdeveloped countries. Cheap and efficient medical techniques, made available under the auspices of the United Nations, helped to lower the infant mortality rate. Today, because fewer babies die in newly developing nations, more youths live to a fertile age when they can beget and bring forth children — hence, the population explosion. Social scientists by their objective analysis of the social changes which have occurred since World War II have helped society to redefine its population problem.

Sometimes social problems are newly recognized without any objective social changes in society. This may happen when a perceptive author or journalist makes the community aware of problems which have long been in their midst. At the turn of this century, novelist Upton Sinclair wrote a scathing attack on the hazardous health and safety conditions in American factories in his exposé of Chicago meat packing plants, *The Jungle*. Sometimes, human interest stories on the front page of a newspaper lead to a redefinition of community problems of crime and delinquency. Again, we are very aware today of the social problem of poverty. This problem existed in 1956 and before. Why weren't we as concerned about it ten years ago as we are today? Why wasn't there a war on poverty then? It is not so much social conditions as men's perceptions of them which have changed. The book cover of Michael Harrington's *The Other American* — a book about poverty in America — claims that "It is clear that this book contributed to Johnson's War on Poverty." The student is cautioned not to attribute a new awareness of social problems entirely to one book or magazine article. Popular journalism is effective only because it brings to the surface problems which were already vaguely recognized as social problems.

Because so much seems to depend on chance, the way in which society defines some problems as important seems arbitrary and unscientific. Can this be avoided? Do you think social scientists should decide for the nation which social problems are worthy of concern?

What Standards Should Society Use to Determine Social Problems?

There are so many problems in a complex society like the United States that it is often hard to decide what standards should be used in determining the importance of social problems. Consider the following examples. There are approximately 8000 murders per year in the United States compared to 50,000 automobile deaths due to careless driving. Since the American people spend more money each year to combat crime than to improve traffic, we evidently think that murder is a greater social problem than reckless driving. Do you think that the American people are correct in this judgment? Again, more money is allotted per year for 600,000 mental patients and 50,000 drug addicts than for the cure of alcoholics who number in the millions. Should our government spend more for the prison population of America or for students in college? As you can see, these are difficult questions to answer. Implicit in these questions is another one: Who should define social problems?

Who Should Define Social Problems?

Americans have a great regard for the principle of majority rule. Majority decisions decide issues in the local PTA or in national elections. Should majority consensus define social problems? Are only those problems social which concern the major portion of the population? There are two basic reasons why the majority may not always be a good judge of social ills. First, the majority may not be keenly aware of the real social problems of minority groups within the country. Negro and Jewish groups have protested about the injustices which they have claimed to suffer without any majority concern.

Second, the majority is often apathetic. During the summer of 1954, sociologist Samuel Stouffer interviewed Americans, asking them the question, "Are there any problems you worry about or are concerned about, especially political or world problems?" During that summer, war was raging in French Indo-China; Senator Joseph McCarthy was conducting a controversial Senate investigation into Communist infiltration in government; the Soviet Union was threatening the peace in the middle East; a large portion of the world was hungry and ill-clothed. Nevertheless, 52 percent of those interview by Stouffer replied that there were no social problems "which worried them or they were concerned about."

Usually a small minority in any country, the intellectuals and religious leaders, have the task of convincing the majority that certain social problems demand solutions. The great religious seers of ancient Israel, almost alone, raised their prophetic voices in outrage against social abuses. Sometimes it took generations before they convinced the populace that there was any problem. Intellectuals, of course, are not always correct in their assessment of social problems. The power of intellectuals and religious leaders lies in their ability to pass moral judgment on the ills of society. The power of the majority lies in consensus. The majority population and a minority of intellectuals and religious leaders must cooperate in defining social problems.

Our answer to the question, "Who should define social problems?" becomes complicated by the fact that one group's problem is often another group's gain. Consider the example of medical-care insurance sponsored by the government. While the American Medical Association considers the existence of government medical programs one of its greatest problems, many citizens over sixty-five years of age see government medical insurance as a great source of security. Most of our pressing problems concern social processes which help some groups and hurt others. Although some workers find themselves permanently unemployed because of automation, business groups view automation as an economic boon. Sociologist Scott Greer treats of this aspect of social problems in an example about the problem of traffic congestion: "Traffic congestion may be defined as a problem by the driver of automobiles but be regarded as a distinct asset by the proprietors of stores along the routes of congestion."

It is very difficult to give a theoretical answer to the question, "Who should define social problems?" Our practical American solution has been to allow open access to government officials for all groups, lobbies, and interests. The government, by compromise and concession, must try to achieve the greatest justice for all.

How Does Society Cause Social Problems?

Widespread unemployment is certainly a social problem in the sense that many people in society are concerned about it. Is it also caused by society? It is necessary here to distinguish between unemployment as a purely personal problem and unemployment as a social problem. Some men do not work because of laziness or ill-health. Society does not cause their unemployment. For good reasons, looking to the humanitarian purposes of government, society may desire to extend welfare to those in need, even if society itself did not cause their need. In other words, there can be social solutions for purely personal problems. By contrast, there are other men who are unemployed in a depression because of tight credit control, risky management investment policies, automation, or an imbalance in trade. Although they are able-bodied and willing, these men cannot find work. Their unemployment is attributed to market forces in the economy over which they have no personal control. In such cases, their problems are social, not purely personal. The New Deal legislation of the 1930's as well as current legislation aimed at combating unemployment are examples of efforts to provide social solutions to these problems.

How does society cause social problems by its very structure? Let us consider an example from the chapter on social stratification in which we saw that our society is so organized as to encourage social mobility, i.e., changing of social class position. Social mobility demands physical mobility. In order to advance up the ladder of success, businessmen must often change companies, moving from town to town. This frequent physical mobility discourages rootedness in a given community; it undermines a sense of belonging. The breakdown of community in America is a serious social problem. Social mobility also complicates the problem of the aged in our society because aging parents cannot rely on their children to care for them in their old age. In fixed agrarian societies with only a minimum of social mobility, the problem of aging is not as acute as it is in America.

One of the most significant social trends in industrial societies is urbanism. Successful industrialization demands that greater proportions of the population live in impersonal, diversified cities in which judgment is passed on the individual's efficiency and work output. Yet, urbanism intensifies the problem of personal loneliness. Because of the variety of opinions tolerated in large cities, urbanism breaks down a consensus on norms concerning what is right and wrong. This may explain the higher rates of crime and suicide in urban areas when compared to rural America. Are urbanism and social mobility evil? By no means! They do, however, cause in their wake many social problems.

Another way in which society itself causes social problems should be considered here. In societies undergoing rapid social and institutional change, there occurs a conflict of loyalties toward different institutions. To take but one example, American women who are working wives are caught between divided loyalties toward their duties as wife and mother and their professional work role. This role conflict is certainly one source of tension which leads to divorce.

Social Problems Defined

Sociologist Robert A. Nisbet has defined social problems in the following way: "Social problems we have defined as breakdowns or deviations in social behavior involving a considerable number of people, which are of serious concern to many members of the society in which the aberrations occur."

The sociologist is on somewhat shaky ground when he treats of social problems. He loses scientific objectivity if he begins special pleading for one cause rather than another. Since one group's problem is another group's gain, he must be cautious in aligning himself too solidly with one faction rather than another. Again, since specific solutions to social problems are usually controversial political issues with a vast array of pro and con arguments, the sociologist is not equipped to prove any given solution to a social problem is the best one. His main task is to array the facts and opinions on both sides, weigh consequences to a given course of action, and promote objectivity in assessing social problems. In the following sections of this chapter we will limit ourselves to a consideration of three major problems in America: crime; juvenile delinquency; and race relations.

THE PROBLEM OF CRIME IN THE UNITED STATES

Crime Defined

In Chapter 2, norms, mores and folkways were discussed. Norms are uniform ways of acting which regularly recur and are expected to occur among the majority of people in a particular society. Sometimes, in a loose style of speaking, every infraction of a norm is called a crime. Strictly speaking, a crime is an infraction only of legal norms defined by the state law and punished by government. Every crime is an infraction of a norm. Not every violation of a norm is a crime. Crime is related only to a limited segment of norms, laws. Criminologist Donald R. Cressey has given a concise definition of criminal law: "Criminal law is defined conventionally as a body of specific rules about human conduct which apply uniformly to all members of the classes to which the rules refer and which are enforced by punishment administered by the state."

There are two main divisions of criminal law: misdemeanors and felonies. In common and statute law felonies are crimes which are in general graver and more serious in their nature and penal consequences than those called misdemeanors. Felonies usually incur penalties of over one year in prison and the loss of certain constitutional rights, e.g., the right to vote in elections, hold public office. Convicted felons in the United States are barred from obtaining civil service appointments and excused from jury duty. Only a personal pardon from the governor of the state in which the felony was committed can restore the rights of a convicted felon.

The Extent of Crime in the United States

It is very difficult to measure the extent of crime in the United States. Most statistical studies of crime are based on recorded crimes or all crimes known to the police, whether or not the culprit is found or convicted. These police records cannot tell us directly about the number of undetected crimes. Table 1 presents a schematic view,

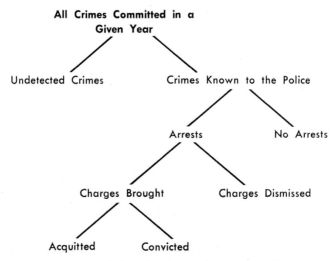

TABLE 1:   Crime in the United States — schematic view.

helpful in conceptualizing the extent of crime in the United States.

Table 1 indicates that the number of convictions for crimes is not a good index of the true crime rate. Many men are arrested but have the charges against them dismissed. Still others are brought to court and acquitted. Again, an increase in the number of arrests in a year does not necessarily reveal an increase in crime. It may be due to stricter police surveillance. Neither the yearly conviction nor the yearly arrest rates are good measures of the true crime rate.

What is the true crime rate in a given year? It is the number of all crimes committed, whether detected or not, per one hundred thousand population. The best index we have to work with for determining true crime rates is listed in Table 1 as "crimes known to the police." This index is the best available index of crimes committed because it is closest to the true crime rate. Even this index, however, presents some difficulties. If the true crime rate includes both undetected crimes and crimes known to the police, we can only use the latter as an index of *true crime* if we make the assumption that the recorded crime rate maintains a constant ratio over the years with the true crime rate. Many criminologists maintain that this assumption is scientifically unwarranted. Hence, in effect, when we talk about crime rates in the United States, we are dealing with recorded crime rates, not necessarily true crime rates. Since 1930 the United States Department of Justice has published *Uniform Crime Reports* in which information on arrests and crimes known to the police are contained.

Table 2, derived from *Uniform Crime Reports,* indicates the estimated crime rates and major crimes known to the police for a recent year.

TABLE 2:   Estimated Crime Rates and Major Crimes Known to the Police

Crime	Number of Crimes	Rate per 100,000 inhabitants
1. Murder and negligent manslaughter	8,599	4.7
2. Forcible rape	16,012	8.8
3. Robbery	91,659	50.1
4. Aggravated Assault	133,020	72.7
5. Burglary	852,506	466.0
6. Larceny, over $50	498,117	272.3
7. Auto theft	326,206	178.3

Some Statistical Variations in Crime Rate in the United States

Careful analysis of statistics concerning crime in the United States reveals that rates of crime vary according to age, sex of offender, race, nationality, size of community, and social class.

Age: The age range of most criminal offenders is 18 to 24. Rates for crime drop sharply for males and females over 40 years of age. They are minimal for the population over 60. Certain crimes are committed more frequently by the younger generation. The majority of convictions for automobile theft and burglary are for youths between the age of 20 to 29. Most convictions for gambling and embezzlement involve those over 30.

Sex: It may not be true elsewhere, but in the world of crime "it is a man's world." Males are arrested 10 times as often as females. Women are 15 times less likely to be sent to correctional or penal institutions. The ratio of male offenders over female crimes increases according to age. Thus, while for the age bracket 15 to 17 there are 13 male convictions for every female conviction, for the age range 60 to 64 the ratio becomes 25 to 1.

Race: The arrest rate for Negroes per 100,000 population is three times the rate of whites. Negroes are six times as likely to be sent to prison.

Nationality: Native born Americans have greater chances statistically to end up in prison than do foreign immigrants who have crime rates which are only half the rate of native whites. The crime rates for children of immigrants, while higher than rates for their parents, is still lower than the rate of the general American population.

The type of crime typically committed differs according to the national origin of immigrant groups. Japanese Americans have the lowest crime rates of all foreign groups. Italian immigrants have a higher incidence of homicide than other foreign migrants. The Irish, who are often popularly pictured as heavy drinkers, bear out this stereotype by having the highest rate of arrests for alcoholism. In the peak years of the Irish and German migrations to this country (1840–1890) the arrest rate of the Irish was four times greater than that of the Germans.

Size of Community: A general statistical rule is that the larger the city, the higher the incidence of crime, both in absolute numbers and in percentages. For example, in 1958 one study indicated that the rate of robberies known to the police was 14.1 robberies per 100,000 population for cities and towns of over 10,000. On the other hand, the rate soars to 112.4 robberies per 100,000 population for cities over 250,000.

Social class: The data concerning the relationship of social class and crime are very easy to sum up. Donald R. Cressey in his book, *Principles of Criminality*, has demonstrated that the poor contribute disproportionate numbers to our criminal population. From 60 to 75 per cent of the men and 90 per cent of the women in American prisons come from the lowest two socioeconomic classes.

The student needs to be cautious about equating statistical variations in crime rates with a theory of crime causation. From what we have said in the preceding paragraphs, the mathematical probabilities are very slight that a foreign born woman over 60 years of age residing in a small town and comparatively well-off financially will be convicted of a crime. Does this mean that it is impossible for her to commit a crime? If statistics indicate that Negroes, the poor, and citizens of large cities have greater crime rates than other members of the population, we should not conclude that members of these groups commit crime *because* they are Negro, poor, or residents of large cities. Many members of these groups — the overwhelming majority — are never convicted of crime. Our main reason for reviewing statistical variations in the crime rate is to gather clues for constructing a theory about crime causation. It is illogical science to turn a statistical correlation into a theory of crime causation. Yet, in our off-guard moments, we tend to do just that. How often have you heard people say that someone committed crime because he was a Puerto Rican or lived in the slums? One of the tasks of the social scientist is to point out the fallacy of this kind of thinking about social problems.

Theories of Crime Causation

Every theory which tries to explain the cause of crime must show why some people rather than others commit crime. There are three major kinds of theories about crime: biological, psychological, and sociological.

Biological theories of crime causation, very popular in the nineteenth century, maintain that all criminals exhibit similar biological traits. Crime is the result of a criminal nervous system or glandular defects. The Italian jurist, Cesare Lombroso, who first espoused the biological theory of crime, held that every criminal had a "long lower jaw, flattened nose, sparse beard, low sensitivity to pain." While the biological explanation of criminal behavior seems ridiculous to us today, it was very popular in the nineteenth and early part of the twentieth century. Even today it is not completely dead. Psychologist William H. Sheldon maintains that criminals all have similar body builds and bone structures. A popular novel and movie in the 1950's, *The Bad Seed,* had a young heroine who was a hopeless homicidal character because of the "bad seed" which she had inherited through her mother. No one has yet been able to demonstrate that special nervous systems, body builds, or glandular structures determine criminal traits. Even if William Sheldon could prove that criminals have typical body-builds (he has not done so to everyone's satisfaction), he would have to show that this fact is more than a mere statistical correlation. He would have to demonstrate that a certain type of body build *causes* crime.

Another popular explanation of crime uses psychological theories. Until the 1930's many held that criminals were feeble minded or had low intelligence quotient scores. There is no evidence that criminals — at least those who are incarcerated — have noticeably low I.Q.'s.

Some psychologists maintain that all criminals are mentally sick persons who use their criminal behavior to solve emotional problems. For example, these men argue, criminals secretly punish their fathers by engaging in crime. Or, again, they use crime to relieve themselves of anxiety or guilt feelings. While there is ample evidence that some criminals are mentally ill, there is not sufficient indication that all of them are. Many criminals appear to be mature, rational men who have freely chosen crime as a way of life. At any rate, not every mentally ill person engages in crime. Some men with anxiety or guilt feelings choose other types of nondelinquent behavior to relieve their tension. Psychological theories of crime causation do not fully explain why some people commit crime while others do not.

There are several sociological theories of crime. We will limit our discussion here to two such theories. Edwin Sutherland, perhaps the most influential criminologist in America's history, propounded a theory of crime causation in his book, *Principles of Criminology.*

According to Sutherland, criminals learn patterns of crime just as they learn lawful patterns of behavior, *by association.* Against those who maintained that crime was biologically determined, Sutherland argued that no man is born a criminal. Sutherland had enough first-hand contact with convicted criminals to reject the theory that all criminals are mentally ill. His theory was called the theory of "differential association." People who belong to groups — whether organized groups, such as the *Mafia,* or informal groups of friends — which engage in criminal behavior, tend themselves, to become criminals if they are isolated from membership in groups which engage in lawful behavior. At first glance, the theory of differential association seems to be a variation of the old adage, "You can tell a man by the company he keeps." Let us consider the example of two young men who live in a slum in which crime is widespread. Both have some knowledge and contact with criminal behavior. According to Sutherland's theory, the young man who has *the greater proportion* of his associations with criminals will become a criminal himself. The other young man, even if exposed to delinquent behavior, will not become a criminal if *the greater proportion* of his associations occur in law-abiding groups. Violence in movies, television, or comic books does not cause crime. The principal part of the learning of criminal behavior takes place in intimate personal groups such as the family and friendship cliques.

Sutherland's theory obviously cannot explain all criminal behavior. In some respects it is a deterministic theory which denies or minimizes freedom of the will by asserting that association in groups, not man's free choice, causes crime. Nevertheless, there are certain truths connected with the theory of differential association. Most criminologists agree that crime is learned in intimate personal groups. As a result, many criminologists question the wisdom of our present prison system of reform for criminals because they feel that prisons only intensify differential association. Whom, after all, they reason, do prisoners associate with, if not other convicted criminals? It has long been a truism among criminologists that institutions of correction, set up for the purpose of reforming criminals, are sometimes breeding houses of crime. Some of the most ingenious crimes have been planned in prison. On the other hand, many released prisoners are never again convicted of a major crime. It is difficult to know for certain whether the fear of prison served as a deterrent for these men from committing further crime. At any rate, no criminologist has yet convinced the American public that there is an efficient substitute for our prison system.

The distinguished sociologist, Robert K. Merton, sees the root of criminal behavior in a conflict between American cultural values of success and blocked access to legitimate means of achieving success. In American culture the value system places great emphasis on material success. Only those who can prove their success by conspicuous, expensive status symbols achieve top positions in the status hierarchy. This cultural goal of success is taught, in subtle ways, to every American boy. The legitimate way to success, of course, is through ambition, hard work, and personal initiative. "Become a success at all costs, but only use lawful means," Americans are told. On the other hand, argues Merton, those who live in the culture of poverty experience frustration in trying to achieve material success. Despite ambition, hard work, and personal initiative, they are unable to overcome the social handicaps of poverty. As a result, while they continue to endorse the *goal* of success, they reject the normative *means* to attain the goal. They expect to achieve material success by engaging in criminal behavior, e.g., stealing, peddling dope, or gambling. Merton's theory, like Sutherland's, although it contains a half-truth, does not fully explain why some people commit crime and others do not. For, not all of those who belong to the culture of poverty engage in criminal behavior. Some simply reject the American goal of material success. Others spend their entire lives in hard work. Only a few turn to crime.

The Cure for Crime

Because no one theory of crime causation gives an adequate explanation of crime, it is difficult to know how to reform criminals or prevent crime. The basic flaw in all three types of theory of crime causation (biological, psychological, and sociological) is that they deny or minimize human freedom. They are deterministic.

There are three major approaches to curing crime. Some hold that the best cure for crime is strict criminal codes, rigidly enforced by police departments and the courts. They reason that severe sentences in prison deter the criminal from further crime. Again, the certain knowledge that a committed crime, if detected, will lead to punitive measures, is seen as a deterrent from the very commission of an initial crime. The effectiveness of this approach to curing crime — the approach most favored by ordinary citizens when they discuss crime prevention — is difficult to assess. We can never be certain just how many people have kept the law from motives of fear of arrest and imprisonment. Common sense would indicate that at least some citizens are included in this category. On the other hand, strict penal codes or fear of punishment does not deter all men from criminal behavior. Even in the strictest police states some men do not obey all laws. The fact that paroled prisoners often are sent back to prison is evidence that imprisonment is not a sure cure for all crime. Probably a persuasive case can be made that swift completion of court trials and definite prescribed sentences for all similar crimes would increase the deterrent effect of strict criminal codes. On the other hand, the often drawn-out court trials and flexible punishments for similar crimes may be the price we have to pay for a democratic system of enforcing justice which tries to be fair in weighing all motives for a committed crime as well as being certain of the guilt of a man on trial before convicting him of crime.

Those who accept the psychological explanation of crime try to use methods of counseling and psychiatry to reform the criminal. They see the cure of crime as a personal problem to be solved by individual therapy. Sociologists tend to view crime as a social problem. They urge that society try to change the associations and social relations of the criminal. According to this approach, crime will be prevented if the greatest proportion of a man's contacts are with non-criminals or if the avenue to material success is not blocked. The cure for convicted criminals in this approach is not prison but supervised paroles in halfway houses by which the criminal can be introduced into lawful associations in his work life and personal relationships.

None of these approaches to the prevention or cure of crime has achieved complete success. A combination of all three approaches seems to be necessary. For those who hold that men have free wills, it may well be that no sure cure for crime is possible.

JUVENILE DELINQUENCY

In many ways theories concerning the cause and prevention of juvenile delinquency parallel theories about crime. Juvenile delinquents are simply young criminals. In most states, a juvenile delinquent is a youth under 18 years old who has committed the kind of crime which, were he an adult, would merit him a fine or imprisonment. On the other hand, the statutes regulating juvenile delinquency in many states are very vague. A youth can be brought to court for actions which would not be crimes for an adult. In some states, minors are labeled juvenile delinquents for such crimes as "truancy," "growing up in idleness," "living without visible means of support."

Is Juvenile Delinquency on the Increase?

We have the same problem concerning the extent of juvenile delinquency as we do with crime. We have no way of calculating the amount of juvenile delinquency which goes on unapprehended or unrecorded. One sociologist has claimed that perhaps every high school student has engaged in some activity during his teenage years which could have resulted in his arrest for juvenile delinquency. Do you think that this estimate is an exaggeration? If we look at juvenile delinquency in terms of reported cases which have come to the courts, then juvenile delinquency is on the increase in the United States. Albert K. Cohen in *Delinquent Boys,* stated that "roughly two percent of all children aged 10 to 17 were involved in court cases each year after 1954 in contrast to 1 per cent in the pre-World War II period."

Statistical Variation in Delinquency Rates

Juvenile delinquency rates in this country vary according to age, sex, and social class. The median age for court referrals in juvenile delinquency cases is 15.8 years. For boys the age is 16.1 years; for girls, 15.6. There are five boys referred to court for juvenile delinquency for every girl. In 1900 the ratio was 50 to 1. These figures are somewhat misleading inasmuch as many girl delinquents have their cases handled by private agencies instead of through court trial. Delinquency, just as crime, is linked statistically with poverty and other social dysfunctions. Albert Cohen has stated this fact clearly when he says that "rates of juvenile delinquency and recidivism (repeat crimes) are highest in inner-city areas characterized by physical deterioration and the concentration of other social problems such as poverty, suicide, adult crime, and mental illness." Sociologists from the University of Chicago have given an impressive indication of the relation of delinquency with poverty. They plotted out areas of the city of Chicago which had high delinquency rates. These areas, labeled "delinquency areas," were studied over a period of several years. During these years some of the areas changed as regards ethnic or racial com-

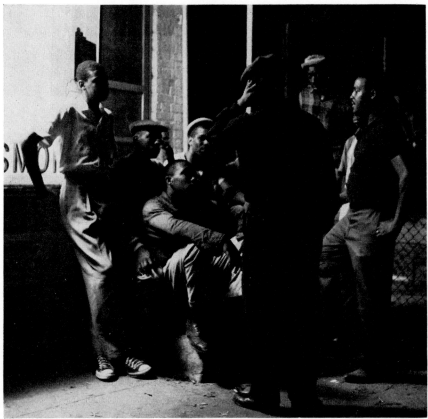

Children's Bureau

Delinquency is linked statistically to poverty and other social dysfunctions.

position. A Polish slum, in turns, was occupied by "Hillbillies" (rural migrants), Puerto Ricans, and Negroes. No matter what its racial or ethnic composition, the poorest sections of the inner city always had the highest delinquency rates.

Theories of Causation

The theories of delinquent causation parallel those of crime. Most Americans see juvenile delinquency as minor-league crime. Albert Cohen has stressed the fact that when juvenile delinquents belong to gangs (not just isolated individuals) they tend to form *contracultures*. Because they come from poor homes, the members of juvenile gangs adopt behavior which is just the opposite of middle-class norms. Virtue consists in defying middle-class morality, orderliness, amenability to adult supervision and guidance, respect for property, polite speech and manners. Delinquents spurn middle-class norms for their new way of life based on violence and criminal behavior supported by group delinquent behavior.

There are really four different types or forms of delinquency. These forms do not relate to one another, except inasmuch as they involve breaking the law. *Apprentice-criminal delinquency* refers to delinquent behavior which is associated directly with adult crime. Groups of teenagers get their apprentice-training by cooperating with adult syndicates for gambling, prostitution, or burglary. Often, these youths know adult criminals personally. In some cases, they hero worship some successful criminal just as other youths admire a great athlete or entertainer. In time, when their apprenticeship is finished, the delinquent criminal graduates into the world of adult crime. Apprentice-criminal delinquency can be a rational, lucrative type of behavior. Edwin Sutherland's theory of differential association helps to explain apprentice-criminal delinquency.

Violence delinquency refers to the destructive, senseless, violent behavior engaged in by juvenile gangs. Since it is unlikely that an entire gang is psychologically disturbed, violence delinquency probably results from frustration with middle-class norms of success. The gangs reflect American values of success and engage in contra-cultural behavior by destroying property. Albert Cohen's theory best fits this type of delinquency.

The third type of delinquency can be called *retreatist delinquency*. This term refers to delinquent behavior which leads young people to retreat from the harsh facts of reality by resorting to drug addiction, alcohol, or promiscuous sexual behavior as a way of escape. Retreatist delinquency probably is rooted in psychological causes. It is a symptom of mental illness.

The fourth type of delinquency, *middle-class delinquency,* is very difficult to analyze. We all know cases of young men from substantial homes who engage in delinquent behavior. Most of their friends are law abiding. Their avenue to success is not blocked by the handicaps of poverty. They use delinquent behavior as rebellion against parental values or as an escape from boredom. Sometimes the cause of middle-class delinquency is psychological. No one of the theories of juvenile delinquency, however, adequately explains middle-class delinquency.

Controlling Juvenile Delinquency

It is probably a mistake to over-emphasize either psychological

St. Charles Boys Home

This home for delinquent boys provides a friendly atmosphere conducive to their rehabilitation.

or sociological methods of curing juvenile delinquency. Imprisonment or retention of delinquents in custody has achieved only 50 percent success in preventing future lapses into crime. Some psychologists have achieved notable success in counseling delinquents, especially if the youth takes part in a group counseling session with his parents and the psychologist. Yet, since delinquency is not always a purely personal problem, individual counseling methods do not achieve 100 percent success. Those who rely on sociological theories of causation have urged the creation of area projects which will provide delinquent areas with adequate recreation facilities, job opportunities, and incentives for poverty-stricken youth. A few social workers have tried working directly with juvenile gangs as adult moderators and go-betweens. Their job is difficult because they must avoid the two perils of "policing" the gang (this would lose for them the confidence of the gang); and of moderating a minor-league crime syndicate (this would weaken the confidence of the law-abiding community in their work). Just as with crime, the perfect prevention and cure of juvenile delinquency has yet to be discovered.

RACE RELATIONS IN THE UNITED STATES

The final social problem we will consider in this chapter is the problem of race relations in the United States. This section of the chapter is entitled "Race Relations in the United States" to underscore the fact that we are dealing neither with the "Negro problem" nor with "the white man's problem" but with the social problem of relations between Negroes and whites.

Although the term, race-relations, immediately suggests Negrowhite relations, Negroes are only one of several racial minorities listed by the United States Census Bureau. Others include Filipinos, Chinese, Japanese, American Indian, Mexican American, Puerto Rican, and Korean. In terms of sheer numbers, however, the dominant race relations problem in the United States concerns the relation of Negroes and whites. There are approximately twenty million Negro Americans, representing over 10 percent of the total United States population.

Processes in Intergroup Relations

Competition: When two or more groups in society come in contact, various group processes emerge which determine relations between the groups. The groups may engage in *competition.* Competition is a process by which groups undertake mutually opposed efforts to secure the same scarce objectives. CBS, NBC, and ABC, for example, are in competition to secure the limited television audience. To some extent, Negroes and whites are in competition for a limited number of jobs and scarce status rewards. Competition, however, does not really characterize Negro-white relations, since the social process of competition demands a degree of equality between the two groups involved. White Americans, by and large, enjoy unequal advantages of access to educational and employment opportunities when compared with Negro Americans. As we shall see, this unequal advantage of white Americans is not simply due to prejudice or unjust discrimination. It is the product of the process of social stratification in America. By reason of their social-class positions, white Americans enjoy, as a statistical group, special advantages of access to political, economic, and social opportunities.

Conflict: When the clash of interests between groups is so intense that these groups do not merely compete for the same scarce goals but seek to injure or destroy each other, there occurs the group process of *conflict.* In some American communities, conflict characterizes Negro-white relations. While conflict minimizes cohesion between the two groups in conflict, it tends to increase the internal solidarity of these groups. Negroes, for example, identify more intensely with their racial group in those communities in which Negroes and whites are in open conflict.

Accommodation: It is difficult for two groups to remain in conflict over a long period of time. Eventually, the groups reach a stage of *accommodation.* Thus, for instance, after a bitter strike, union and management reach a working agreement. They may continue to be hostile to one another, however, and to be prepared to engage in open conflict at a later date The process of accommodation is the mutual adjustment of groups which retain their own interests and identity. By accommodation, conflicts between two groups are reduced so that at least a minimum of cooperation is achieved. Accommodation between conflicting groups can be either temporary or stable. After a bitter race riot, for example, at least some temporary accommodation must be achieved. In the summer of 1965 there occurred a prolonged and destructive riot in the Watts area of Los Angeles. The National Guard was called in to quell the riot. Discussions took place between leaders of the Negro community in Watts and the political and business leaders of the white community of Los Angeles. Accommodation was reached when spokesmen for the Negro community were allowed a channel for voicing their grievances against the municipal government.

Cooperation and assimilation: When two groups agree upon joint action there occurs the process of *cooperation.* Cooperation between groups admits of degrees. Minimal cooperation is the same as accommodation. When cooperation between two groups becomes so intense that the identity of the groups is fused, we encounter the process of *assimilation.* The barriers to communication between the groups are broken down. Most of the immigrant groups which came to the United States experienced a cycle in their relation to the dominant majority which began with conflict, moved to accommodation, grew to cooperation, and finally arrived at assimilation. The general rule has been that it takes three generations before an immigrant group becomes assimilated into the dominant American culture.

Superordination and subordination: The relationship between two groups may be based on equality. Thus, for instance, the Irish and German immigrant groups which migrated to the United States about the same time, enjoyed relative equality in their competition for successful assimilation into American culture. When one group, however, enjoys economic, political, or numerical dominance in the community, while another group is a numerical minority, lacking equal access to political or economic control, the relationship between the two groups is characterized by *superordination* and *subordination*. The dominant group has more favorable access to status, political control, and economic and educational opportunities. The minority group is subordinate to the wishes and values of the dominant group.

Intergroup Processes in Negro-White Relations

Which of these group processes characterize Negro-white relations in the United States? There are very few American communities in which Negroes are the dominant group. Even when they enjoy numerical superiority, they rarely have political or economic control of their community. Negroes, as a group, are not fully assimilated into American society. They retain a separate identity based on race. A few light-skinned Negroes "pass" into white society. They, as well as their families, become assimilated. Despite newspaper accounts of racial tensions in the United States, there is evidence that in most American communities there is accommodation and cooperation between Negro and white communities. Certain men serve as liaison men between the two communities. As the historic march on Selma, Alabama, in 1965 made clear, some Negro and white groups cooperated in attempting to further the interests of American Negroes. In certain American cities — not limited to the Southern section of the United States but, perhaps, mainly centered there — there is open or concealed conflict between Negroes and whites. The student should realize that it is impossible to give a picture of Negro-white relations which would be equally valid for all communities in the United States. Relations vary by region and from community to community within the same region. They vary over a span of time. An intense study of race relations in many United States cities is needed to determine whether at a given time conflict, cooperation, or temporary accommodation is most characteristic of Negro-white relations.

In order to understand the processes involved in Negro-white relations in the United States, it will be helpful to get some idea of the geographic, occupational, and educational distribution of Negroes in the United States.

Distribution of Negroes in the United States

Tables 3, 4, and 5 present data concerning the distribution of Negroes by geographical area and occupational rank. Table 4, based on data gathered from the U. S. census, over-represents the number of Negroes in the South. Since the last decennial census in 1960 many Negroes have migrated from Southern states into cities in the North or Far West.

TABLE 3		
Year	Percentage of Negroes in South	Percentage of Negroes in rural areas
1900	90	75
1950	65	38
1960	60	34

As Table 3 makes clear there has been a dramatic shift of the Negro population since the turn of the century away from the rural South.

% Distribution of Negro Population by Geographical Area

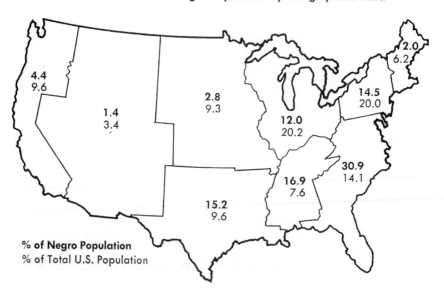

% of Negro Population
% of Total U.S. Population

TABLE 4:   Distribution of Negro Population by Geographical Area

Geographic area	Percentage of Negroes of total population of geographic area	Percentage of total U. S. population living in geographic area
New England	2.0	6.2
Middle Atlantic	14.5	20.0
East N. Central	12.0	20.2
West N. Central	2.8	9.3
South Atlantic	30.9	14.1
East S. Central	16.9	7.6
West S. Central	15.2	9.6
Mountain	1.4	3.4
Pacific	4.4	9.6

If Negroes were perfectly distributed geographically throughout the United States the percentages in the column in the far right
of Table 4 would coincide with the figures in the middle column.
As Table 4 illustrates, the American Negro population still resides
largely in the South, though this distribution is rapidly changing.

TABLE 5:   Distribution of Negroes by Type of Occupation

(Based on 1960 Department of Labor Statistics)

Type of occupation	Percentage of Negroes in occupation	Percentage of Whites in occupation
Professional, technical and kindred	4.0	11.3
Managers, officials, proprietors	2.7	14.6
Highly skilled industrial workers	9.0	20.0
Semiskilled mass production	48.0	25.3

Distribution of Negroes by Type of Occupation

(Based on 1960 Department of Labor Statistics)

Type of Occupation

1. Professional, technical and kindred — 4 / 11.3   Percentage of Negroes
2. Managers, officials, proprietors — 2.7 / 14.6   Percentage of Whites
3. Highly skilled industrial workers — 9 / 20.0
4. Semi-skilled mass production — 48 / 25.3

We can conclude from the data presented in Table 5 that fewer Negroes than whites belong to the middle or upper classes. The Negro population comprises a large segment of the culture of poverty. In New York City, for example, 50 percent of the Negro families earn less than $4,000 a year compared to 20 percent of the white families who earn less than that amount. Again, Negroes in New York City represent less than 12 percent of the population but account for 40 percent of all families on public assistance. United States Department of Labor statistics consistently show that unemployment rates for Negroes are twice those of whites. In 1964 average non-white income was 56 percent the amount of average white income. This percentage has not changed substantially during the last decade. Table 6 presents data on comparative education standards of whites and nonwhites in the United States.

TABLE 6.   Comparative Education Standards of Whites and Nonwhites in U. S.

(Compiled from Census of the Population: 1960)

Education Level	White	Nonwhite
College graduate	17.4%	7.9%
High school graduate	45.1%	32.5%
5–8 years completed	30.9%	36.2%
4 years or less	6.7%	23.4%

Since relations between two groups in a society are affected by the history of their dealings with one another, it will be instructive to consider the history of Negro-white relations in the United States.

Brief-History of Negro-White Relations in the United States

The first Negro slaves were imported to this country in the first decades of the 1600's. Only the American Indian and the descendents of *The Mayflower* have been in America as long as the Negro. In 1661 the Virginia Parliament passed a law authorizing lifetime slavery. During the eighteenth century many Americans agitated for the abolition of slave trading. Finally, in the early years of the nineteenth-century congress outlawed further importation of slaves.

The Negro slaves were concentrated in the agrarian South where the harvesting of "King Cotton" demanded cheap hand labor. From 1810 until the beginning of the Civil War bitter disputes raged between Northern "free" states and Southern slave states, briefly as-

The Negro slaves provided the cheap labor needed for harvesting cotton.

Department of Labor

suaged by the Missouri compromise. It is difficult to assess what life for the slaves was like in the pre-Civil War South. Harriet Beecher Stowe in her famous polemical novel, *Uncle Tom's Cabin,* portrayed the Southern slave owner as a ruthless, cruel tyrant who misused his slaves for personal gain. Without defending slavery as a social institution, we must, however, be cautious in picturing all Southern plantation owners as tyrannical Simon Legrees. There is evidence that many Southern slave owners had a warm, if paternalistic, feeling for their slaves. Harriet Beecher Stowe's *Uncle Tom's Cabin* needs to be balanced by the picture of kind slave owners in the antebellum South presented by Margaret Mitchell in her novel, *Gone With the Wind.* After the Civil War, many Negroes chose to remain with their former slave owners.

In 1861 the Civil War began. Like any complex historical event, this war was caused by a variety of factors. The rivalry between the northern and southern states was not merely a humanitarian battle over the question of slavery. It was rooted in regional economic and political conflicts which had a century-long past. When the southern states seceded from the union, President Lincoln refrained from freeing the slaves because several border states which remained in the Union such as Maryland and Missouri allowed slavery. Finally, he issued in 1863 *The Emancipation Proclamation,* freeing the slaves in the Confederate states. This historic document was probably motivated both by humanitarian motives and by the concrete political motive of introducing internal division into the ranks of Lincoln's southern enemies. After the Civil war, Congress enacted the Thirteenth, Fourteenth, and Fifteenth Amendments to the Constitution, which abolished slavery, guaranteed the Negro full legal citizenship, equal protection under the law, and protected his right to vote.

Immediately following the Civil War, unscrupulous northern politicians, known to history as "carpetbaggers," invaded the South. Many of these politicians played on the ignorance and fears of the former slaves. For a time after the Civil War some Negroes held prominent public offices in the South, placed in these offices by northern politicians. Much of the natural resentment felt by defeated southerners was displaced in the direction of these Negro office holders who were seen as tools of the northern politicians. Again, some Negroes after the war abused their new-won freedom in destructive activity. In some ways, despite legal and political gains by southern Negroes, Negro-white relations were more tense during the period of Reconstruction than they were before the Civil War.

After the southern states regained political control over their internal affairs, Negro-white relations in the South returned to a predominant relation of superordination and subordination. Negroes were subordinate to whites in status and opportunity. Grandfather's clauses, all white primaries, segregation of public facilities and separate schools — all were attempts to maintain a subordinate position for the Negro in the South. Because of differential cultural, educational, and economic backgrounds, there was an intense social distance between Negroes and whites. The principle of equal protection under the laws, guaranteed by the Fourteenth Amendment, was tested in the Supreme Court of the United States in the famous Plessy *vs* Ferguson case of 1896 in which the plaintiff disputed the constitutionality of segregated schools. The Supreme Court ruled that schools could be separate so long as facilities were equal.

For most of the period between the end of the Civil War and the turn of the century, Negroes, for whatever reason, accepted their socially defined subordinate position. They were not militant for integration. Booker T. Washington, famed Negro leader in the nineteenth century, espoused the principle of the separation of the races. By the turn of the century, Negroes began to migrate from rural areas to cities. They also began to leave the South. In 1901, the first Negro newspaper, *The Boston Guardian,* went to press. Race riots in Springfield, Illinois, in 1909 led to the formation of *The National Association for the Advancement of Colored People.* For over fifty years the NAACP has championed the cause of advancing the Negro race, especially by challenging the constitutionality of laws which they considered discriminatory. Most of the NAACP's battles have been fought in the law courts of America. With the emergence of a Negro press and the formation of the NAACP, Negroes in America began to challenge the traditional subordinate relation of the Negro. They were joined in this challenge by many whites.

During World War I, many Negroes left the South to take better paying jobs in the industrial North. Their northward migration was not always welcome, especially by industrial workers who felt that Negroes were anti-union replacements for their jobs. In a few cases, Negroes were imported by northern industrial firms to act as strike breaking "scabs," anti-union employees in an industrial plant. After World War I, bloody race riots took place in Detroit and East St. Louis, Illinois, between white and Negro industrial workers. When the depression hit this country in the late 1920's, Negroes were unemployed in large number. Many Negroes, rallying around a popular demogogue, Marcus Garvey, agitated for a separate state of the union for Negroes. Still others joined a "Back to Africa" movement. The majority of American Negroes, however, did not want to go back to Africa nor to set up a separate state. They wanted legal equality and social integration of the races.

A major step toward obtaining Negro equality took place during World War II when President Franklin Roosevelt set up a Fair Employment Practice Commission to regulate federal government hiring practices. After World War II a quiet Negro revolution began. In 1946 New York State passed the first state Fair Employment Practices law. Soon, other states followed the example. Before the Korean War began, President Truman integrated the armed forces of the United States.

The Supreme Court decision in the Plessy *vs* Ferguson case came under attack in the early 1950's. In 1950 the court ruled in the Sweat *vs* Painter decision that the state of Texas was required to admit a Negro to the Texas University Law School. About the same time, Oklahoma was required to allow a Negro to attend its state university. Finally, in 1954 in the Brown *vs* State of Kansas decision, the court ruled that segregated primary and secondary schools could never be "equal." Invoking the "equal protection under the laws" clause of the Fourteenth Amendment to the U. S. Constitution, the court overruled segregation in public education.

Throughout the 1950's and 1960's Negro groups became more

Ebony Magazine

Negroes are using sit-ins, freedom marches, and economic boycotts to register their desire for legal equality and social integration.

militant. They used sit-ins, freedom rides, economic boycotts, and protest marches. In 1964 the United States Congress, following the lead of the Supreme Court, outlawed segregation in public accommodations (restaurants, hotels, swimming pools open to the public). In 1965 it passed the historical voting rights legislation which provided federal intervention in those states where Negroes were hindered from registering to vote. Joining the NAACP in leadership in the Negro revolution were newer, more militant Negro groups such as the Congress of Racial Equality (CORE) and the *Student Nonviolent Coordinating Committee* (SNCC).

In the latter part of the 1960's there are probably as many shades of opinion and attitude in the Negro community concerning perceived and desired Negro-white relations as there are in the white community. Some Negroes, notably the Black Muslim group, support a policy of social separation of the races. Others accept the Negro-white relations which exist in their communities. Still others are militant for integration on all levels of social life.

The history of Negro-white relations in the United States reveals social distance between the races and patterns of separate association in marriage, friendship groupings, occupation, education, residential location, and religion. The trend toward social distance and patterns of separate association is a fact. Its explanation is not simple. Rhetoric and emotional appeals might explain this trend either by the "inferiority" of Negroes or by the "bigotry" of the white majority. Neither explanation does justice to the facts. Before exploring the fact of social distance and patterns of separate association between

Negroes and whites, it will be necessary to define carefully the vocabulary used to describe relations between the races.

The Vocabulary of Negro-White Relations

Segregation: The first key term in the vocabulary of social relations between Negroes and whites is the term, *segregation.* Segregation is an emotion-laden word which can have several meanings. In the sense in which we will define it, segregation refers to a policy or norm of behavior which excludes or isolates a particular group of people from joint participation in social life. Segregation as a norm is enforced either by law or custom. Segregation can be total —as, for example, the enforced segregation of America's prison population — or partial. Full or total segregation is not possible if a minority group is large enough, in physical proximity and contact with the dominant population. There was never total segregation of Negroes and whites in the United States. As a policy of action enforced by the dominant group in social relationships, segregation is designed to create and maintain social distance and patterns of superordination and subordination between the dominant group and the minority.

In a loose sense of the term, segregation may be used to refer to patterns of separate association between two groups. Hence, for example, many immigrant groups which came to this country lived in self-imposed separate residential units. They belonged to separate voluntary associations. Again, Protestant and Catholic groups in this country are segregated on Sundays in the sense that they worship in separate churches. Members of various social classes are segregated inasmuch as they tend to marry and choose friends within their class level. Residential and voluntary association, as a rule, does not cut across class levels. Self-imposed separate patterns of association based on personal choice or economic class factors do not constitute segregation in the strict sense. Since segregation has become a value-laden word, the student should restrict his use of the term to refer to policies or norms of behavior, enforced by law or custom, which *deliberately* exclude a group from joint participation in social life as a means of fostering relations of superordination and subordination between two groups. He should use a term such as "patterns of separate association" to refer to the isolation of a group because of self-choice or socioeconomic factors where there is no deliberate policy of exclusion toward that group. Why is this distinction important? We sometimes meet in the rhetoric of race relations claims of segregation where there is no deliberate policy of

Negro exclusion. For example, the religious group in America with the smallest number of Negro adherents is the Jewish faith. This is obviously not a result of segregation.

A society such as the Union of South Africa which chooses a deliberate policy of racial segregation must pay a social price for its choice. Segregation involves a costly reduplication of facilities such as schools and hospitals. It minimizes communication between the dominant and subordinant group. It impairs the cohesion of society by lessening consensus on society values. It is wasteful of human talent inasmuch as many talented members of a minority group are excluded from certain occupations or government positions. Finally, it demands the expenditure of effort and manpower to maintain a pattern of subordination, especially when the minority group refuses to accept this pattern of relationship with the dominant group.

Integration: The correlative of segregation is *integration.* Integration refers to policies of action which permit minority groups and dominant groups — whites and Negroes — access to areas of community life on the basis of free and equal association. Integration can be total or partial. It can extend to education, occupation, or residential location. It can also include informal social relationships such as friendship groups. The cessation of deliberate segregation and policies of integration need not lead to patterns of equal association. For example, although many states have outlawed miscegenation marriage laws which forbid interracial marriage, the majority of marriages in these states continue to be between members of the same race. The stressed phrase in the definition of integration is "*access* to free and equal association." No barriers, legal or customary, are placed to equal association. There is no guarantee that policies of integration will eliminate patterns of separate association. Thus, many of America's exclusive private college preparatory schools have adopted deliberate policies of integration. Nevertheless, for financial, academic, or cultural reasons, few Negroes attend such schools. Some groups in America advocate what can be called planned or manipulated integration. They desire to go beyond the removal of barriers to equal association. They wish to plan deliberate ways of bringing about interracial association. Some Americans object to planned integration as a denial of constitutional freedoms. Others views it as a necessary step for achieving good race relations. The wisdom of planned integration as a public policy is a matter of debate which each citizen must decide for himself. The student should carefully discriminate between deliberate and planned interracial association and integration as a policy which permits *access* to all groups on a basis of free and equal association.

Communities which choose a policy of integration, especially after a prolonged history of segregation patterns, must also pay a social price for their choice. The policy of integration in such cases introduces strains and instabilities into customary racial relations. For a time, communication between the races may be reduced to explicit areas bearing on formal or legal race relations. An awareness of racial differences may be intensified. Those who support segregation as well as those who favor integration should be aware of the social price of each choice.

Discrimination: Another value-laden word in the vocabulary of race relations is *discrimination*. In its neutral sense, discrimination is a policy of preference and exclusion of members of one group as compared to members of another. When we discriminate we make a difference in our treatment of one person compared to the way we treat others. We favor some people. All of us practice discrimination in our everyday life. We choose some people as special friends and exclude others. Catholic parochial schools discriminate between prospective students who are members of the Catholic faith and those who are not. The Ancient Order of Hibernians discriminates between Americans of Irish descent and members of other ethnic groups. Do you think that discrimination is a natural process in social living? How would you distinguish between just and unjust discrimination?

When used as a value word in race relations, discrimination refers to unjust attitudes of preference and exclusion based on race. Every human has certain rights which accrue to him either from his basic humanity or from his constitutional rights due him as a citizen. Refusal to respect these rights because of race is unjust discrimination. Most Americans agree that racial factors are not a just basis for preferential treatment in public transactions such as buying and selling, and hiring and firing. What constitutes unjust discrimination in private social transactions is currently a matter of debate and discussion by social scientists and students of ethics.

An example of discrimination in race relations can be seen in the traditional southern etiquette of race relations. The following generalizations are derived from social science studies such as Bertram W. Doyle's, *The Etiquette of Race Relations in the South*. As generalizations, they have validity. The student is cautioned from concluding that all southern Negroes or whites accepted the traditional etiquette. Customary etiquette forbade hand shaking between whites and Negroes because this was a sign of equality. It was the white man's prerogative to initiate any interracial conversation. Whites never addressed Negroes as Mr. or Mrs. Instead, they used the first name or last name without any title. Sometimes, if the white man did not know the Negro's name, he used a term like "auntie," "boy," "nigger," or "sister," depending on the sex of the Negro whom he was addressing. When speaking, the white man expected attention and deference from the Negro. The Negro should look at the ground. Negroes were to address whites respectfully, using titles like "boss," "sir," "captain," or "Mister." In his play, *Blues for Mister Charlie,* Negro author James Baldwin recalls this etiquette of race relations. Mother Henry, one of the characters, is in court being cross-examined about the mysterious shooting of her grandson. When the prosecuting attorney addresses her as Mrs. Henry, she snaps back: "No white man never called my husband Mister neither, not as long as he lived. Ain't no white man never called me *Mrs.* Henry before today. I had to get a grandson killed for that."

Prejudice: Segregation, integration, and discrimination refer to actions or policies of action. In Chapter 2 we defined policies of action as norms. Prejudice is a matter of belief or attitude. It is a way of thinking which is accompanied by emotional overtones. Prejudice is irrational thinking. Whereas discrimination refers to outward behavior, prejudice involves the inner feelings of a man. Like discrimination, prejudice is a natural phenomenon in social living. Every man has certain prejudices which operate in his everyday life. To prefer the San Francisco Giants as a baseball team to the Los Angeles Dodgers is probably a matter of prejudice, not rational choice.

Racial prejudice is a fact of social existence. It may or may not lead to unjust discrimination. A man can unjustly discriminate on the basis of race without being prejudiced, out of fear, human respect, timidity. Conversely, a person can be prejudiced without practicing discrimination. He checks his irrational prejudice before it overflows into action. The real social evil of prejudice is that it often leads to overt acts of unjust discrimination. There are two major forms of prejudice: attitudes of social distance, and belief in stereotypes.

Social distance: Those with attitudes of social distance feel that some group or category of persons should maintain a social distance from them, i.e., avoid social contact. This attitude is usually based on an irrational fear of contamination or threat if social distance is eliminated or reduced. In an intensive study of race relations in 100 American cities conducted by Cornell University, sociologist Robin Williams attempted to measure attitudes of social distance by a questionnaire in which he asked white respondents to answer whether they objected to eat at the same table as a Negro, dance with a Negro, attend a party in which most of the guests were Negro, have a relative marry a Negro, or live next door to a Negro. To object to social contact in everyone of these relationships was evidence of extreme attitudes of social distance. Williams found that the intensity of prejudice increases as social distance decreases. Thus, while people in Elmira, New York, overwhelmingly approved of the practice of Negroes eating in white restaurants (71 percent approval), when social distance was minimized by asking the question, "would you want to eat at the same table as a Negro," 57 percent answer that they would not wish to do so.

Stereotypes: A second form of prejudice is the belief in *stereotypes.* Stereotypes are labels or identities which we assign to people that show what we believe these people are like and how we think that they will behave. Stereotypes are illogical generalizations which predicate certain qualities about *all* members of a group such as "all redheads are quick tempered" or "all Italians are gangsters." Usually, there is some basis in fact for the stereotype. Thus, we would not believe that all Italians are gangsters unless at least some of them were. Stereotype thinking can lead to unjust discrimination. Many whites avoid all Negroes because they believe that all Negroes are dirty In turn, some Negroes resent all whites because they believe that all whites are cruel. Stereotype thinking minimizes social communication between the races.

The terms in the vocabulary of race relations apply both to Negroes and to whites. There are both Negroes and whites who support policies of segregation and integration. Both groups include members who practice unjust discrimination and prejudice.

In the next section of this chapter we will consider patterns of separate association in residential location, education, and occupation. The phrase *patterns of separate association* is deliberately chosen because the cause of these patterns is complex. Customary segregation and unjust discrimination are certainly one major factor. Other factors include self-segregation by Negroes and economic and cultural differences between Negroes and whites.

Patterns of Separate Association in Housing

The Supreme Court ruled in 1948 in *Shelly* vs. *Kramer* that restrictive covenants— legal contracts which forbade home owners to sell their property to Negroes — would not be enforced in the courts. Several of our cities and states have passed fair housing legislation which aims at giving Negroes equal access to the housing market. As the legal barriers to fair housing have been broken down, customary restrictions remain. Separate patterns of housing, if anything, may have increased in recent years. Consider the example of Chicago. In 1910 there were no census tracts in which Negroes represented over 61 percent of the population. Two thirds of Chicago's Negroes lived in census tracts which were at least 50 percent white. A full 33 percent lived in tracts in which Negroes represented only 10 percent of the population. By 1920 87 percent of Chicago's Negro population was located in residential areas over 50 percent Negro. By 1960 this figure reached 90 percent. Sixty-three percent lived in census tracts which were 90–99 percent Negro.

The causes for patterns of separate association in housing for Negroes and whites are many and complex. One cause is the economic inability of many Negroes to purchase homes in middle-class neighborhoods. Another is the economic fear of white homeowners who are afraid that sales to Negroes will lower property values. A careful study conducted by the department of sociology at the University of California, Berkeley, demonstrated that in those areas of the San Francisco Bay region in which the dominant white population did not panic and sell their homes at a loss when Negroes began to move into their area, there was no reduction in property values. Another cause of separate association in housing is the self-segregation by Negroes who either wish to live in all Negro areas or who refrain from moving into dominant white sections because of real or imagined fears of white hostility. Unjust discrimination is at least one factor in explaining separate Negro housing areas. Many white owners simply refuse to sell to Negroes.

The first Negro to move into an all-white area is often the source of curiosity. In the late 1940's there was a bitter racial flare-up when a Negro family moved into a predominantly white section of Ciccro, Illinois. Lorraine Hansberry in her play and movie, *Raisin in the Sun,* has portrayed the conflict and tension felt by both whites and Negroes when a Negro moves into a middle-class white neighborhood.

The various fair housing ordinances are attempts to overcome unjust discrimination in housing sales. Proponents of these laws see them as a way of increasing housing opportunities for Negroes. Opponents of these laws argue that fair housing transactions are properly the business of voluntary efforts, not legal restraints. Fourteen states and over a hundred municipalities have enacted fair housing ordinances. Even states and cities with such laws, however, continue to exhibit patterns of separate housing between Negroes and whites.

Patterns of Separate Association in Schools

Legal segregation in public schools was ruled unconstitutional in 1954. At the time of the Supreme Court ruling, 17 southern and border states and the District of Columbia maintained school segregation based on race. Ten years after the court decision, there were 6000 school districts in the 17-state area. Half of these districts included both Negro and white students. In one third of these biracial districts, schools had been desegregated. In the District of Columbia and three border states, no biracial school districts were still segregated. In three states there were no integrated schools. By November, 1962, about 255,000 Negroes attended school with whites in formerly segregated school districts. This represented one fourth of all Negro students in desegregated districts. Eighty-five percent of the school districts involved integrated voluntarily, without court intervention. But many problems still exist. The process of school integration is slow, particularly outside of the border states. In many school districts there is token integration which involves only a few Negro students.

In the mid-1960's Negro leaders coined the phrase *de facto segregation* to refer to patterns of separate association in non-southern school districts. In most American cities public school districts correspond with neighborhood boundaries. Children attend the public school closest to their homes. Since most Negroes live in predominantly Negro neighborhoods, they attend schools which are as a matter of fact (*de facto*) "segregated." The student should note the quotation marks around the term segregated. Unless there is a deliberate policy by school boards to keep Negroes in separate schools, it would seem advisable to refer to "patterns of separate association in schools" rather than to use the more value-laden term, segregation.

Some racial leaders complain that the policy of neighborhood schools relegates the majority of Negro students to the oldest, least well-equipped, and most over-crowded schools in the community. They claim that the best teachers avoid teaching in all-Negro schools. In the summer of 1965 Negro protest groups picketed school boards in Chicago and Oakland, California, to fight *defacto* segregation. In some cities they withdrew their children from public schools to protest against neighborhood schools.

The problems involved in assessing the policy of the neighborhood school are complex. As the movie *The Blackboard Jungle* makes clear, it is not an easy task to teach in a slum school. Yet, many good and dedicated teachers pass up offers to teach in middle-class schools in order to dedicate themselves to underprivileged youth. Again, while in some cities, all-Negro schools have inadequate facilities, in others special educational funds are allocated for Negro schools. The Ford Foundation has made grants available for school districts which initiate special educational programs for culturally deprived minorities. The United States government has sponsored Operation Headstart, a prekindergarten educational enrichment program for underprivileged children.

Some groups who want to eliminate patterns of separate association in public schools argue for bussing service for Negroes to schools in middle-class districts and reverse bussing of middle-class whites to predominantly Negro schools. Others desire changes in the policy which draws school boundaries to coincide with neighborhood units. Proponents of these plans maintain that interracial association at the school-age level is an essential part of the education process. They feel that separate patterns of association in school necessarily lead to inferior education for Negroes despite enrichment programs. Opponents of these plans argue against the expense and hardship for children in forced bussing programs. They maintain that the mere proximity of Negroes and whites in the same school does not guarantee interracial association. They point to self-segregation patterns in technically integrated schools. The wisdom of forced bussing or the elimination of the residential school district is, therefore, a controversial question of public policy which each American citizen and school district must settle for himself.

Patterns of Differential Employment

Table 5 of this chapter indicated the occupation distribution of Negroes in the United States. There is some evidence that differential employment opportunities for whites and Negroes is due to unjust discrimination. It is also due to other factors such as educational attainment. One third of all employed Negro women work as domestic servants. Only 1.69 percent of the apprentices in highly rewarded skilled crafts are Negro. In the summer of 1964 the bricklayers' union in New York City ran advertisements in several cities of the United States searching for qualified applicants for apprentice jobs. No New York Negro was accepted by the union. The Cornell study on Negro-white relations discovered that in Bakersfield, California, over 80 percent of the bricklayers' helpers (an unskilled, low-paying job) were Negro. There were no Negro journeymen or apprentice bricklayers. The same study indicated that in Steubenville, Ohio, "There are no Negro carpenters, plumbers, or painters (only one Negro electrician)." The skilled crafts unions in America follow a nepotism system by which relatives and close friends of union members are sponsored as apprentices. The absence of large numbers of Negroes from craft unions may be due more to nepotism preference than policies of Negro exclusion. CORE and other Negro groups have attempted to persuade employers to institute fair hiring codes which eliminate race as a factor in choosing prospective employees. The federal government and many state governments have set up Fair Employment Practice Codes for firms seeking government contracts. We will conclude this chapter with Table 7, based on 1960 census data representing the income differential between nonwhite and white groups in the United States. It gives some indication of patterns of differential employment for white and nonwhite groups.

TABLE 7

Income per year	Percentage of whites	Percentage of nonwhites
1. $10,000 +	7.2	0.7
2. $ 7,000–$9,999	11.8	2.1
3. $ 6,000–$6,999	9.3	2.9
4. $ 5,000–$5,999	13.2	7.0
5. $ 4,000–$4,999	12.8	11.3
6. $ 3,000–$3,999	11.0	14.2
7. $ 2,000–$2,999	9.8	17.2
8. $ 1,000–$1,999	11.3	18.0
9. Less than $1,000	13.5	26.5

Major Concepts in Chapter 12

1. *Social Problem:* Breakdowns or deviations in social behavior involving a considerable number of people which are of serious concern to many members of the society in which the aberrations occur.

2. *Criminal law:* A body of specific rules about human conduct which apply uniformly to all members of the classes to which the rules refer and which are enforced by punishment administered by the state.

3. *Felony:* Grave, serious crime subject to penalties of over one year in prison and the loss of certain constitutional rights.

4. *Misdemeanor:* Any crime, subject to fines or imprisonment, which is less serious than a felony.

5. *True Crime Rate:* The number of all crimes committed in a given year, whether detected or not, per one hundred thousand population. Sociologists work with the recorded crime rate, i.e., crimes known to the police.

6. *Theory of Differential Association:* A theory about crime causation, first propounded by Edwin Sutherland, which maintains that those men become criminals who have the greater proportion of their contacts with criminals and who are relatively isolated from contacts with lawful behavior.

7. *Competition:* A process by which groups engage in mutually opposed efforts to secure the same scarce objectives.

8. *Conflict:* A process by which groups seek to injure or destroy each other.

9. *Accommodation:* A process by which groups, retaining their own interests and identity, achieve a mutual adjustment, which is at least temporary.

10. *Cooperation:* A process by which groups agree upon joint action.

11. *Assimilation:* A process by which the separate identities of groups become fused and barriers to communication are removed.

12. *Segregation:* Policies or norms of behavior, enforced by law or custom, which deliberately exclude a group from joint participation in social life as a means of fostering relations of subordination and superordination between two groups.

13. *Integration:* Policies of action which permit minority groups and dominant groups *access* to areas of community life on the basis of free and equal association.

14. *Discrimination:* Policies of preference and exclusion of members of one group as compared to members of another.

15. *Prejudice:* Attitudes or ways of thinking which are emotional rather than rational. There are two major types of prejudice: attitudes of social distance and stereotype thinking.

16. *Attitude of Social Distance:* A feeling that some group or category of persons should maintain its social distance. An attitude which discourages social contacts between groups.

17. *Stereotype-Thinking:* Illogical generalizations which predicate certain qualities about all members of a group. Stereotypes are labels or identities we assign to people that show what we believe these people are like and how we think that they will behave.

Review Questions

1. Distinguish between social problems and personal problems.
2. Give at least two reasons why the majority is not always a good judge of social problems.
3. How does society cause social problems?
4. What are some of the problems involved in trying to compute the true crime rate?
5. What age group statistically contributes the largest number of criminal offenders?
6. What is the relation between size of community and the crime rate?
7. *Identify:* Cesare Lombroso, Robert K. Merton, William Sheldon, Edwin Sutherland.
8. Define: "a deterministic theory of human behavior."
9. *Identify:* delinquency area, contraculture, apprentice-criminal delinquency, violence delinquency, retreatist delinquency.
10. In what type of occupations are Negroes mainly found? Using the Warner classification for social stratification, in which classes would you find the majority of U. S. Negroes?
11. *Identify: Plessy vs. Ferguson; Shelly vs. Kramer; Brown vs. State of Kansas.*
12. Distinguish between "policy of segregation" and "patterns of separate association."
13. Distinguish between "policy of integration" and "deliberate and planned interracial association."
14. What is the social price of segregation? Of integration?
15. Define: "de facto segregated schools."

Discussion Questions

1. Discuss: "One group's problem is another group's gain."
2. State and criticize the biological and psychological theories of crime.
3. What do Edwin Sutherland's and Robert Merton's theories of crime causation have in common?
4. Re-read the section on the history of Negro-white relations and describe each period in terms of cooperation, conflict, accommodation, competition, and assimilation.
5. Discuss: "Discrimination and prejudice are natural to man."

Bibliography

Cohen, Albert K., *Delinquent Boys: The Culture of the Gang* (Glencoe, Ill.: The Free Press, 1955).

Fortune magazine, *The Exploding Metropolis* (Garden City, N. Y.: Double-day & Company, 1958).

*Frazier, E. Franklin, *Race and Culture Contacts in the Modern World* (New York: Alfred A. Knopf, 1957).

*Griffin, John Howard, *Black Like Me* (New York: New American Library, 1960).

*Hansberry, Lorraine, *Raisin in the Sun* (New York: Random House, 1959).

Merton, Robert K., *Social Theory and Social Structure*, rev. ed. (Glencoe, Ill.: The Free Press, 1957).

Kefauver, Estes, *Crime in America* (Garden City, N. Y.: Doubleday & Company).

Morris, Terrence, *The Criminal Area* (New York: Humanities Press, 1958).

*Myrdal, Gunnar, *An American Dilemma,* 8th ed. (New York: Harper & Brothers, 1944).

McDonaugh, Edward C., and Eugene S. Richards, *Ethnic Relations in the United States* (New York: Appleton-Century-Crofts, 1953).

Nye, Francis I., *Family Relationships and Delinquent Behavior* (New York: John Wiley & Sons, 1958).

Queen, Stuart A., and David Carpenter, *The American City* (New York: McGraw-Hill Book Company, Inc., 1953).

Simpson, George E., and J. Milton Yinger, *Racial and Cultural Minorities* (New York: Harper & Brothers, 1953).

Stowe, Harriet Beecher, *Uncle Tom's Cabin* (New York: Dodd, Mead, 1952).

*Sutherland, Edwin H., *White-Collar Crime* (New York: Dryden Press, 1949).

Sutherland, Edwin H., and Donald R. Cressey, *Principles of Criminology,* 6th ed. (Philadelphia: J. P. Lippincott Co., 1960).

Warner, W. Lloyd, and Paul S. Lunt, *The Social Life of a Modern Community,* Vol. I of Yankee City Series (New Haven: Yale University Press, 1941).

Williams, Robin M., Jr., *Strangers Next Door: Ethnic Relations in American Communities* (Englewood Cliffs, N. J.: Prentice-Hall, Inc., 1964).

* Also published in paperback edition.

Index